*Improving Outcomes for*
*Children and Families*

*Child Welfare Outcomes*
*Series Editor: Harriet Ward, Centre for Child and Family Research, Loughborough University, UK*
This authoritative series draws from original research and current policy debates to help social work managers, policy makers and researchers to understand and improve the outcomes of services for children and young people in need. Taking an evidence-based approach, these books include children's experiences and analysis of costs and effectiveness in their assessment of interventions, and provide guidance on how to develop more effective policy, practice, and training.

*also in the series*

**How Does Foster Care Work?**
**International Evidence on Outcomes**
*Edited by Elizabeth Fernandez and Richard P. Barth*
*Foreword by James K. Whittaker*
ISBN 978 1 84905 812 4

**Costs and Consequences of Placing Children in Care**
*Harriet Ward, Lisa Holmes and Jean Soper*
ISBN 978 1 84310 273 1

**Young People's Transitions from Care to Adulthood**
**International Research and Practice**
*Edited by Mike Stein and Emily R. Munro*
ISBN 978 1 84310 610 4

**Babies and Young Children in Care**
**Life Pathways, Decision-making and Practice**
*Harriet Ward, Emily R. Munro and Chris Dearden*
ISBN 978 1 84310 272 4

**Safeguarding and Promoting the Well-being of Children, Families and Communities**
*Edited by Jane Scott and Harriet Ward*
ISBN 978 1 84310 141 3

*of related interest*

**Child Well-Being**
**Understanding Children's Lives**
*Edited by Colette McAuley and Wendy Rose*
*Foreword by Gillian Pugh*
ISBN 978 1 84310 925 9

**Enhancing the Well-being of Children and Families through Effective Interventions**
**International Evidence for Practice**
*Edited by Colette McAuley, Peter J. Pecora and Wendy Rose*
*Foreword by Maria Eagle*
ISBN 978 1 84310 116 1

**The Developing World of the Child**
*Edited by Jane Aldgate, David Jones, Wendy Rose and Carol Jeffery*
*Foreword by Maria Eagle*
ISBN 978 1 84310 244 1

# Improving Outcomes for Children and Families

## Finding and Using International Evidence

*Edited by Anthony N. Maluccio,*
*Cinzia Canali, Tiziano Vecchiato,*
*Anita Lightburn, Jane Aldgate and Wendy Rose*

*Foreword by James K. Whittaker*

Jessica Kingsley Publishers
London and Philadelphia

Table 5.1 is adapted with permission from *SIGN 50: A Guideline Developer's Handbook* by the Scottish Intercollegiate Guidelines Network © 2008 Scottish Intercollegiate Guidelines Network.

First published in 2011
by Jessica Kingsley Publishers
116 Pentonville Road
London N1 9JB, UK
and
400 Market Street, Suite 400
Philadelphia, PA 19106, USA

*www.jkp.com*

**Library of Congress Cataloging in Publication Data**
Improving outcomes for children and families : finding and using international evidence / edited by Anthony N. Maluccio ... [et al.] ; foreword by James K. Whittaker.
    p. cm.
Includes bibliographical references and index.
ISBN 978-1-84905-819-3 (alk. paper)
 1. Child welfare--Evaluation. 2. Family services--Evaluation. 3. Evaluation research (Social action programs)  I. Maluccio, Anthony N.

HV713.I47 2010
362.7--dc22
                            2010010008


**British Library Cataloguing in Publication Data**
A CIP catalogue record for this book is available from the British Library

ISBN 978 1 84905 819 3

Printed and bound in Great Britain by
MPG Books Group

# Contents

## List of Tables

## List of Figures

# *Foreword*

Despite the impressive growth of research-based knowledge in child and family services, particularly in child mental health, its utilization and dissemination have lagged, pointing up what some have termed the 'science-to-service' problem (Hoagwood, Burns and Weisz 2002). Kimberly Hoagwood, a highly regarded child mental health policy analyst and researcher in the US, cites several potential reasons why research-based knowledge is not being more widely used. These include a lack of consensus on what constitutes evidence-based practice, the relative paucity of research on effective service solutions for children with severe and co-occurring mental health problems, and the fragmented and uncoordinated state of much of the current service system with its differing funding, administrative, training and organizational features.

In combination, the above challenges create obstacles to the systematic, planful review and adoption of empirically validated interventions on the part of child mental health agencies. Nonetheless, the need for testing of clinical interventions in more 'real world settings' is only underscored by the growth of managed care and managed revenue initiatives in behavioral health in the US, which pose additional challenges for clinicians and consumers alike (Armbruster, Sukhodolosky and Michalsen 2004).

What is needed, Hoagwood and other eminent researchers argue, is a 'new direction' for services research that includes development of agency-based 'intervention development and deployment models' (Hoagwood, Burns and Weisz 2002, pp.327–338). Hoagwood's comments suggest both new roles and a set of emergent challenges for a select number of child mental health service agencies desirous of adding research-based knowledge, development and dissemination to their core function of delivering high-quality child mental health services. As Kazdin and Weisz note:

> Testing treatments under conditions more and more like those of actual practice in mental health service settings may be a way to build especially robust treatments and a way to build an evidence base that supports their use in everyday clinical care. (2003, p.448)

Recent contributions from a variety of international investigators and commentators have underscored the fact that the 'science-to-service' gap in children's services is not limited to North America and, indeed, will benefit from cross-national perspectives as many governments struggle with defining and measuring meaningful outcomes for children in care as well as in implementing what might be termed evidence-based or 'best practices'. Recent examples of such international contributions include Fernandez and Barth (2010) on foster care, McAuley, Pecora and Whittaker (2009) on evidence-based practices, Munro, Stein and Ward (2005) on transitions from care in differing cultural and political contexts, and Whittaker (2009) on factors impeding and enhancing the adoption of evidence-based practices in children's services. As many of the contributions to this present volume attest, two ingredients will be critical to closing the science-to-service gap in services for families and children:

1. Identification of creative pathways for integrating evaluation and research activities right in the heart of the service enterprise.

2. Learning from critical cross-national analyses about the most effective organizational structures and service stratagems to achieve desired outcomes for vulnerable children and their families.

The work of the International Association for Outcome-Based Evaluation on Family and Children's Services (IaOBERfcs), as well as other international groups, holds great promise as a vehicle for deepening and extending our knowledge on what works in child and family services and how to bring effective programs to scale in differing cultural, political and organizational contexts. To be sure, this is all very much 'work in progress': it remains to be seen whether evidence-based interventions can successfully be adapted to meet cultural and political milieu separate from those in which they are developed. What is encouraging is that researchers, policy makers and practitioners from differing countries and contexts are engaged in increasingly sophisticated conversations about fruitful pathways for improving outcomes for vulnerable children and families.

This latest contribution by Maluccio, Canali, Vecchiato, Lightburn, Aldgate, Rose, and their contributors extends this critical conversation in ways that will be helpful to those who plan, implement and evaluate services for children, youths and families. The contributions within this volume shed light on important issues of policy, research and evaluation, and bring together useful insights from a variety of international perspectives. As Weisz and Gray (2008) note, renewed attention must be given to the contexts of usual care and services and their compatibility or lack thereof with model, evidence-based interventions. Taken together, the rich and varied contributions to this present effort bring us closer to understanding the critical contextual elements in effective service delivery. They point the way to future research endeavours, including those making use of routinely collected data. One hopes that what is presently a modest cross-national literature in the area of child and family services will expand in scope and scale. This volume is both a catalyst to such expansion and an important step in the right direction.

One final note. Cross-national discussion of research topics pertinent to child and family services is at one level stimulated and sustained by the very power of the questions themselves. Can model interventions be transplanted from one cultural context to another? Can service 'quality' be measured accurately and by what indicators? Can routinely gathered administrative data be 'mined' through systematic analysis and thus yield important insights for both policy makers and practitioners? Such questions have indeed served as both catalyst and reinforcement to the members of the previously noted international association – IaOBERfcs – some of whose contributions make up this present volume. In truth, however, any fairly conducted multivariate analysis would uncover one additional explanatory variable, or 'active ingredient', at play here. I speak of the inspiration and enduring leadership of our small company provided by our founding president, Professor Anthony (Tony) Maluccio, whose vision, energy and personal encouragement literally caused this particular international discourse to begin and whose felt presence continues to sustain it. We salute Tony for the power of his vision of cross-national collaboration, long before it was deemed either fashionable or feasible. We are, all of us, in his debt, and it is to his abiding faith in the added power of shared ideas that this present volume is humbly dedicated.

*James K. Whittaker*
*Seattle, Washington*
*February 2010*

# Part I
# Evaluating Outcomes for Children and Families

## Improving the Evidence Base

# Chapter 1

# *Improving the Evidence Base*

Anthony N. Maluccio, Cinzia Canali, Tiziano Vecchiato,
Anita Lightburn, Jane Aldgate and Wendy Rose

## Introduction

> The true measure of a nation's standing is how well it attends to
> its children – their health and safety, their material security, their
> education and socialization, and their sense of being loved, valued,
> and included in the families and societies into which they are born.
> (UNICEF 2007, p.1)

The United Nations and its member states are committed to creating
a 'world fit for children' in which 'all children have the best possible
start in life' and 'all have ample opportunity to develop their individual
capacities in a safe and supportive environment' (UNICEF 2002, p.5).
As children told the United Nations, 'We want a world fit for children,
because a world fit for us is a world fit for everyone' (UNICEF 2002,
p.9).

In order to ensure that all children are given the opportunity of
doing well, it is acknowledged that special attention has to be paid to
those children who are likely to face particular obstacles as they grow
up and who will need support to overcome them. Services for children
and their families, therefore, have broadly two roles to play: to deal with
the consequences of difficulties in children's lives and, perhaps more
importantly, to prevent problems arising in the first place. Increasingly

the focus is shifting away from predominantly remedial services to developing community-based services that identify when children are vulnerable, enable them to grow up in their own families wherever possible and support them to do well in every aspect of their lives.

With a bewildering array of approaches and repertoire of service programs available, policy makers, commissioners and service agencies are asking searching questions about which approach or which services work best, for whom and in what circumstances. They understandably want to know which services make a difference and support the changes needed for children to flourish. For the answers, they turn to research to find evidence of effectiveness. There are multiple audiences for the answers. Policy makers seek detailed information for policy and planning purposes about evidence-based programs that can be implemented with confidence in different contexts and with different populations.

Practitioners want to know the evidence about best practices so that they are better informed in case planning with individual children and their families. In a context where significant amounts of money and resources are spent on public and private child and family services, and where funding is under pressure, increasingly service agencies are expected to evaluate and justify their effectiveness to their funders. Continued funding for innovative services depends on outcome data that attests to the efficacy of these services. Finally, but not least, a critical audience is children and families who are using the services. They are no longer seen as passive recipients. The consumer and empowerment movement has resulted in an emphasis on clients' rights to quality assurance and a voice in shaping the services that they need.

As a result, researchers carry a heavy responsibility in meeting the expectations of these different audiences, particularly their responsibility to children and families. The findings on impact and effectiveness are likely to have a profound influence on some of the difficult decisions to be made about which services continue to be funded. Improving the evidence base for children and family services is, therefore, the important focus of this volume. Exceptional progress has been made in the art and science of evaluation over the past two decades to make the evaluation process more accessible and readily understood for consumers, participants and evaluators. Evaluation should be about empowerment, as we build knowledge about more effective ways to help families stay together and to prevent child abuse and neglect. It is about making evaluation relevant, something an agency owns and that still attends to accountability, but is disseminated and understood by those with responsibility for making decisions about service provision (Fetterman and Wandersman 2004).

Often the evidence available tells part of what must be understood to provide the most responsive and effective services, as demonstrated by the contributors to this volume. On the other hand, evaluations can answer researchers' questions without their process and findings having relevance to service providers and consumers. In the quest to find and use the best evidence, researchers in this volume offer their perspective on systematic, theoretical and common-sense evaluation of the types of evidence available and promote utilization-focused evaluations that best meet the needs of stakeholders and consumers (Patton 2008).

An arduous journey is ahead to make evaluation synonymous with good service provision. For progress to continue, service providers, children and families, and evaluators need to work together to answer several critical questions:

- Is the program being implemented as planned to meet service objectives with the resources available? If not, why not?

- How can change be part of the evaluation process in response to feedback from consumers, administrators, practitioners and others?

- How do we know we have improved the well-being of children and families based on the outcomes in our evaluations?

- How do our interventions result in change for children and families?

- Are we cost-effective in our work?

- How do our evaluation results contribute to ongoing evaluation practice in agencies, changes in policy and improvements in service provision?

- How do we invest in cross-national evaluations to broaden perspectives and possibilities?

These questions are not confined to a single country but are being asked across the world. There is a growing commitment to the use of outcome evaluation for the purpose of improving quality and developing the most effective services to meet the needs of families and children. With this commitment comes the experience of evaluators who are concerned with improving the evidence base through choice of the right paradigms to guide evaluation practice.

## Introducing this volume

The authors of the following chapters are part of the IaOBERfcs learning community, introducing evaluation practice from eight countries, including cross-national studies, with proposals about how to improve the evidence base to advance children and family services. Authors present their work from the field, addressing real-world concerns, identifying the implications in addressing the serious challenges in the prevention of child abuse and neglect, the reunification of families when children are placed in out-of-home care, family support and early intervention for high-risk families, and implementation of evidence-based programs. Authors offer new ways of thinking and approaching complex assessments, with guidance for evaluation and practice, emphasizing the evaluator's role in improving outcomes through documenting the process of change and collaborating with practitioners (and with children and families) in observing what works for clients.

Contributors have valued learning from each other, and share here how their understanding of outcome evaluation has been enlarged from understanding the varied contextual realities in different countries. Current issues are addressed which speak to our collective concern that we wisely participate in the knowledge-building process, responsible in our collaborations with providers and policy makers, and accountable to the children and families in need of services.

The book is structured in three parts. The first part of the book considers some of the major issues in improving the evidence base in evaluation. The next part explores methods for designing and using evaluation. The third part gives examples, from across the nations of IaOBERfcs members, of evaluation in the real world of policy and practice.

In Part I of the book, Nina Biehal's chapter on demystifying evidence in child welfare challenges the evidence that is available in the US and UK based on systematic reviews, asking whether relevant research questions central in understanding outcomes have been addressed. Biehal demonstrates how findings from well-developed studies from the US have to be cautiously compared because of different definitions for the same outcomes, different evaluations, time periods, and outcomes that occur after the evaluation, all of which influence the meaning of the evidence. Biehal then reviews three qualitative studies from the UK that examine outcomes for this population, focusing on important ingredients in reunification that have the potential to explain outcomes based on service provision and child and family characteristics. Consumers of research need to look at studies that qualify for comparisons in systematic reviews, such as randomized control trials (RCTs), as well as attend to case studies and pre/post-test evaluations that expand the questions to be answered, reviewing more nuanced outcomes.

This chapter demonstrates how, in adapting principles of systematic review for child welfare, research evidence is assessed based on appraisal of relevance, design and quality of studies. It is an example for researchers on how better to design their studies, and to help consumers understand what is important and known, and the gaps that need to be addressed. Biehal is also instructive in pointing to what should aid digesting studies that are done in different countries. It is obvious from this review that it is important for researchers to prepare evaluation reports so that they will be useful across culture and countries.

Barbara Pine and Robin Spath's chapter on 'unlocking the mysteries of program evaluation' discusses a comprehensive, five-year evaluation of a model program to reunify families. ('Model program' is not a term used in every country and refers to a well-tried and tested intervention.) A key feature of the program evaluation was the partnership with program staff in all facets of the process that included process and summative evaluation, with multi-level and multi-method, quantitative and qualitative evaluative methods. From a case-study design that includes development of a logic model to show relationships between program components and outcomes, the authors detail study questions and hypotheses that guided the evaluation. Major findings and their relevance are outlined with the authors' reflections on lessons learned in successfully completing a user-friendly, relevant evaluation that provided a foundation for continued program assessment to improve services.

For evaluators, this open review helps demystify process and summative evaluation, with clarity about how to be relevant to the program through an ongoing collaborative process. For consumers, particularly agency leadership and policy makers, it is a clear example of what can be included in an evaluation and how to relate the evaluation to what needs to be known for program development and accountability. Finally, this model is relevant around the world as we work to improve children and family services.

Anita Lightburn and Chris Warren-Adamson open Part II of the book, on finding methods and using evidence, with their chapter on evaluating complexity in community-based programs. Based on complexity theory, the chapter emphasizes evaluations that attend to the whole system, where the interworking of all relevant agents and factors results in the sum of the whole program being more than the sum of the parts. To bring applications of complexity theory to life, the authors use illustrations of patterns of integrative processes that occur in family centers across the globe. Design and methods are discussed which involve new and old approaches to data collection and analysis based on a constructivist, collaborative, participatory orientation to research. A brief introduction to the tenets of complexity theory is outlined, with implications for evaluations that are concerned with understanding change and transformation in complex community programs. The key for understanding pathways to change emphasizes identifying steps on the way to major program outcomes as means to document the linear and non-linear ways in which changes occur. Recommendations include giving attention to integrative processes that are important to all outcomes, such as the culture of care, containment and synergy, all processes that can be identified, measured and evaluated as they contribute to quality programs and hence effectiveness.

This chapter offers evaluators new ways to think about evaluation of programs where the whole is more than the sum of the parts, moving us beyond reductionism, opening up possibilities of more adequately representing what happens in community programs, which by their very nature are extraordinarily complex. For consumers, this approach to evaluation documents the realities of context, their stories and feedback that has been offered over the years without adequate representation in outcome studies. For practitioners, this approach documents intervention in new ways, so that interventions are more fully described, and this means that there is potential for new program theory to emerge, as does new understanding of 'what works'. It is the authors' hope that the complexity approach opens new ways of thinking, conceptualizing and doing evaluation that can be shared, building studies that can be compared across the globe because of the emphasis on patterns contributing to change.

The difficulties in implementing outcome-based evaluation are highlighted by Cinzia Canali, Anthony Maluccio and Tiziano Vecchiato's approaches to evaluation in services for families and children in

Chapter 5. Evidence-based approaches developed in more experimental or laboratory conditions may discourage investment in outcome evaluation: in real life it is difficult to find advantages for their use because these approaches tend to be so sophisticated that they lose contact with the complex problems of the children at risk and their families. The chapter considers the difficulties encountered by evaluators and by professionals. It proposes exploring different designs, mainly focusing on those that can take into account the multidimensional nature of the problem that is to be tackled. Instead of selecting a small number of variables, incapable of representing all the dimensions of the problem to be confronted, the authors suggest considering many more variables, so as to avoid the risks of simplification. This results, first, in an experimental design that is more complex and demanding to sustain; second, the greater the number of variables, the less 'artificial' the experimental design will be. Also, the chapter describes a case study on a multi-site research on children at risk of unnecessary placements, proposing tools for better monitoring changes over time.

Considering its international value, this chapter suggests a way for redefining the strength of scientific recommendations and for discussing at different levels the usability of evidence-based research which requires multidimensional situation (researchers, professionals, users and service managers).

In Chapter 6, Mary Berry and Colleen Reed focus on family support centers. They provide an organizational scheme to guide the conceptualization and operationalization of family support center research. They focus on three essential and interdependent elements of family support centers – nature, structure and contexts – as a way of assisting program evaluators and researchers to develop evaluations useful for program development and to promote understanding across national boundaries. The variations in approaches to family support center research point to a need for more sophisticated, rounded methodologies and multidimensional techniques, in order to capture the complex nature of such services. The authors point to the advantages of such an approach to evaluations, as, for example, the greater transparency in the evaluation of outcomes.

From an international perspective, they also identify the benefits of cross-national research, which can illuminate previously overlooked dynamics in programs, suggesting that cross-national approaches have the potential to improve the development of family resource centers and to provide opportunities to learn from successful centers.

In Chapter 7, Anne Nicoll and her colleagues present an evaluation in the clients' own words, demonstrating a very different perspective that considers how service users' views can be used to inform and improve services for young people. The focus is on the transition of young people from foster care to independent living, including the potential outcomes for youths at the completion of various types of transition services. There are barriers for a successful transition to independent living where youths may lack self-care skills, independent living competencies and a safety net of supportive resources. Evaluators give voice to these young people. The chapter shows how, by using qualitative approaches, the views of young people can provide invaluable guidance to practitioners and policy makers organizing leaving-care services. Excerpts, both from interviews from foster care alumni who used leaving-care services, as well as those who did not use any services, reveal the main components of a smooth, abrupt or poor transition into independent living. Common themes that emerge are translated into recommendations.

More and more youth need to be listened to in order to improve the outcomes of services provided for them. For an international audience, this is an example of how to create a set of recommendations involving young people that can be transferred across cultures while recognizing complexity and cultural differences.

The final chapter of Part II gives suggestions on the usage of administrative data. June Thoburn underlines how administrative data sets can contribute to the evaluation of services in cross-national evaluations. A summary of lessons learned from earlier work using administrative data on a large population of children in out-of-home care in England is presented. These illustrate how such data can provide the necessary context to assist policy makers who are looking at initiatives in other states or countries in order to improve outcomes for their vulnerable children. The central objectives of these linked studies are to help increase the appropriateness of comparisons of available data, within and between jurisdictions, to guide the improvement of information systems, and to alert policy, practice and research communities to meaningful comparisons that can guide their work. The hypotheses underlying this work are that high-quality administrative data sets have an important contribution to make to the evaluation of outcomes for children in care.

Their strength is that they provide data on whole cohorts and large numbers of children.

At an international level, the author suggests that the search for evidence of what works at lowest cost across national boundaries is to be welcomed, provided that due care is taken to understand the similarities and differences between the in-care populations and systems in the country where a particular innovation has been developed and the one into which it is being imported. A failure to understand differences can lead to failed policy initiatives, poor use of resources and further harm to individual children, their parents and carers.

Part III of the book considers some international evidence from community-based practice.

Jane Aldgate and Wendy Rose, in their chapter on taking standardized programs to different cultural contexts, show how a mixed methods approach is most helpful in evaluating complex center-based projects implementing an internationally recognized evidence-based program by Webster-Stratton. The evaluation of process as well as outcomes is needed. Some factors have to be explored in some depth, such as drop-out rates to understand the diverse reasons why children and families are unable to complete the program and to put in place creative and sensitive strategies to overcome this.

The chapter suggests to practitioners and those setting up evaluations that account has to be taken of local circumstances and local context. Some adaptations to the program may need to be made to ensure that the terms and language can travel across cultures. It is also clear that it is important to engage children and families in the evaluation to improve the fit of services for them, so that center staff and families become partners with researchers in finding out if interventions are providing the help that is needed. It shows that it is not necessary to remain purist when using a program developed in a different culture, as long as the main intentions and elements of the program are retained. They conclude that improvization and a developmental evaluation design are important to program success.

Hans Grietens reviews his study on child abuse and neglect with the development of an assessment instrument and a systematic review of such programs. Grietens shows that, although it is generally thought to be a good thing to have targeted intervention in cases of child abuse and neglect, there is still a problem about knowing how to target those families most in need of prevention. Screening devices such as those used in Flanders, developed from this study, may help identify those most in need of targeted help, but this is not without its problems. How the screening device is implemented is as important as the screening device itself.

Alternatively, universal prevention programs such as Triple P could be used, but does this universal program reach those most in need early enough and what is the cost-effectiveness of such programs? The chapter reminds us that we must not forget how politically sensitive child maltreatment is. Inevitably, cases of fatal abuse and neglect will influence priorities for intervention.

Marion Brandon's chapter on identifying outcomes at a family center shows that if evaluation wants to understand the impact of relationships in service delivery, it is important to assess the emotional as well as the structural and policy climate of a setting. Qualitative methods can provide data which offer a good barometer of the health of an agency. In terms of practice, the study found that it is the impact of managers and staff on the outcomes that is most important. Staff were able to take care of their own emotional needs and each other, and subsequently they were able to be more sensitive to the needs of children and parents. The quality of relationships between staff and families led to a sense of containment that helped prevent drop-out for participant families.

The value of this study internationally is that it confirms what others have found: that it is difficult to find a single turning point when change takes place, and there is a staged approach to change. The study also emphasizes taking account of the contribution of staff in evaluating a center's outcomes. Such evaluative work needs a range of methods to explore this in sufficient depth.

Anat Zeira, in Chapter 12 on the importance of professional relationships, provides an interesting case study in one distinctive cultural setting. The messages are clear that evaluators have to take account of the cultural context and, more importantly, real-world factors such as the shortage of resources for workers that may impede the progress of intervention. The messages for practice are that evaluators can help identify the constraints on workers and that progress with families could have been speeded up if workers had been supervised regularly, as the reflective process is important in supporting effective interventions. Evaluators can act as a catalyst by helping workers when they are stuck in their thinking in relationship to the dynamics in the helping relationship.

Looking at the international value, this chapter endorses the view that the future of evidence-based work in children's services requires as much attention to how an intervention fits within the local cultural, structural and economic context as to *what works*.

Chapter 13, with Robyn Munford, Jackie Sanders and Bruce Maden as co-evaluators, shows that there is great merit in evaluators being in tune with the values and principles of the programs they are evaluating. This provides an ethical base for evaluation, by evaluators being aware of the positive role they can play in helping practitioners and families achieve the outcomes they want. Their developmental approach to evaluation was consistent with the culture of the community center, enhancing and synchronous with the native Maori customs of family.

In terms of helping practice, this evaluation showed the complexity in working simultaneously at the level of individual families and, at the same time, influencing the health of communities. What can be learned from this study is the importance of looking at the processes of work and at the value of the ethical foundation of a strengths-based and empowerment approach. Building relationships between staff and families, confronting what empowerment means and being inventive all contributed to the success of the program. This study is important internationally because it helps to create a clear set of principles that are transferable across cultures, while recognizing the complexity of the specific cultural context.

Patricia McNamara, in Chapter 14, reviews her study of assessing practice in a child and family center and suggests that, within a single case-study design, the collaboration of practitioners, managers and researchers can help to identify and focus sensitive outcomes of intervention.

The message for practice is that the presence of evaluators can raise the confidence of practitioners to recognize the powerful role they can have in effecting positive change with families. The discussion and exchange of knowledge between practitioner, researcher and family was useful in identifying turning points in the change process.

Internationally, this chapter reinforces the view that evaluating complex family interventions can benefit from looking at the processes in detail as well as the outcomes.

# Lessons learned from this volume to improve the evidence base

There are a range of lessons from this diverse group of studies that can be used to guide how we find evidence and promote its use. We highlight those lessons that have emerged across chapters and that merit attention as central to all of our efforts to improve outcomes for children and families.

1. *Empowerment approaches for evaluation are valued* through promoting collaboration and participation of all stakeholders in order to promote agency buy-in that contributes to quality assurance, among other outcomes. The essence of empowerment is in the co-constructing with practitioners and clients evaluation designs, measures and findings that result in long-term benefits in improving services (see, for example, chapters by Aldgate and Rose; Lightburn and Warren-Adamson; Nicoll *et al.*; Spath and Pine; Brandon; Zeira; Munford, Sanders and Maden; McNamara). This is one of the ways of meeting the challenge of involving practitioners in systematic evaluation. The empowerment approach to evaluation has been demonstrated to increase ownership of the evaluation design with description and choice of outcomes, and promotion of findings. These studies aim to involve those in the evaluation process who are closest to the delivery of services, including administrators, practitioners and consumers. In the tradition of Fetterman and Wandersman's (2004) empowerment approach to evaluation, collective work involves partnerships with evaluators to arrive at the most productive focus to produce evaluations that contribute to sustaining programs that work.

2. *A comprehensive approach to evaluation includes process and summative evaluation* that is based on a developmental design, where continual input for program improvement is possible. Both types of evaluations are critical to improving outcomes based on identifying the most relevant and useful evidence. Evaluators' work is beneficial when it contributes to clarity about program function (identifying needs, goals, evidence-based practice that furthers best practice, theories of change and logic models to guide program design, and outcomes that are relevant to all involved (Spath and Pine)). The importance of this approach has been

established through evaluation of the evaluation process 'Getting to Outcomes' similar to Spath and Pine's design in Chapter 3 (Chinman *et al.* 2008).

3.  *Context matters as important evidence that shapes programs*, influencing outcomes in substantive ways (Berry and Reed). New paradigms that guide evaluation include complexity theory that recognizes that the sum of a community program, for example, is more than the sum of the parts of the program. That being the case, it is important to develop evaluation methods that represent the whole (context and program) as a valuable way of describing factors that determine implementation, such as synergy and improvization (Lightburn and Warren-Adamson; Aldgate and Rose). Context is also critical in interpreting program functioning from a cross-national perspective (Thoburn; Grietens; Zeira). Methods that described the agency context evident in active program implementation demonstrate how critical contextual factors, such as staff and administration, contribute to positive outcomes (Brandon), and are essential to attend to in improving outcomes in children and family services.

4.  *Clarifying the usefulness of evidence – from science to practice* – is a challenge to all who work to improve outcomes. An insightful review of the applicability of evaluative studies based on scientific rigor is developed through extending the scope of systematic reviews. From digesting systematic reviews of studies that contribute to the knowledge about what works across countries, (Biehal; Grietens), to implementation of standardized programs, such as Webster-Stratton (Aldgate and Rose), and the challenges to applicability of studies across national boundaries (Canali, Vecchiato and Maluccio; Thoburn), contributors present evaluative wisdom as we translate practice guidelines and best practice. In particular these are contributions that evaluators can bring forward in the formative stage of evaluations, as demonstrated by Spath and Pine, where evidence for practice can strengthen program offerings and outcomes. It is important to recognize the evaluators' role as advocate regarding the usefulness of theory and evidence that can transform practice (see Thomas, Chenot and Reifel 2005).

5. *Choice of the right paradigm for evaluation practice matters. Evaluators now have a range of paradigms from which to choose.* As Patton suggests, it is incumbent on the evaluator to understand what programs need, what is to be evaluated, and the appropriate paradigm to use as a framework for evaluative work (Patton 2008). A developmental design, based on the tenets of complexity theory, for example, can guide development of a theory of change and provide useful information to improve program design and the improvisation needed when implementing a standardized program in a different cultural context (Lightburn and Warren-Adamson; Rose and Aldgate). Similarly, a collaborative/participatory design will guide evaluation work where culture is a major factor that influences the development of evidence and ongoing program renewal (as Munford, Sanders and Maden demonstrate). And, from yet another perspective, theory can influence how we evaluate the evidence available, as well as provide basic support for assessment and measure development (as shown in examples from Biehal; Grietens; Canali, Maluccio and Vecchiato).

6. *Evaluations need to recognize pathways to change, steps on the way,* emphasizing proximal outcomes as a means to documenting achievements. Quality evidence needs to describe developmental processes for participants and for the program. These proximal outcomes often need to be discovered through ethnographic methods that reveal otherwise unrecognized client and program achievements. They are in and of themselves important outcomes that contribute to the achievement of program goals and long-term client outcomes (Brandon; Aldgate and Rose; Munford, Sanders and Maden; Lightburn and Warren-Adamson; McNamara).

7. *Cross-national research depends on planning and conducting evaluative studies among researchers from different countries and collaborating with researchers from a variety of disciplines* (Thoburn). There is a need to inject rigor into the design and execution of these cross-national evaluation projects. Clarity about definitions, improvement of information systems, use of administrative data sets with contextual information is essential as an orientation to what works in different countries (Zeira).

## Conclusion

As this volume illustrates, cross-national collaboration on outcome evaluation for human services – especially child and family services – is a worthwhile endeavor. As such, it requires continuing, collaborative and determined efforts on our parts. Collaborative strategies include replication of successful programs across countries, sharing knowledge of methodology and approaches that can be adapted, explaining implementation problems that we encounter in conducting outcome-based research, circulating information about program innovations and their effectiveness, and conducting parallel studies in various countries regarding the outcomes of diverse approaches to similar problems. We strongly believe that cross-cultural comparison and collaboration can help to improve the well-being of children and families.

These and other lessons, detailed in the following chapters, present opportunities to shape guidelines for evaluation practice in diverse countries that are at different stages of conceptualization and development. We appreciate that evaluation is increasingly regarded as fundamental for accountability and quality assurance across human service agencies around the globe. We recognize that, although each country presents different priorities, there is much to learn from each other as we work with established pathways to achieve quality evidence that has the potential to transform children and family services.

# Chapter 2

# Demystifying Evidence in Child Welfare

## Nina Biehal

In recent years, the increasing pressure to ensure that public policy is evidence-based has been manifest in the demands of policy makers for evidence as to *what works?* Alongside primary research studies, reviews of research can offer one way of answering such questions, but traditional research reviews may sometimes be selective or may uncritically report the findings of studies which have been poorly designed or conducted. In contrast, systematic reviews employ strategies for avoiding the risk of bias in selecting studies for review and have clear, predefined quality criteria for studies that may be included.

Systematic reviews have most often been used to address questions about the effectiveness of interventions and have typically regarded only experimental and quasi-experimental studies as having the minimally acceptable study design (Macdonald 2003). There is growing acceptance, however, that they may also be useful in assessing the evidence on other types of research questions and, in doing so, they may need to draw on studies using a broader range of research designs. This chapter discusses the adaptation of systematic review procedures for use in child welfare, drawing on a recent review of research on reunification which was guided by the principles of systematic review (Biehal 2006a, 2006b). This review adapted the procedures of systematic review but the resources available precluded a full systematic review. These are normally undertaken by a review team, advised by an expert panel, whereas this review was conducted solely by the author within a relatively short period of time. Using a number of the studies reviewed as illustrations, the chapter also explores some of the issues involved in making sense of research evidence, both in relation to the effectiveness of interventions and to a broader set of research questions.

## Background to the review

During the 1970s, the permanency planning movement emerged in both the UK and the US in response to concerns regarding the problem of children who 'drifted' in foster care. The permanency planning approach encouraged a focus on finding a permanent home for children in care. Rehabilitation with families was the placement of choice but, failing that, adoption or permanent foster care were recommended (Maluccio and Fein 1983). However, in the UK there has been a greater emphasis on finding permanent substitute families for children than on planned work to return them home.

A number of studies conducted in the UK during the 1980s revealed that children continued to have unplanned admissions to care and, once admitted, to 'drift' in care for lengthy periods due to a lack of proper planning (Department of Health and Social Security 1985). For those who did return, the return process was fraught with difficulty and little attention was paid to preparation for children's return home (Millham *et al.* 1986). During the 1990s, researchers continued to find a laissez-faire approach to return and a lack of proactive planning for the rehabilitation of looked-after children, referred to children in care in the US (Bullock, Little and Millham 1993; Farmer and Parker 1991; Sinclair, Garnett and Berridge 1995).

Increasing concern with the prevention of placement led to a dramatic decline in numbers of children in the care system between the mid-1970s and mid-1990s and, as a result, children with more extreme difficulties now constitute a higher proportion of those placed. The English care system is increasingly populated by children who have been abused or neglected (Department of Health 2000b). In this context reunification is not self-evident in itself as a safe policy, and therefore a careful appraisal of the evidence on reunification is needed.

# Criteria for inclusion in the review

Since 1973 there have been numerous studies of reunification in the US but relatively little research specifically on this topic in the UK. However, the extensive literature on substitute care in the UK has often touched on the subject of reunion. Studies of children in care published since the implementation of the *Children Act 1989* were therefore scrutinised for data on reunification. Since the review was conducted, two new English studies of family reunification have been completed (Biehal *et al.* 2010; Farmer, Sturgess and O'Neill 2009). Studies were included in our research review if they met the following three criteria: first, they had to address clearly specified research questions; second, their study design had to be adequate to answer these questions; and third, they had to meet the quality appraisal criteria designed for the review.

## *The research questions*

Much of the literature on reunification has reported on the numbers who return home from care or who subsequently re-enter placement, exploring the factors that predict the likelihood of returning home or re-entering care. These studies have often had a stronger emphasis on service outcomes (asking, for example, how many were reunified) than on outcomes at the level of the individual child, such as re-abuse. Few studies have questioned whether return is necessarily a good outcome in all circumstances. It may well be beneficial for many children to be reunited with their families, but it is important to consider carefully *which* children are likely to benefit and in what circumstances. Therefore, the focus of our review was on both child and service outcomes. Only publications that addressed one of the following research questions were included:

- What is the effectiveness of specialist interventions in reunifying children?

- Which children are most likely to be reunified?

- What is the evidence on the stability of these reunifications?

- What are the developmental outcomes for children who are reunified?

This is a broader set of research questions than is typical for true systematic reviews, which tend to be more narrowly focused. Only studies of outcome were included in the review. Descriptive studies of process and the many essays published on reunification were excluded.

## Assessing study design

The review critically evaluated studies that employed a range of methodologies to explore reunification. Systematic reviews typically use the concept of a hierarchy of evidence to rank study designs according to their ability to minimise bias, with randomised control trials (RCTs) as the 'gold standard', followed by quasi-experimental studies, cohort studies and so on – with descriptive studies at the lowest level of the hierarchy (see www.cochrane.org and www.campbellcollaboration.org). Although proponents of evidence-based practice do not claim that *only* RCTs can provide evidence about the effectiveness of interventions, they argue that these provide the most robust evidence. In some fields of enquiry, such as medicine, it is sometimes the case that only RCTs are considered sufficiently 'robust'. However, this approach has been criticised as being both narrow and rigid, and the transferability of this model to a social policy context has been questioned (Boaz, Ashby and Young 2002; Dixon-Woods, Fitzpatrick and Roberts 2001). Indeed, the Campbell Collaboration has acknowledged that process evaluations using qualitative or mixed methods may provide the best means of answering certain types of research questions, providing evidence on issues such as the acceptability of services or the ways in which professional or service-user behaviour can help or hinder the implementation of services (Popay and Dunston 2001).

In the UK researchers on child welfare have, until relatively recently, tended to view quantitative and experimental approaches with a degree of hostility (Boaz *et al.* 2002; Fisher 2002). Until the later 1990s, much of the research on child welfare in the UK was characterised by a concern with needs and process, with relatively little direct attention to outcome evaluation, and experimental studies of social work were rare. If studies meeting the 'gold standard' of experimental design had been the only ones to be included in this review, then *all* UK studies on this topic would, de facto, have been excluded. However, there is a danger of underestimating the value of evidence if the research methods used are 'lower' in the hierarchy, since studies that are more modest methodologically may nevertheless offer important findings (Baldwin *et al.* 2002).

Although it is harder to draw conclusions on effectiveness from studies without control groups, alternative designs may nevertheless be useful in providing insights into outcomes for children and into the ways in which interventions come to be associated with particular types of change. For example, theory-driven models, which try to explain how, why and in what circumstances interventions produce change, may often be appropriate to the constantly shifting service context of social work (Connell and Kubisch 1999; Pawson and Tilley 1997).

## Quality appraisal

The issue of study quality is arguably even more important than the issue of study design. Indeed, some experimental studies may be flawed, despite their use of random sampling (Biehal 2006b). It is, however, all too easy to pick holes in other people's research, and in any case in the real world of research it would be hard to find many studies which do not have imperfections of one kind or another. There is a real tension between setting the evidential threshold so high as to exclude the majority of studies and following a laissez-faire approach that obscures real gaps in the research (Macdonald 2003).

How, then, should quality be assessed? Although there are widely accepted standards with respect to the scientific rigour and credibility of studies using quantitative methods, which can be assessed in terms of the reliability and validity of the measures used and of the possible bias arising from sampling strategies or sample attrition, no consensus exists as to the criteria by which qualitative research should be judged. This issue has been hotly debated, with positions ranging from a rejection of the need for any quality criteria at one extreme to the retention of concepts common to quantitative and qualitative research at the other. There is fairly widespread support for the idea that all qualitative studies should be conducted in a rigorous and transparent manner so that others can judge their methodological validity. There is more controversy, however, about whether or not validity in terms of credibility or truth claims can be judged, reflecting the wide range of philosophical positions underpinning different approaches to qualitative inquiry (Mason 1996; Silverman 1993; Spencer *et al.* 2003).

The above discussion illustrates the difficulty of devising a simple set of criteria to appraise the quality of studies using a variety of methods and designs. Baldwin and colleagues have argued that studies should only be included in research reviews if they meet essential criteria regarding the clarity of the research question, description of the population and the intervention, the use of appropriate sampling strategies and the rigour with which data are analysed (Baldwin *et al.* 2002). Studies were therefore included in this review only if they met these pre-specified criteria, resulting in a list of just over 70 studies of sufficient relevance and quality (see Biehal 2006b).

## Comparing outcomes across studies

It might be thought that comparing the results of studies on a discrete topic such as reunification would be reasonably straightforward. However, comparing outcomes across studies posed considerable problems due to differences in study design and sampling methods. Different studies have reported on samples of children who differ in important ways, either including children of all ages or only younger children, children in all types of placements or only those in foster placements, children placed for a variety of reasons or only those placed as a result of abuse.

These sampling decisions inevitably have an impact on findings. For example, it is extraordinarily difficult to synthesise the findings of the numerous studies that have examined the question of how many children return home. Some samples include children who have only just entered the care system and, since most children return home in a matter of weeks, rates of return are higher than in studies that sample only children placed for at least three, six or even 12 months. To muddy the waters further, some studies define reunification as a return to biological parents, whereas others include a move to other relatives and are, as a result, likely to report higher rates of reunification. Policies, services and hence rates of reunification may also differ between countries, making international comparisons particularly difficult.

The rest of this chapter first illustrates the difficulty of comparing research findings across an apparently similar group of studies, examining the findings of four randomised control trials of specialist family reunification services in the US. It then considers the evidence on the return process from studies with quite different designs, to illustrate the contribution made by non-experimental studies (that is, studies which do not have control groups). Although non-experimental studies may be of limited value in assessing the *effectiveness* of interventions, they may nevertheless provide valuable evidence on other aspects of services and outcomes in the complex field of child welfare.

## Assessing effectiveness

In considering studies of effectiveness, it is important to ask: what do we mean by *effective* and what do we count as evidence of effectiveness? Since neither the way in which social problems are defined nor the way in which the limits to knowledge are explained is value-free, what counts as evidence cannot be seen as a neutral question. Equally, what works for children may not be the same as what works for parents or, indeed, for society (Glass 2001).

Our review identified four randomised control trials which investigated the effectiveness of specialist interventions to reunify children, all of them from the US. All four compared outcomes for children using specialist reunification services with those for children receiving routine services. Three of them, the Alameda project, the Family Reunification Service (FRS) project and the Preventive Services Demonstration (PSD) project, found that intensive, specialist services were more likely to reunify children, but the fourth, the Charleston Collaborative Project (CCP), found the specialist service to be no more effective than routine services either in returning children home or in improving psychosocial outcomes (Swenson *et al.* 2000).

Length of follow-up is an important issue when assessing outcomes, but as the studies used different follow-up periods it is difficult to compare like with like. The FRS study showed a higher rate of return for those receiving the specialist service (93% were reunified after 90 days, compared to 28% of the control group). However, six months after the service ended 30 per cent of the FRS children had returned to care whereas additional control group children had returned home. By the 12-month follow-up, more of the FRS group had returned to care than those in the routine services group (21% compared to 17% of control group) (Fraser *et al.* 1996; Lewis, Walton and Fraser 1995; Walton *et al.* 1993). The PSD project found that after six months 62 per cent of project children had been reunified with their families, compared to 43 per cent of the control group, but after five years there was no difference between the groups in the proportion reunified (Jones 1985). The Alameda project found that just one child in each group had returned to care by one-year follow-up (Stein and Gambrill 1979).

The proportion of children who returned home clearly varied dramatically across these specialist projects, although it is difficult to compare findings when different follow-up periods are used. Furthermore, apparent differences between intervention and control groups may be due not only to possible *real* differences in the effectiveness of the services but also to the different samples and methods used. All the children referred to the CCP were in protective custody due to maltreatment, as were virtually all of the Alameda project children. These might be considered a higher-risk group for long-term placement than those in the FRS study, of whom 28 per cent were placed due to concerns about child behaviour. It was precisely these older children with behaviour problems that the FRS was particularly successful in returning home. Furthermore, the FRS project only worked with children for whom a plan for return home had already been made, whereas the Alameda project and the CCP service recruited children for whom no case plan had yet been made. The latter groups were clearly more likely to include some children for whom a return home was unlikely to be possible. As for the PSD project, it is important to note that the definition of reunification used in this study encompassed children who returned to other relatives as well as those returning to parents, and this may account for the higher rate of return compared to most other specialist projects.

Bearing in mind these caveats regarding the interpretation of findings from these studies, the crucial question remains: what did these specialist services offer and which features of these services were associated with their success? A common element shared by all of them was the intensity of service provision, with low caseloads allowing workers more frequent contact with families than the usual services could offer. However, the Alameda study found that treatment intensity was not predictive of a child's return home, although the other studies did not explore this issue. It did find, however, that among parents in the experimental group, those who agreed to sign written contracts were more likely to be reunited with their children. This suggests that parental motivation and willingness to engage with workers were important ingredients of success. Other common features were purposeful case planning and the specification and agreement of clear goals with families.

An important issue that arises from the FRS study is that, although this project was spectacularly successful in returning a high proportion of children to their parents (93% within 90 days), significantly more of the FRS group returned to care compared to those who received routine services. Older children (usually with behaviour problems) were more likely to be returned home by the intensive service, but this was also the group most likely to re-enter care. These older children with child-related reasons for placement could probably be returned home with less risk of maltreatment – but paradoxically it was possibly these child characteristics that contributed to the instability of some reunifications.

Intensive services thus rapidly returned children home, but for some this return was perhaps precipitate and hence unstable. This also raises questions as to whether return was in the best interests of *all* of these children and whether outcomes at the level of the individual child, such as developmental outcomes, were positive for all.

## Investigating the return process

Although they may be less appropriate for measuring the effectiveness of interventions, studies which use single-group designs or include the use of qualitative methods can also produce valuable evidence on other aspects of reunification. If we consider, for example, three English studies that examined factors associated with the return of children to their families, we find a subtle exploration of a number of complex issues. Thoburn selected a purposive sample of 34 children from a larger qualitative sample, excluding children placed due to parental illness or homelessness (Thoburn 1980). Bullock and colleagues undertook an intensive study of 31 children in the context of a larger quantitative study (Bullock, Gooch and Little 1998). Cleaver similarly carried out an intensive study of 33 children alongside a case file analysis of a much larger group (Cleaver 2000). These studies explored in depth some of the factors associated with return home. Of course, this has been a topic of interest for many quantitative studies with samples of hundreds, or even thousands, of children and these can provide statistically significant evidence on factors associated with return, such as demographic or placement characteristics, length of placement or parental contact. However, these studies do offer insights on complex issues such as parental ambivalence and the quality of relationships.

For example, the association between parent–child contact during placement and the likelihood of reunification has been much discussed in both the UK and the US (Aldgate 1980; Biehal 2006a; Quinton *et al.* 1997). Cleaver's intensive study explored some of the ramifications of this. She argued that contact was an ingredient of successful return if it was purposeful, had the clear aim of improving the parent–child relationship and was a positive experience for the child. It was also important for contact to be adequately resourced and supported by social services (Cleaver 2000). Bullock and colleagues (1998) noted the importance of such aspects as whether a child has a sense of belonging to her or his family, whether the family regards itself as a unit, and whether both parents and child expect that the child will stay, once returned. These findings echo Lahti's contention that it is the *perception* of permanence that is key, and evidence from a recent study of permanent placements supports this view (Biehal *et al.* 2010; Lahti 1982).

The quality of parent–child relationships has also been found to be an important ingredient in reunification, although relatively few studies have addressed this issue. Cleaver (2000) rated the quality of mother–child attachment on the basis of case file data and found that, where a strong attachment relationship appeared to exist, children were significantly more likely to return home. Analysis of qualitative data in Cleaver's intensive study added further weight to this finding and highlighted the importance of direct work with families to help improve relationships. Related to this, Bullock and colleagues (1998) found that where children were expected to return but did not do so, parental ambivalence was often a factor, and this ambivalence was often accompanied by only intermittent contact with the child.

Looking at this issue another way, Thoburn (1980) argued that parental determination to have a child home was perhaps the most important factor in determining who actually returned. She found, as other studies have done since, that when social work plans changed this was usually as a result of pressure from parents or children (Farmer and Parker 1991; Fisher, Marsh and Phillips 1986). However, Bullock and colleagues (1998) argued that once a child had been in placement for several months, whether a child returned home depended less on the parents than on social work activity, or lack of it. They also offered insights into the problem of re-entry to care, finding that a substantial number of the children who returned home subsequently oscillated in and out of care without ever achieving stability. Older adolescents sometimes oscillated between members of their extended family and their friends, staying with people who perceived an obligation to shelter them but provided few controls – a phenomenon identified in a recent study of adolescents at risk of placement (Biehal 2005).

Clearly, reunification may not be a positive experience for all children and there is evidence that some children may be ambivalent about it (Sinclair *et al.* 2005). A more recent study has also explored the nature and impact of children's own views about reunification (Wade *et al.* 2010). There is some evidence that those who do go home may suffer re-abuse or further neglect, or display poor educational adjustment and social behaviour (Farmer and Parker 1991; Hensey, Williams and Rosenbloom 1983; Hunt and Macleod 1999; Sinclair *et al.* 2005; Taussig, Clyman and Lands 2001; Terling 1999). As Maluccio and his associates have suggested, a broader conceptualisation of reunification in the child welfare field may be more helpful than extreme commitments to returning children to their families. They suggest that reunification is best viewed as a continuum ranging from full re-entry to the family to occasional contact to maintain children's sense of connectedness and involvement with their family of origin (Ainsworth and Maluccio 1998; Maluccio, Pine and Warsh 1994; Maluccio, Abramczyk and Thomlinson 1996).

## Conclusion

Adapting the principles of systematic review to the field of child welfare may offer a useful means of assessing research evidence, based on an appraisal of the relevance, design and quality of studies. Research reviews may help end users of research to negotiate a path through evidence from numerous studies conducted in different ways and addressing a variety of research questions with varying degrees of rigour. In a complex and rapidly shifting social world, research evidence is likely to be situational and contextual; this makes the application of evidence a complex process (Frost 2002).

A research review may not only summarise the available evidence but may also highlight gaps in research. In the field of family reunification, much is known about which children are most likely to return home to their families, but further research is needed to establish for which children, and in which circumstances, the outcome of such return is most likely to be positive and when the risks to children's health and development are likely to be too high.

# Chapter 3

# Unlocking the Mysteries of Program Evaluation
## Lessons from a Comprehensive Evaluation of an Innovative Program to Reunify Families

Barbara A. Pine and Robin Spath

## Introduction

'Program evaluation is the use of research approaches to assess program goals, implementation, interventions, and results' (Pine, Healy and Maluccio 2002, p.87). There are three common types of evaluation: need, process, and outcome. The approach or type chosen is based on the questions one wishes to answer. For example, needs assessment/ evaluation answers questions such as: Is the planned program needed? By whom? What interventions are likely to be more successful with the target population? Process evaluation answers questions such as: Is the program being implemented as planned? Is it reaching the intended audience? Are resources being allocated as planned (including staff, funds, space, equipment)? Finally, outcome evaluation answers questions about the changes and/or benefits for program participants resulting from the program (Mika 1996).

Answers to these questions are often necessary for accountability to funding sources (Ginsberg 2001), accrediting bodies, and, most importantly, clients and communities served by the program. Evaluation helps program managers make better program decisions and modify and redesign programs, assuring the best use of resources for improving clients' lives (Royse *et al.* 2006). Evaluation helps clients to understand how they have changed and grown, it contributes to the knowledge base of services in the field (Turner 1993), and information on outcomes helps to motivate staff interest and commitment to services that achieve results (Poertner 2000).

In this chapter, we present and discuss a comprehensive, five-year evaluation of a model program to reunify families separated by a child's placement in foster care. The evaluation was a collaborative endeavour between university-based researchers and program staff, incorporating both qualitative and quantitative methods in process and outcome studies. A key feature of the study was the partnership with professional staff in carrying it out, which involved constant communication and collaboration and regular, specially planned feedback sessions. Here, we walk the reader through the various steps and processes undertaken throughout the evaluation, with emphasis on how the research was made user-friendly for agency staff. The goal is to demystify program evaluation as a tool for designing and improving programs that make a difference in the lives of children and families.

## Overview of the program model

The Family Reunification Program (henceforth referred to as 'the Program') was initiated by a not-for-profit child welfare agency serving urban areas in two northeastern states in the United States, and was a substantially revised model of an earlier program. The Program is aimed at reunifying families within six months through the provision of specialized case management and clinical intervention services that go beyond the normal range of services offered by the local public child welfare agencies in each location. Among the key features of the Program are targeting of families experiencing a first-time removal, referrals from the public agency within five to 15 days of a child's removal, concurrent planning toward other possible permanent plans, and close collaboration and joint service planning with staff in the public agencies who also continue to work with families. Families in the Program are involved in intensive, home-based services, frequent visits with their children, and groups with other parents. The Program was designed based on evidence-based practice which has been defined as the judicious use of the best information available that pertains to clients' needs and well-being (Barsky 2009).

In the United States, the Adoption and Safe Families Act of 1997 (ASFA) greatly shortened the time that parents had to make needed improvements for the return of their children who had been removed from their care. Reunification with birth parents is still the outcome of choice; however, child welfare agencies are now required to seek termination of parental rights sooner and find adoptive families for children in care. We recognize that policies on permanence and adoption differ across countries. For a comparison of UK and US policies, for example, see Selwyn and Sturgess (2003). The evaluation included 135 families and 254 children who were served by the Program. For the most part the families typified those involved with child welfare agencies. Children were removed because of abuse and/or neglect. Families were poor; more than half were headed by single mothers, and they tended to be young as did their children.[1] Racially, when taking the two sites into account, just over half of the parents were white, nearly 30 percent were Hispanic, and 9 percent were African American.[2]

## The evaluation design

### Process evaluation

The process evaluation was a study of the design and implementation of the Program as a model for reunifying families. It consisted of a variety of qualitative approaches,[3] including a case study, a quantitative–descriptive study, and an examination of three key components of the Program model: the use of groups with parents, parent–child visiting, and the partnership with the two state child welfare agency partners. Additionally, researchers worked with staff to develop a logic model of the Program, and a program design in which goals and process and outcome objectives were specified in measurable terms. A logic model is a graphic representation of a program that shows the relationship between its components expected outcomes; it also shows a conceptualization of a series of events within the program that can serve as a tool for both program planning and evaluation (Mulroy and Lauber 2004). A program design is a narrative format showing the theory or hypotheses of the program[4] and its relationship to program objectives. The design also delineates program goals, and all of the process and outcome objectives of the program in measurable terms, as these are a precondition for evaluating outcomes (Pine, Healy and Maluccio 2002).[5] Development of these tools assured both researchers and Program staff that the Program was indeed ready for evaluation, and that the plan for evaluation 'worked' for the Program (Mancini *et al.* 2004). These study approaches in the process evaluation sought to answer the following questions:

- Is the Program being implemented as it was designed and within the planned time frames?

- What factors facilitate or impede implementation?

- Are the interagency collaborative relationships developing as planned?

- What are the characteristics of the families and children in the Program?

- Are these the families the Program had intended to serve?

- What are the risk factors to child safety and family integrity at case intake?

- What protective factors/family strengths are present?

- What aspects of the program need further development?

## *The case study*

The case study was exploratory in nature and involved data from multiple sources including archival records and documentation, open-ended interviews with 46 key informants from across all three agencies involved as well as staff from other child welfare agencies, and observation of Program team and administration-level meetings. A strength of the case-study approach is that data from various sources can be triangulated, that is integrated together to examine one phenomenon, in this case, the Program (Snow and Anderson 1991). The data analyses compared actual developmental milestones and program structures to models proposed in either Program descriptions or exemplary models. The results provided a description of the development of the Program, its congruence with best practice models, and an interpretation of forces inhibiting or facilitating implementation. Findings were published that included a set of recommendations for strengthening the Program (Spath *et al.* 2002). In keeping with the overarching goal of an evaluation partnership with professional staff involved in the Program, and administrative staff, results were shared and discussed at a specially planned meeting as soon as they were available.

### The quantitative–descriptive study

This study was launched on completion of the case study to determine what families and children were receiving services through the Program. Carried out across several months, it entailed a review by the researchers of all cases open at the time to detail the reasons children come into care, family and child demographics, and services provided. From this review, an instrument for use in gathering child and family case data was developed that could be applied to all closed cases by the end of the study.

### Sub-study on the use of groups

This study and the two additional studies described below were undertaken to delineate more clearly the important components of the Program. The examination of parent groups included focus groups and interviews of Program staff, a focus group with parents attending a group at one Program site, and observation of two seven-week group sessions by the researchers. Meetings with an expert on social work with groups assisted in the development of a set of principles and guidelines useful in both data gathering and analysis. Findings and a set of six recommendations on group-related issues, such as membership, format, curriculum, and evaluation, were published and shared at a specially planned meeting of Program staff (Pine *et al.* 2004). Recommendations led to a re-vamping of the group at one site, including use of a new curriculum with attending parents.

### Sub-study on the use of visiting

Since the most convincing evidence available in foster care research in the United States is that regarding the relationship between parent–child visiting and successful outcomes for children and families, it was important for the research to gain as much information about visiting as was possible. The researchers began this phase of the study with a careful review of the literature on visiting. Findings affirmed that the Program's plan for a minimum of one weekly visit ranging from one and a half to two and a half hours each was congruent with available evidence. As families in the Program moved closer to reunification, visits became longer and more frequent, often in the parents' home.

Information about visits and visit planning was gathered through focus groups with Program staff and administrators in both sites. In addition, researchers observed three lengthy parent–child visits, using a specially developed instrument to guide and record activities and interactions. As with other sub-studies of Program components, findings and recommendations were published as well as shared at an open forum (Pine, Spath and Jenson 2005).

### Sub-study on collaboration

This study involved use of a 20-item questionnaire on inter-organizational partnerships (Center for the Advancement of Collaborative Strategies in Health, New York Academy of Medicine 2005) and eight open-ended questions to interview 41 key informants drawn from the three participating agencies: Program and administrative staff in the two sites, and line and supervisory staff in the two partner state child welfare agencies. Those informants at the administrative levels of their agencies were asked to identify leadership qualities they thought were important for leading inter-organizational partnerships. The results of this sub-study underscored the centrality of the collaboration between the Program and its partners and highlighted implications for practice. As with the others described above, results and recommendations from this study were published and shared and discussed at a special meeting with study participants and other stakeholders (Pine *et al.* 2006).

These qualitative study approaches offered many hours of interaction between researchers and Program staff that had a number of benefits. They helped build solid relationships, develop researcher credibility, and foster staff buy-in to the research; staff felt empowered by their active involvement in designing and carrying out the various approaches. The case study, in particular, enabled a clear specification, in measurable terms, of the Program's practices and intended benefits (Spath and Pine 2004), allowing for a specification of outcomes on which all stakeholders could agree, and laid the groundwork for selecting measurement tools and approaches for the outcome study.[6]

## The outcome evaluation

The outcome phase of the study was fully launched within one year of the study's inception. It sought to answer the following questions about the effectiveness of the Program:

- Are families being reunified?
- Are risk factors for families and children reduced?
- Do families remain safe and stable over time?
- Which families are likely to be reunified and stay together?
- What other permanent plans are made for children who cannot return home?
- Is the Program more effective in reunifying families, or in achieving permanency for children, than standard reunification services offered by state agencies?

Eight outcomes were identified, some of which were mediating variables, meaning that these outcomes affect the ultimate achievements of the Program. These included:

- worker–family alliance (the strength of the helping relationship)
- interagency collaboration
- level of client participation in the Program's services
- family satisfaction with the services.

Other outcomes used to measure the Program's effectiveness included:

- improved parenting skills
- improvement in the family's situation
- increased child safety
- permanency for children.

To measure these outcomes, the study employed both standardized instruments and specially designed questionnaires. Program staff were involved in the selection (or development) of all measurement tools.

## Worker–family alliance

To measure the relationships between the Program staff and parents, which earlier research had shown was critical to successful outcomes, the Research Team gathered data at six months after intake using the Worker–Family Alliance (WAI) to interview each parent in the Program and the staff members providing services to them. This study hypothesized that stronger alliances would lead to better outcomes.

Horvath and Greenberg (1989) conceptualize the helping alliance as consisting of three dimensions: (1) goal – how well the client and helper agree on the goals of treatment; (2) task – how well the two agree on how to reach the agreed-upon goals; and (3) bond – the degree of mutual trust and acceptance they have for each other. Since the Program emphasized goal-directed service planning and intensive work with parents to carry out service plans, measuring agreement on goals and tasks seemed essential (Jenson *et al.* 2009). Moreover, the use of standardized instruments strengthens study findings because of reliability, the extent to which a measure achieves the same result each time it is used, and validity, the extent to which it measures the behaviours that the program is seeking to influence.[7]

### Client participation in the program

In addition to the above measures, the study also measured the level of participation by clients in the Program, since engagement in the intervention has been shown in earlier research to affect outcomes. See, for example, the study by Frame and her colleagues (Frame, Berrick and Brodowski 2000). The Level of Participation Questionnaire used a Likert-type scale to measure a client's extent of participation in visiting, parent groups, clinical services, and concrete services. When a case closed, the social worker completed the Level of Participation Questionnaire for the family, based on their overall participation in these four key components of the Program.

### Family satisfaction with services

The research team also obtained information on client satisfaction through interviews with parents in the Program at 12 months after intake using the 12-month Client Satisfaction Questionnaire. This instrument also was used to obtain data on parents' views on interagency collaboration, how well the Program and its partner child welfare agency worked together to help the family solve its problems and reunify.

## Improvement in the family's situation

Data on change in the family and child's situation was gathered by Program staff using two standardized instruments that were selected by the staff: the North Carolina Family Assessment Scale for Reunification (NCFAS-R) and the Adult-Adolescent Parenting Inventory (AAPI-II). These two assessment tools provide information on improved child safety, children's well-being, and improved parenting skills. The NCFAS-R is a seven-domain scale that was especially developed to measure family strengths and needs in cases involving reunification. Recently, the NCFAS-R was ranked as a top assessment tool for use in child welfare in a review of standardized instruments (Johnson *et al.* 2006) and is used widely in child welfare services in the United States.

The AAPI-II is an instrument that examines parents' attitudes in five areas: parental expectations, empathic awareness of children's needs, use and value of corporal punishment, role reversal, and children's power and independence. AAPI-II was designed as an index of risk for abusive and neglectful parenting attitudes and practices. The AAPI-II was already in use at one Program site, and during the collaborative planning process for the outcome study, the staff elected to use this tool in the other Program site as well. Progress was measured using these instruments at intake, six months, and 12 months following referral to the program. Due to their use in the study, these tools have become part of the Program's comprehensive assessment and service planning process.

## Permanency for children

Permanency and stability for children was measured in several ways. This was done first through a review of Program case records for information on permanency outcomes and timelines. This review showed which children went home and which went to other placements, how long children were in care before achieving a permanent placement, and how many moves a child experienced in care. Second, the research team conducted interviews with children's caregivers using the 24-month Follow-up with Family Where Child Resides Questionnaire. Finally, for cases where these families could not be reached, a review was made of the state child welfare agency's records to determine whether or not another referral to authorities had been made during the 24-month period following the family's entry into the Program.

## The comparison study

In addition to looking at outcomes for families and children in the Program, the study included a comparison sample of families also experiencing a first time removal, who were matched to Program families on a number of characteristics including reasons for removal, age, calendar year of removal, and other similarities. This enabled the researchers to look at outcomes for a group of families who looked like Program families but who received the standard public child welfare agency reunification services in the two states where the Program operated. Record reviews of these families produced the necessary information. The study hypothesized that:

- Families in the comparison group would experience longer separations than families in the Program.

- Fewer children in the comparison groups would be reunified with their birth families than children in the Program.

- Within 24 months of their first removal, more reunified families in the matched comparison group would become re-involved with child protection authorities and would re-enter foster care than those in the Program.

- Fewer children in the comparison groups who cannot be reunified would be placed in other permanent placements.

- Children in the comparison groups would experience longer waits for alternative permanent placements than children in the Program.

Data were analyzed using bivariate and multivariate approaches. A detailed discussion of research methods and findings goes beyond the purposes of this chapter, but can be found in Pine *et al.* (2009). For our purposes here, the following findings are reported for 197 children who had a permanent plan at the time their family's case was closed:

- Children were reunited with their families. Over 60 percent returned home.

- Program children achieved permanency when they couldn't go home. Forty-one were placed in an adoptive home; 19 were placed with a legal guardian.

- Children who were reunified went home in 39.1 weeks; on average they achieved a permanent placement in 44.2 weeks.

- Children in the Program experienced fewer moves while in care; nearly two-thirds moved only once; 12.4 percent moved three or more times.

Did Program children and their families fare better than those receiving standard child welfare services? Yes and no. Overall, the two public agencies did quite well in reunifying families experiencing a first-time removal. In terms of reunification, 57.2 percent of children in the comparison sample were reunified. Children in this sample also received other permanent placements at the same rate as those in the Program. However, of major significance are the differences in length of time to achieve permanence – 66 weeks for children in the comparison sample. In addition to length of time in care, another major contributor to children's stability and sense of permanence is the number of placements they experience while in care. Forty percent of children in the comparison sample had only one placement; over 35 percent had three or more. Additionally, with respect to stability, in the 24-month period following reunification, Program families experienced slightly fewer re-referrals to child welfare authorities – 25.2 percent as compared to 32.5 percent for comparison families – and slightly lower rates of substantiated abuse or neglect reports – 40.7 percent versus 42.1 percent.

Parents in the Program also experienced reduced risks and improved safety during their involvement with the Program, as measured by the NCFAS-R and the AAPI-II. Changes over time as measured by these instruments included improved family interactions, parental capabilities, safety, and readiness for reunification. Parents also were found to modify their expectations of their children and their use and value of corporal punishment over the time-points of the evaluation.

## Lessons learned

A number of lessons for evaluators and program administrators can be drawn from the above description of a complex and comprehensive program evaluation.

1. Regardless of whether the evaluators are internal or external to the program being evaluated, the involvement of program staff is key to its success. Staff are the experts about their program. Without their input and collaboration, evaluators would miss or overlook important information about the program and its interventions

(Mancini *et al.* 2004). Moreover, as was the case in this study, instruments chosen to measure client change were selected in partnership. Therefore, since the staff assisted in selecting these tools, they had a strong investment in using them due to their clinical as well as evaluative utility. In addition, these clinical tools continue to be in use long after completion of the study.

2.  Educating staff on the nature of program evaluation is critical to a study's success. The close involvement of staff in evaluation planning and implementation provides an ideal opportunity to educate staff. As Cousins and his colleagues have noted, 'Intended users' direct participation in doing the evaluation helps to develop their skills and abilities to do systematic inquiry and enables them to understand more fully specific features and aspects of their program' (Cousins, Donohue and Bloom 1996, p.208). For an evaluation to be successful, it is critical that staff understand the reasons for evaluation, and the benefits of the evaluation process for the program, as well as for the clients. With staff intimately involved in the planning of the evaluation, they are more likely to understand and appreciate the merits of the evaluative process and support the implementation of the evaluation.

3.  Evaluation should mirror the major tenets of the program being studied (Green *et al.* 1996). In this case, the Program was based on family strengths, not deficits, and sought to partner with parents to work collaboratively with them to address needed changes. The evaluation was also strengths-based and collaborative.

4.  The process evaluation is essential to understanding what programs actually do. It helps link what was done to outcomes, and helps evaluators to decide when to assess outcomes (Wandersman 2001). Programs and interventions need time to evolve and mature (Gelles 2000). This study used a variety of methods to understand better the Program, its goals and objectives, and the theory behind the intervention including a case study, a logic model, and a program design, before launching the outcome portion of the study.

5.  Constant communication between evaluators and program staff, as well as with agency administrators is essential (Torres, Preskill and Piontek 1997). In this study, communication took many forms, including written reports, the earlier mentioned Research

Advisory Committee meetings, many feedback sessions, a regular newsletter, and on-going communication by phone and email. The latter was particularly critical for maintaining contact as researchers were at some distance from one of the sites. In addition, throughout the evaluation, many feedback sessions included agency-wide workgroup meetings, which often included the state agency partners, to discuss key findings and their implications for the agency. These meetings provided the opportunity for the Program staff involved in the evaluation to see the benefits of their participation in the process, and for them to play an active role in making programmatic changes based on the findings.

6. Close working relationships between evaluators and program staff can suggest a lack of objectivity in the research. This is the value of using standardized instruments and measures that place some objective distance between the researcher and the work being studied. The other benefit to using standardized instruments is the ability to compare outcome findings with other studies.

## Conclusion

This chapter has aimed to demystify the process and product of program evaluation by presenting and discussing a comprehensive, five-year evaluation of a model program to reunify families separated by a child's placement in foster care. This collaborative endeavour between university-based researchers and Program staff used both qualitative and quantitative methods to conduct a process and outcome study of the Program. Several lessons that both administrators and evaluators can benefit from were learned during this study. First, the involvement of staff in the evaluation process is critical for a number of reasons. Furthermore, conducting a process evaluation in addition to an outcome evaluation is essential in understanding what programs do, and helps to link practice to outcomes. Finally, using standardized instruments provides a level of objectivity and allows comparison of findings with research of similar programs.

## Acknowledgements

The authors would like to thank the Program staff, their state agency partners, and the families for their time and willing participation in the study. Special thanks to Stephanie Gosteli for providing feedback on the lessons learned during this study. This project was funded by Casey Family Services, which operates as the direct service agency of the Annie E. Casey Foundation. The views expressed are those of the authors.

## Notes

1. The Program worked with families experiencing a first-time removal, which tend to be younger than families with multiple experiences with child welfare authorities.

2. Racial demographics are skewed because the Program in one site emphasized services to Hispanics using bicultural, bilingual staff, and because there was less diversity in the population served by the other site.

3. Qualitative approaches rely on listening, interviewing, recording, and reading, and bring the researcher closer to the respondent than quantitative approaches that rely on more structured 'at a distance' approaches such as standardized tests and measures and surveys (Chambers, Wedel and Rodwell 1992).

4. Program theory is an assumption about what will work to solve the problem or create the needed change. Selecting the intervention(s) implies a theoretical model that explains the link between the problem, the proposed intervention, and the expected outcomes (Pine *et al.* 2002). It can be cast as an 'if...then...' situation – for example, if parents receive parent education, then they will improve their ability to parent.

5. Goals are general statements about the direction of change the program seeks – for example, increase the rate of reunification; process objectives are the measurable activities of clients involved in the program; and outcome objectives are the measurable changes that will result from the program's interventions.

6. In addition to regular, planned feedback meetings with Program staff and administrators, three other vehicles enhanced collaboration, coordination, and communication throughout the study. The first was a research advisory committee made up of staff from all three participating agencies and the research team, which met quarterly. Second was a monthly newsletter from the research team, focusing on developments in the study and featuring success stories from the Program. A third mechanism sought to put findings to use as soon as they were available. The agency funding the study founded an agency-wide workgroup on family reunification to incorporate study findings and recommendations into its programs as they became available. As Torres, Preskill and Piontek (1997) have said, 'no aspect of evaluation is more fundamental than its use' (p.105).

7. Readers might think of a scale as reliable if it shows 150 pounds each time that weight is placed upon it; scales have validity for measuring weight, but not height.

# Part II
# Methods for Finding
# and Using Evidence

# Chapter 4

# Evaluating Complexity in Community-Based Programs

## Anita Lightburn and Chris Warren-Adamson

This chapter will review evaluating community-based programs based on complexity theory, attending to the whole system, where the interworking of all relevant agents and factors results in the sum of the program being more than the sum of the parts. To bring applications of complexity theory to life, we draw upon evaluations of community-based family centres from a cross-national perspective that has contributed to an integrative model for family centre practice (Warren-Adamson and Lightburn 2006).

## A new/old orientation to evaluation

Central characteristics in community-based services across the globe are consumer involvement and empowerment practice, with responsiveness to the realities of context. Models of practice include community development and capacity building, educational and clinical methods, and the melding of formal and informal services provision with productive collaboration and partnerships. Consistent with these community-based service characteristics are the tenets of the complexity theory paradigm and constructivist evaluation approaches that emphasize participatory and empowerment models for evaluation (Dore and Lightburn 2006).

From a complexity perspective, a community is recognized as a dynamic network of diverse agents interacting with one another and the environment to co-evolve over time (Mathews, White and Long 1999). The majority of community-based programs function with participants with diverse talent, motivation and supports. Success depends on contributions from community residents, volunteers, parents and professional staff trained in different disciplines. It is relatively easy to imagine the myriad ways that these contributors interact to meet program and participant needs. The challenge for the evaluator is to account for this complexity, as a considerable menu of program components and processes are important to consider. Our goal is to introduce ways that the complexity paradigm will assist us in more adequately building knowledge about what works for participants and staff in these programs. Complexity does not mean that evaluative methods need to be overly complex. However, the complexity paradigm does take us in new directions, with implications for understanding change and transformation. Complexity theory emphasizes the centrality of relationships; therefore, how to study process becomes key. There needs to be a developmental evaluation design with openness to emergence with respect to documenting outcomes and consideration of the unpredictable (Patton 2008).

A brief review of the tenets of the complexity paradigm is set out below, followed by methods and study design. We then draw from international family center studies emphasizing the importance of studying holism and how major processes can be identified across centers that contribute to our understanding of change. We suggest that there are integrative mechanisms important to the whole that are synergistic, contributing to all outcomes, although rarely described in practice protocols or espoused practice theory.

## Complexity theory, paradigm and assumptions

Complexity theory, a contemporary evolution from chaos theory, is the study of complex systems and is concerned with transformations – negative and positive – which arise from the fusion of biological activity. So, A + B is not AB but becomes C. Complexity theory engages the tantalizing idea that understanding the link between a transformed 'whole' and its original constituent parts is not easily made. The connections are observed and described as non-linear. *Complex* systems – such as the weather and the brain – are classic examples that are irreducible, or at least difficult to disaggregate. These complex systems can be distinguished from *complicated* systems – for example, the motor car and a laptop, which can, by and large, be reduced from their recognizable states (motor car) and then be reassembled to that same state (motor car). In this domain, therefore, complex is different from complicated.

Complexity is all but commonplace in the physical sciences, introducing us to a number of concepts which by analogy and metaphor we may employ in seeking to understand social interventions. So, for example, complexity theorists focus on the phenomena of *emergence*, generally the appearance of higher-level features of a system – for instance, a children's center is an emergent feature of its component parts. Or of *synergy*, which is from the Greek 'sunergos' – the whole is greater than the parts. The whole is different than the parts and the whole can do things which the parts cannot. The parts may be unaware or partly aware of their contribution to the whole. Synergy involves transformation, and synergy is everywhere, from the aggregation of subatomic particles to the collective endeavours of women and men (Corning 1993; Lasker and Weiss 2001). And complex systems are said to have a self-organizing capability – *autopoiesis* – and with this capability a system can change spontaneously according to or despite the intentions of the agents within the system. It means unpredictability and small changes can have big impacts (Goldspink and Kay 2003). Proponents of complexity theory challenge research and practice discourse to move beyond *reductionism* – of identifying the subsystems or features of the system whilst taking no account of the relationships between them. The point is that we have gained understanding of the parts through Newtonian science that led to identifying the atom and subatomic particles. The challenge remains to understand what happens 'in relationships' to advance understanding of change and transformation. The significance of such theoretical notions is readily recognized by practitioners in complex community programs, where there are a multitude of factors that influence daily programming and clients' experiences. A community-based program is also responsive to a context that is rarely fixed or static. In fact, the strength of community programs depends on the responsiveness to context. As Patton (2008) has pointed out, administrators and practitioners in such programs depend on information that helps them to continue to change programs in response to new conditions and insights, so development is a constant. Development intrinsically reflects the dynamics of emergence or self-organizing that influences successful service delivery (Stacey 2003).

Central tenets of complexity theory applied to evaluation are (Friedman and Israel 2008, p.695):

*Evaluation objectives*
a) To understand how change happens to improve programs.
b) To develop patterns of process that can be compared across sites.
c) To develop models for practice based on process descriptions.

*Assumptions*
- Causal relationships are primarily non-linear and complex.
- Responsiveness to contextual issues is key.
- Effective systems are iterative, evolving, changing, dynamic, always emerging.
- Therefore, relationships/connections/integrative mechanisms between agents and components are critical.
- Values, principles, culture, and goals are also important.
- Understanding systems requires focusing on relationships, recurring patterns, implicit as well as explicit rules.
- The 'system' exists in the eye of the beholder.

So when thinking about evaluating community-based family centres as complex systems of care, specific methods are consonant with these tenets of the complexity paradigm.

## Design and methods

The shift to working with the complexity paradigm has major implications for research design and methods. Basic to these designs are action research and collaborative inquiry approaches that develop understanding through description and shared reflection with stakeholders (Heron and Reason 2001; Patton 2008). The quality of the data depends on participants' involvement, since the full meaning of the data can only be known through interaction with those who contribute to – and experience – change. Complexity theorists emphasize use of new approaches, combined with traditional methods that create a picture of the whole. Therefore, use of mixed methods, structured interviews, focus groups, document reviews, thick description, and quantitative measurements all contribute to a multifaceted perspective (see, for example, the US national study of systems of care, Friedman and Israel 2008). The process for knowledge-building is iterative, recursive and adductive.

Where knowledge-building is a primary goal, a case-study design is useful to guide evaluation process (Spath and Pine, Chapter 3). A theory of change or logic model can be developed during this case-study process, as a working model that will be refined throughout the evaluation. Since one of the reasons for working with the complexity paradigm is to document and understand change, developing a theory of change will provide the means to show components, relationships, connections and integrative mechanisms between agents and components. This approach sets the stage for developing program theory. Grounded theory approaches to data analysis to inform theory construction done in collaboration with stakeholders in the community will increase the relevance of the theory (Dore and Lightburn 2006). The value of program theory has been underscored in a meta-study of prevention initiatives for families, where theory-driven programs and practice were the most effective (Small, Cooney and O'Connor 2009). An enduring concern in evaluations of family centers has been limited description of the 'black box of practice'. A theory for family center practice, based on elucidating the black box of practice, would definitely contribute to the development of these programs as viable systems of care for vulnerable families (see examples from Brandon, Chapter 11; Hess, McGowan and Botsko 2003; Warren-Adamson and Lightburn 2006).

The complexity paradigm's emphasis on the importance of relationships to emergence and transformation means that a theory of change should show how multiple relational pathways, in linear and non-linear ways, lead to desired outcomes. To achieve this, describing 'steps on the way' as short-term outcomes, captures a more sensitive stage of the change process, such as a parent learning to provide and receive mutual aid. Short-term outcomes or sensitive outcomes are discovered within a case-study process. Pathways, goals and achievement emerge that are steps on the way to longer-term goals. These short-term outcomes may not be initially apparent, yet they are important to identify as part of the evaluation story that speaks to both a parent's and a program's emergence, which is credible evidence of progress toward long-term goals (Lightburn and Warren-Adamson 2006). Undoubtedly non-linear pathways will emerge when illuminating pathways to change that will clarify the complex inter-relationships and factors that need to be understood for their part in the theory of change.

Another approach to studying complexity is agent-based modelling that offers a visual representation of a system in order to comprehend it in holistic terms. The dynamic and evolving nature of the system is illustrated through a series of 'runs' of the system, tweaking the number of agents, the levels of various agent characteristics, and environmental conditions in a series of virtual experiments (Axelrod and Tesfatsion 2006). The complexity alternative design model also depends on what Snowden and Boone (2007) have called 'Sense-Making'. Complex systems are said to develop in fractals, meaning that patterns of approximate self-similarity are recognizable at multiple scales. Storytelling has that same capacity. The aim is to look at clustering, identifying patterns and recurring themes in one story (Baskin 2004). In research methods, to make meaning through sense-making requires both qualitative and qualitative methods. This invites use, for example, of ethnography, agent-based modelling, storytelling, participatory methodologies, and companion modelling. Cognitive Edge software provides pattern analysis across a great many stories (Snowden and Boone 2007).

Ethnography traditionally studies the holistic, emergent nature of an organization or a community. Although limited resources determine what is possible, Agar (2004, 2006) advises that doing rapid ethnographies can be useful in identifying patterns based on an intense involvement with a system at different intervals, from different places in the system, representing different participants' experiences. Use of narrative process – that is, posing questions that facilitate the development of story and identification of critical incidents – can provide process detail of pathways of change, illuminating interconnections among parts of the system. In particular, rigor and clarity can be gained through the use of dialogical analysis of interventions and stories about helping experience and processes of change. Chambon (1994) describes dialogic analysis as a negotiated exchange where the exploration of the change process for parent or practitioner is expressed in their stories during the interview, conceptualized by the researcher/practitioner and responded to by the parent. In this exchange, the process of change, including clarity about goals, is co-constructed. For example, the researcher assists service providers or parents to tease out and describe the critical steps in their process. Often the process of naming what is happening contributes to ongoing change.

Participant observations with field notes that describe interactive incidents in context capture activities that may not be included in narratives. A collection of critical incidents can also be drawn from stakeholders' and providers' observations, and combined with narratives; they provide a rich source for analyzing patterns of synergistic or mediating activities (Lightburn 1992, 2002). These patterns are equally important for a theory of change, as they describe integrative factors that contribute to both short- and long-term outcomes. Integrative factors can be recurring relational patterns, such as culture or collaborative synergy. We provide examples of these patterns from family center case studies later in this chapter, illustrating their significance for program effectiveness and parents' outcomes. It is worthwhile noting that similar to this co-constructive work that contributes to change is the study of critical intervention events in the history of a community program (system) that leads to the evolution of new structures of interaction and new shared meanings elaborated on by Hawe, Shiell and Riley (2009, p.267), that has significant implications for how interventions should be evaluated. In line with this approach, companion modelling developed in France (Barreteau 2003) is an approach where a multidisciplinary research group constructs an agent-based model, tests it by playing it out with local agents, returning to the field to gather more information, then refines the model and repeats the process until reaching a satisfactory fit.

Evaluations based on complexity science in education, health and business show promise in addressing some of the enduring challenges in accounting for the complexity in community-based programs (Anderson *et al.* 2005). Lessons learned from this frontier of evaluation practice provide new ways of seeing and using data that can be equally useful. From these examples it is evident that considerable work has been progressing across disciplines in developing approaches to work with data and methods for analysis that are consistent with our growing understanding of ways to work with complexity theory and particularly suited to program evaluation in community-based family and children services.

## How to understand change based on the complexity paradigm

The following examples drawn from our review of studies of family centers in many countries illustrate the usefulness of the complexity paradigm. Specifically, we focus attention on these centers as complex adaptive systems with common integrative patterns (the culture of care, containment and synergy) that are shared by programs in different national and local contexts that suggest productive avenues for further exploration. An integrative relational pattern involves exchanges that results in influencing or shaping change and transformation. We anticipate that each of these integrative patterns share similarities that point to fundamental ways change happens in community-based programs. At the same time, the differences in these patterns can be examined in relationship to context and a family center's goals and components that can offer insight into alternative ways of providing these services that advance cross-national applications and research (Berry *et al.* 2006).

## Complex adaptive systems

First, it is important to the evaluation design and choice of method to recognize the characteristics that define community-based program as complex adaptive systems. A brief review of what is known about family centers makes the case. Family centers are lively, dynamic and organic, changing to respond to their communities, and changing with the staff and families who participate in them. Across the globe these programs have provided important resources for high-risk families that are frequently involved with the child welfare and mental health systems as early intervention, which typically includes co-located services and a network of supportive resources in the community. Case studies describe the extraordinary interplay between all components in response to changes in context, demands and resources, showing how centers are complex adaptive systems that are more than the sum of their parts (Fernandez 2006; Hess, McGowan and Botsko 2003; McMahon and Ward 2001; Munford, Sanders and Maden 2006; Palacio-Quintin 2006; Tunstill, Aldgate and Hughes 2007; Warren-Adamson 2001; Wigfall and Moss 2001).

A snapshot of family centers provides a sense of how a family's experience or the staff's experience is not based on any one aspect of the center, but rather how the whole works. Complex relationships flourish: staff with administration, staff with families and service providers in the community, families with staff and other families and natural helpers. These centers support and nurture therapeutic alliances, collective learning and collaborative action, partnerships, friendships, mentoring and mutual aid, all through multi-faceted relationships to meet families' needs and ensure safety (Tunstill *et al.* 2007; Canavan, Dolan and Pinkerton 2000; Hess *et al.* 2003; Lightburn 2002; Warren-Adamson 2001).

Centers are characterized by holism – the fusion of activity which is both practical and emotional, embraces short- and long-term interventions, and melds individual, group, family and community approaches. Participant and staff experience engagement in a host of collaborations within the center and broader community – for example, education programs, job training, health services and child welfare protective services. Centers offer complex, multi-purpose resources and opportunity for involvement which is accessed simply and often informally. Anchored in community, centers occupy a physical and symbolic presence as community beacons which add to the social glue of neighbourhoods because they are a unique integrative resource that brings together educational and therapeutic approaches with support, and thereby build community.

These centers are seen as a valuable system of care supporting early child development and protection while attending to the complex needs of parents (Tunstill *et al.* 2007; Warren-Adamson and Lightburn 2006). As complex systems of care, centers function as a hub for integrating a range of services based on a set of values and practices which influences the development of a network of provision to meet individual family needs. Designation as a system of care is a significant characterization of family centers that has critical policy and practice implications and equally critical implications for choice of evaluation methods, including the right theoretical paradigm to guide use. An approach to evaluation which only considers a program component in the center, such as parent training, reduces the focus, whereas consideration given to how the whole family center functions with the parenting training component shows a realistic picture of how the whole influences engagement, motivation, retention and achievement. In all there is a complicated set of relational factors contributing to a parent's increased competence (Rose *et al.* 2009).

## Integrative patterns that influence change
### The culture of care
Although therapeutic relationships and specific interventions are often viewed as the major means by which a parent's development is supported and enhanced, such relationships and interventions appear to be only part of the picture. There are other dimensions of center life, such as the culture of care. The ways the community works together to support staff and families is a major process that forms a distinct pattern of how people relate, influencing outcomes. The culture of care includes how staff members work with each other and how they are supported

by administration, as well as how families relate to each other and to staff. Each family experiences the culture of the center; that is, they are recipients of the culture of care (Brandon, Chapter 11; Munford, Sanders and Maden, Chapter 13). There is evidence of contented, mixed, long-term staff groups which has a noted influence on the centers' functioning (Brandon 2006; Fernandez 2004; Hess *et al.* 2003; McMahon and Ward 2001; Pithouse *et al.* 2000, 2001; Smith 1996). At the same time, each family is a participant in this culture; each family is influenced by, and influences, the norms and rituals through involvement in activities and contributions to the daily life. The centers' accepting, welcoming culture is noted as a factor which influences engagement. Program components and center activities support the nurturance and protection of children. The culture mitigates the stigma experienced by parents who have had difficulty meeting their mental health needs in outpatient and agency programs or in working with protective service agencies. For example, parents offer 'glowing' testimony of satisfaction – often in circumstances where parents face major stigma and have been subject to the compulsory powers of the state (Tunstill *et al.* 2007). Of further import is how safety is a shared concern, influencing respectful ways of relating inside the center and advocacy for strong boundaries regarding personal care and means for protection in the neighbourhood and in the family home, including value-based practice where family strengths are promoted through mutual aid, active roles in decision-making and citizenship in the center. A powerful reflection of this culture is families' description of centers as 'their' family, a safe haven they can depend on as a place of retreat and acceptance.

The quality of the culture of care is integral to most outcomes: staff retention, staff satisfaction and development; parents' engagement, satisfaction, and motivation to keep taking on challenges that lead to educational achievements, employment, restored relationships and more competent parenting. This brief review introduces the centrality of culture to the whole family center as a integrative mechanism for the internal workings of the center and its program, as well as partnerships and collaborations within the community. A measure for the culture of care in these programs would advance both practice and program accountability.

## Containment

Containment is another construct that describes an integrative pattern of relationships integral to outcomes (Ruch 2004; Warren-Adamson 2001). It is a concept that is associated with ongoing positive development. As we have suggested elsewhere (Warren-Adamson and Lightburn 2006), the idea of containment in this sense implies a holding environment that supports *and* challenges. Containment, a familiar descriptor from object relations theory, has been used by parents in describing how centers are helpful when life is overwhelming (Brandon 2006; Fernandez 2006; McMahon and Ward 2001; Warren-Adamson 2001). As these researchers point out, the idea of containment belongs to a number of respected theoretical traditions that offer a valued point of reference, particularly when connected with the well-developed understanding of a therapeutic milieu that has been related to family center programs that emphasize community (Warren-Adamson and Lightburn 2006). For example, drawing from Haigh's (1999) description of the therapeutic milieu, there is a focus on relationships that foster attachment and belonging, where 'staying connected' is critical to families joining and long-term engagement. In order for families to stay connected, the center needs to offer the same quality of *containment* (and holding) that Haigh emphasizes as a 'sensuous and nurturing environment', with a 'play space' alongside rules, boundaries and structure. It seems logical that consideration should be given to these two relational patterns involving complex integrative processes that are generative for families and center staff. The quality containment that families need has been shown to require both time (more than crisis intervention and brief treatment affords), as well as a range of nurturing relationships supported by experienced practitioners, anchored in a geographical place, with nurturing that includes structure, boundaries and support. As with the culture of care, further study of containment as an integrative process would lead to a measure useful in program evaluations to further models of practice that would have cross-national relevance.

## Synergy

It is helpful to think about synergy in family centers as another vital integrative process, where the 'sum is more than the sum of the parts'. This synergy has been frequently characterized by researchers as working in a more or less robust fashion (Hess *et al.* 2003; Lightburn and Kemp 1994; Warren-Adamson 2001). We hypothesize that synergy is catalytic, influencing the capacity of the family center to meet family and staff needs. Synergistic processes include network facilitation that has been identified as a central social support in community-based, family-focused practice. Synergy, like network facilitation, will benefit from conceptual clarity regarding the form of intervention on the part of practitioners and evaluators. Negotiation, influencing, supporting, advocating, mediating and collaborating are all synergistic activities that occur between service providers, staff and parents, administration and staff and so on. These synergistic activities happen in a complex web of relationships that influences, enables and shapes the outcomes of central relationships for parents, helping them manage risk while promoting their resilience. Identifying how synergy works and measuring synergy is a substantive means for representing these instrumental processes. Lasker and Weiss (2001, 2003) have developed a measure of synergy based on successful collaborative community health partnerships across the United States. Such a measure reflects the basic tenets of complexity theory, as there are multiple factors which come together through communication, decision-making, participation and contributions to creative problem-solving that depend on collaboration to bring different resource, perspectives and talents together. Again, this pattern of collaboration has been identified as a major contributor to successful family center programs that functions as a connector and is reported to enhance motivation and result in solutions to difficult problems. Further study of this process and its role as an integrator would further explanations of process that contribute to transformation and change, and consequently desired outcomes for programs and the families they serve.

## The future

There is much to be learned from cross-national comparisons of community-based programs, such as family centers, that seek to mediate the stressors, negative life experiences, risks and challenges facing families. Such centers have unique potential as a system of care and constitute a valuable resource in child welfare, mental health and education. To further our understanding of community-based programs, such as family centers, we advocate for a complexity paradigm as a basis for evaluation, leading to more useful ways of understanding change through identifying patterns of relationships and process in the whole system, as well as pathways for participants that we consider steps on the way or sensitive outcomes that lead to desired long-term outcomes.

Adopting a complexity perspective as a paradigm to examine complex community programmes has a number of implications for the researcher and practitioner/researcher. It requires an elision of 'voice', grounded theory and (new) theory (Patton 2008). For example, the 'black box' of practice in family centers needs further description. It is also important to attend to the mediating factors (integrative) that 'support or augment' specific interventions and combinations of interventions identified in such a black box, within a theory of change. We hope that synergy, a mediating process, which we believe facilitates change and represents the creative energy of the center, will be considered in future evaluations. We look forward to a new generation of community-based, complex adaptive systems evaluations, developing outcome measures that are sensitive to change and valuable indicators for stakeholders and practitioners alike. There is no shortage of complexity-inspired researchers internationally, with whom we should make alliances without delay.

# Chapter 5

# Approaches to Evaluation in Services for Families and Children

Cinzia Canali, Anthony N. Maluccio
and Tiziano Vecchiato

The chapter considers the relationship between evidence-based research and professional choices. The level of evidence and the strength of recommendations are discussed in order to define a new paradigm for representing the problems of real populations and their severity. The authors present the research available on this theme and explore the possibility of defining models that consider the multidimensional nature of problems. This design is at present part of an Italian study, the main elements of which will be described in this chapter.

## Risk assessment and placement prevention

Many difficulties influencing the development of children are related to family problems that prevent parents providing children with the care they need. There are many issues that can contribute to family difficulties, including change in status and income of the remaining parent following death, divorce or separation, low parenting skills, conflicts between the parents, psychological problems. For a long time, the response to such difficulties was to take the young children away from their homes and place them in out-of-home care. Numerous Italian studies from the mid-1960s and subsequent decades provide evidence on the failure of large institutions to provide rehabilitation, education and individualised care (Moro 1991, 2006; Palmonari 2008; Provincia di Torino 1984).

Since the 1980s, the Italian legislation has promoted the creation of regional services aimed at supporting families and helping children return to their birth families. Thanks to this effort, residential institutions began to be closed down in 2001. The consequent reduction in the number of children separated from their families has been the focus of various Italian research reports (Belotti 2009; Palareti, Berti and Bastianoni 2006). This was not just an Italian trend; other countries also followed in the same direction (Berry 1997; Colton, Roberts and Williams 2002; Durning 1992, 2007; Fablet 1993, 2005; Fraser, Pecora and Haapala 1991; Knorth 2008; Lindsey, Martin and Doh 2002; Maluccio and Whittaker 2002; Moran, Ghate and Van der Merwe 2004; Utting, Monteiro and Ghate 2007).

Recent discussions in Europe are based on the assumption of the need to search for new solutions to guarantee a more effective protection for children who live in at-risk situations, where abandonment, maladjustment and severe marginalisation often co-exist. It is also widely acknowledged that indiscriminate out-of-home placements are to be avoided. It is, in fact, necessary to justify if the choices made for an individual child are appropriate to meet the child's needs, and whether the decision improves or worsens the outcome for the child (Aldgate *et al.* 2006; Aldgate, Rose and McIntosh 2007; Biehal 2005; Van Bueren 2008; Gutbrandsson 2006; Mazzucchelli 2008; Stradling and MacNeil 2007; Thoburn 2007; Zeira *et al.* 2008).

Children and families who ask for help are best served by being evaluated using instruments that result in a comprehensive assessment and understanding of strengths and difficulties. An all-round understanding is achieved when various dimensions are considered together: organic and functional, cognitive and behavioural, social–environmental, relational and value-based. Thus, it is necessary to bear in mind that each professional can provide a valuable contribution, with instruments that are appropriate to the problems to be tackled, and are necessary to help throw light on the relationship between needs and outcomes. An emphasis on diagnosing the needs and on the instruments to manage them in an appropriate way must not pre-empt, or push into second place, the importance of appropriate care. Research must look at these problems as a whole transforming evaluation of need into decision-making and action for providing effective help.

At a recent international workshop (Oxford, July 2009) dealing with this issue, experts from different continents shared ideas on the relevance of these processes and on how to make them effective. Even before this meeting, on different occasions, the International Association for Outcome-Based Evaluation and Research on Family and Children's Services had looked at this problem (Berry *et al.* 2006; Biehal 2008; Canali, Vecchiato and Whittaker 2008; Maluccio, Canali and Vecchiato 2002; McAuley, Pecora and Whittaker 2009; Vecchiato, Maluccio and Canali 2002; Zeira *et al.* 2008). The need to seek new professional and service solutions has been strengthened by these debates, with a view to guaranteeing a more effective protection for children who are exposed to at-risk situations. Also, evaluation on the basis of qualitative and quantitative assessments, not only of the changes but also of the conditions that made them possible, is much needed. Questions on how to achieve this are pressing and must take into account those works that in recent years have dealt with evidence-based approaches.

## Evidence and professional choices

In past years, a debate has developed about how professional choices can be based on evidence-based criteria. The debate first began in the health sector and then spread into the social service sector (Gambrill and Shlonsky 2000; Donzelli and Sghedoni 1998; Liberati 2005; Roberts and Yeager 2006; Rosen and Proctor 2003; Sackett *et al.* 2000; Straus *et al.* 2005). The question is not an easy one. It has traditionally been dealt with through the dialogue between 'science and practice wisdom', combining the recommendations provided by scientific research with daily experience. Professional wisdom is called upon to integrate ethical dilemmas and practical knowledge in order to pursue 'the best possible outcomes'.

However, many recommendations from traditional research favour the analysis of the problems and devote less attention to how to solve them. They are more interested in the 'what' and the 'why' and less generous on the 'what to do'. It is not by chance that diagnostic capacity has grown substantially, also thanks to technological development, but the ability to treat and care has not necessarily improved at the same rate. Indeed, many complain of a growing gap between the knowledge based on diagnostic techniques and the outcomes of an effective treatment, not only in the field of evidence-based medicine (Grimshaw and Russell

1993; Grahame-Smith 1995; Horwitz 1996; Hampton 1997; Littell 2005; MacDonald 2003; Sacks *et al.* 1996; Straus and McAlister 2000; Timmermans and Mauck 2005).

The treatment in real-life conditions is different from experimental conditions. It is not at all automatic and taken for granted that the results obtained in theory may provide an answer for those in direct contact with real people, their needs and their problems. The needs of children and families who daily ask the professionals for tangible help are real-life ones. In other words, the usefulness of research findings for real-life situations can be up for debate.

If the problems of research are seen only in terms of experimental design, there is reason to be worried. The question of 'what to do' to achieve effective results applies to every treatment or intervention, because in every single case one should consider: Is what I am doing effective? Does it match the individual's needs? How likely is it that the intervention I have chosen will produce useful results? Am I sure that it does not induce further suffering? Integrity and good faith are not sufficient to reduce the seriousness of this question. Good practice wisdom calls for a breadth of responsibility that not all health and social professionals can handle. Many results achieved with randomised studies are poorly applicable to these situations. In fact, many of them are based on restricted inclusion criteria that limit the external validity of findings.

If a different way of approaching complex problems is seen as the answer, we should support it all the more for use in evaluation of social services. This would lead us to accept an elitist approach with a small number of rules and sophisticated treatments for a selected few, relegating research to a simplified and artificial world far from daily experience.

## Level of evidence and strength of recommendations

The strength of scientific recommendations, achieved through experimental practice, can be ranked, but this ranking is usually defined on the basis of the nature and the complexity of the experimental design and not nearly enough on the basis of the multifactorial nature of the problem we are facing. As an example, Table 5.1 refers to some models, including the SIGN method (Phillips *et al.* 2001; Scottish Intercollegiate Guideline Network 2008).

TABLE 5.1 Level of evidence and strength of recommendations: examples

| SCOTTISH INTERCOLLEGIATE GUIDELINES NETWORK | CANADIAN TASK FORCE/US PREVENTIVE TASK FORCE | US AGENCY FOR HEALTHCARE RESEARCH AND QUALITY | | |
|---|---|---|---|---|
| *Level of evidence* | | | | |
| 1++ | A | Ia | ↑ | High evidence |
| 1+ | B | Ib | | |
| 1- | C | IIa | | |
| 2++ | D | IIb | | |
| 2+ | E | III | | |
| 2- | | IV | | |
| 3 | | | | |
| 4 | | | | Low evidence |
| *Strength of recommendations* | | | | |
| A | I | A (Ia, Ib) | ↑ | High strength |
| B | II-1 | B (IIa, IIb, III) | | |
| C | II-2 | C (IV) | | |
| D | II-3 | | | |
| Good Practice Point GPP | III | | | Low strength |

*Source:* Adapted with permission from the Scottish Intercollegiate Guidelines Network, Edinburgh

As suggested by Table 5.1, the strength of recommendation (for example, grade D) relates to the level of the evidence (for example, level 3 or 4) on which the recommendation is based. If a recommendation depends on the opinion of an expert (or a consensus group), it is placed in the lower position. This category, that we can call 'points of view', could include many recommendations approved by public authorities with formal mandates or adopted by private organisations.

For years, the Italian national guideline programme (PNLG) for health has been the main basis for actions carried out by the Agency for Regional Health Services. The PNLG has favoured research based on consensus groups. On closer consideration, the added 'strength' (according to the opinion of the experts) depends almost entirely on the way recommendations are adopted, based on normative provision. However, the binding nature of an administrative act is no guarantee as to the reliability of its contents. One result of using consensus groups, however, is certain: more uniform professional behaviour, fewer available options and a less discretional approach to choices. For contexts in which variable and discretional approaches prevail, this can be a good result.

For the service users, however, this does not necessarily entail a greater likelihood of getting help, but for those faced with similar problems, at least there is a greater transparency in the answers they can expect from the service. Additionally, for a services manager, transparency is conducive to better processes in government and improved monitoring. Taking this step towards transparency, however, does not go far enough to become an evaluation of the outcomes. It is a sort of preamble towards evaluation that is undeniably useful but still not enough. It helps the governance of services but is not enough to support professional outcome-based choices. The latter, by nature, are concerned with the relationship between needs and effectiveness. Any evaluation, therefore, is done from within this relationship, considering the impact of any actions on the original need.

## Contributions from the experimental approach

The idea that the experimental approach can contribute to dealing with complex problems is challenged by some who consider it an approach distant from real life, alien to the care of the person and oversimplifying the variables to be considered (Dagenais *et al.* 2008; Vecchiato 2007; Zeira *et al.* 2008). There is some evidence in support of this idea, given that the medical science is seriously reconsidering the relationship between real-life practice and practice research. Practice research selects components of problems, reducing their real extent. Nevertheless, the problem remains. The road is not as easy as it may seem, for at least one reason: the dissemination of knowledge today is more accessible and, paradoxically, less useable.

Scientific dissemination is too often aimed at a dialogue and debate between researchers, instead of supporting those who work in the field (Neve and McNamara 2007). Sometimes the dissemination is based on deliberate publicity, often fuelled by economic interests and/or the interests of research centres to sustain their image. The line between interests and evidence is not clearly visible. The consequence is that debate does not produce a better service to people – that is, to the health and social professionals who need information to help them in their jobs and the users of their services who need to be able to choose between the possible options. There is, then, a compelling reason to reconsider the equation between the strength of recommendations and the level of effectiveness. To summarise: results obtained in a social and relational vacuum run the risk of being proxies without any substance, not being rooted in facts, and therefore of dubious efficacy.

The debate tells us that 'crystal clear' certainty does not always have adequate confirmation in real life. It can be reasonably claimed that numerous clinical trials are, at times, of limited value, in particular when they are financed by, for example, manufacturers of drugs or technology, for whom experimentation is useful only in as much as it allows their products to be sold on the market. Once the benefits and side effects are out in the open, the problem, in the eyes of the manufacturers, appears to be resolved (Grimshaw and Russell 1993; Grahame-Smith 1995; Horwitz 1996; Hampton 1997; Sacks *et al.* 1996; Straus and McAlister 2000; Timmermans and Mauck 2005). Experimentations in social services have less commercial relevance, but this does not imply that such research is independent of political or other influences (Littell 2005; MacDonald 2003).

Recently some experimental studies have suggested a different direction to the traditional experimental design (Vecchiato 2007; Whittaker 2008). Instead of selecting a small number of variables, which are incapable of representing the dimensions of the problem to be confronted, they require more variables to be included, so as to avoid the risks of oversimplification. This results in an experimental design that is more complex and demanding to sustain. But it also means that the greater the number of variables, the less 'artificial' the experimental design will be.

These considerations may discourage research in this direction because it lacks commercial value. However, the research would be of value for the final recipients of the results, the people with needs, who are often disempowered (Dagenais *et al.* 2008). The consequence of the perceived lack of esteem for more complex research methodologies by the experimentalists is to condemn the research done in real-life contexts to be systematically underestimated, to be chronically short of funds, and to be an 'orphan', as is often the case for problems that do not 'pay back'. This is a shame because it means that the results achieved with restricted trial designs will necessarily be of less validity in terms of their applicability in real-world situations.

Do we have to take the favouring of experimental design totally for granted, or do we need to develop a new paradigm? By what right does an experimental design, that is technically a means, become an end that everyone has to work by? By what right can the design of a study that includes many variables be considered as valid as a 'simple' experimental design? Those who adopt a simplifying attitude in their work place themselves in a rarified position that is separate from the social and scientific value of the results that they produce. Is it sensible to guarantee a competitive advantage that has so little connection with outcomes?

## Beyond the paradigm

Having in mind the contents of Table 5.1, it is possible to draw a figure in which the vertical axis (level of evidence or nature of the design) is a nominal scale that goes from 4 to 1++ (Figure 5.1). It represents the current hierarchy of the level of evidence, as described in Table 5.1. Nothing prevents us from associating a second axis, set up from an ordinal scale, that describes the ability to focus on the target population using a number of variables that appropriately explain it (we call it 'number of variables').

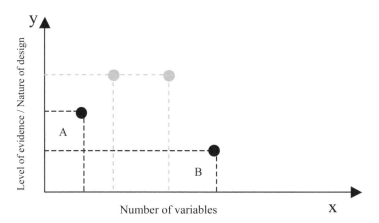

FIGURE 5.1 Value and number of variables

A small number of variables apparently depicts a 'virtual' population that is not the one we are interested in (area A in Figure 5.1). If we increase the number of variables (that is, the ability to focus on the target population), we have more likelihood of depicting the multidimensional characteristics of a real population (area B in Figure 5.1). The paradox is that the area B, which includes more variables and has more likelihood of helping more people in need, obtains a low level of 'evidence' of the traditional kind.

Should we not question how valuable a complexity index (characterising a multifactorial study) may be? Should we not question the value of a complexity index that does not depend *only* on the vertical axis (the degree of complexity of the study) but also on the horizontal axis (the number and the nature of the variables that the study can manage).

If the debate concerning the value of evidence and the failure of evidence-based medicine to keep its promise can help overcome simplistic views, the benefits will be considerable. The greater advantages will favour those in greater need of help from the welfare services. Without the constraints mentioned above, research will be freer but also subject to exacting rules and therefore more likely to provide results. For example, it will be authorised to venture into almost unchartered territories, where so far it has not been recommended to make forays because of mainstream certainties. Relying only on such certainties ends up obstructing the development of knowledge.

Therefore, we suggest that the 'science and practice wisdom' relationship could be reinforced by a systematic use of the best knowledge without becoming enslaved to it, but verifying the hoped-for results with those actually achieved. The proposed revision of the criteria regarding the level of evidence can therefore represent a necessary basis for opening new areas of research and experimentation, to achieve a better service to people and to advance outcome-based practice.

## Searching new solutions: an Italian case study

The RISC study is an Italian-based initiative aimed at assessing the risk of unnecessary placement in out-of-home care for children living with their parents. The study combines issues related to the 'evaluation of needs' and the 'evaluation of effectiveness'. The question is: has what we have done been really effective? It is the same question that the Ministry of Welfare asked when promoting the project and when appointing the Fondazione Zancan to carry it out.

In order to ask the question, a multi-site research project was designed in six regions in Italy, with a target and a control group in each region. Selection of the participants (children living in multiple-problem families at risk of out-of-home placement) was done using the inclusion criteria set out in the grid in Figure 5.2.

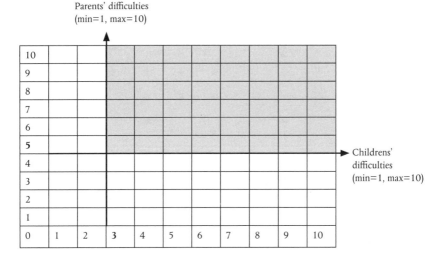

FIGURE 5.2 Grid for the pre-assessment of parents' and children's difficulties

Using this grid, professionals were asked to respond to two questions using a 1–10 scale, where 1 indicates minimum difficulties and 10 maximum difficulties: (1) 'In your opinion (or opinions when dealing with a multi-professional evaluation), what is the index for parental inadequacy and inappropriate relationships within the family?' (2) 'In your opinion, what is the degree of suffering (abandonment, maltreatment, etc.) that the child/adolescent is experiencing?' As can be seen in Figure 5.2, families where parents scored 5 and higher and children scored 3 and higher were included in the study. Professionals were aware that this was not yet a comprehensive assessment of the needs and risks, but it did provide inclusion criteria and prepared the successive analysis of the severity of the situation as a basis for defining the individualised project. For example, Figure 5.3 illustrates the preliminary assessment done by professionals in one region: 12 families were eligible to be included in the study.

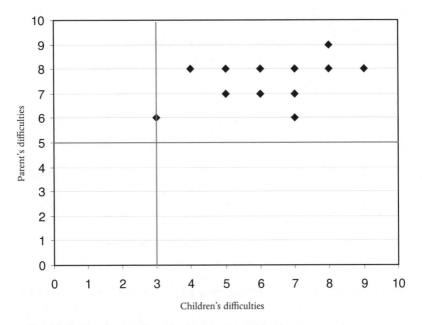

FIGURE 5.3 Pre-assessment by workers in one region

Once included in the study, the children at risk living in these families were assessed using a methodology called the polar scheme (Figure 5.4). This methodology helps professionals to visualise a diagram divided into three domains of children's lives: the cognitive and behavioural domain, the physical and functional domain, the socio-environmental domain. Each domain has rays that represent rating scales, which may vary depending on the subject under investigation. The outer part of the circle corresponds to the individual's best condition (strength and resources), the centre to the worst (need and risk). The gap between the outer part of the circle, corresponding to the best condition, and the line indicating the actual recorded scores can be easily identified: sharing the polar scheme, professionals are forced to look at vulnerabilities but also strengths. It can be used at different levels of analysis (at single-case level or at group level, as in Figure 5.3).

Our research highlighted that the polar scheme is a flexible and powerful tool because it helps to handle complex needs and multidimensional outcomes. It facilitates communication among professionals working in different settings and services, allowing a fertile dialogue. Information is exchanged in real time and professionals access a central database (that is accessible to all authorised professionals). This facilitates the cooperation and integration among different disciplines. Another important element is the possibility of measuring changes over time, comparing and overlapping different polar schemes. The polar scheme helps also to communicate with service users, to share outcomes and motivate children and families' involvement in the care process.

## Discussion

The average profile of two groups of at-risk children living in different regions is illustrated in Figure 5.4. One is represented by a line (line-group) and the other by a coloured area (grey-group). In this way, it is possible to compare the profile of the children living in two different regions. Children were assessed using nine measurement tools: two pertaining to the cognitive and behavioral domain (min-cog, min-app), three to the functional domain (min-org, min-psi, min-aut) and four to the socio-environmental domain (min-soc, min-aff, sr, lpsvr).

All tools starting with 'min' – which stands for 'minor' – pertain to an instrument called 'Scale for observing the child' (Canali and Rigon 2002). The scale is composed of seven areas that are subdivided in 36 sub-areas and related items. Two additional tools are the scale of responsibility (sr) and the level of protection of life space (lpsvr). The scale of responsibility measures the capacity to share responsibility in respect to the problem of the person and his/her family. The level of protection of life space measures the ability of action and collaboration in building the personalised plan. Both tools are based on the 'map of subjects and resources', which considers the persons who can be involved in the personalised project. These persons are placed in the four squares of the map. The position in the map depends on the level of responsibility that each person takes/shows in the problem. The 'subjects' are the ones who have a wider and deeper degree of responsibility, not only about things to do but also in the search for solutions; the 'resources' can take specific responsibility and are therefore helpful in the fulfilment of certain objectives (Canali and Vecchiato 2010). All these tools are represented as rays of the polar scheme.

**TABLE 5.2 List of measurement tools**

| TOOL | DESCRIPTION |
|---|---|
| *Cognitive and behavioral domain* | |
| Min-cog (cognitive functions) | Cognitive functions, communication, memory and attention, practical abilities |
| Min-app (learning functions) | Reading and writing, mathematics, painting, other learning capacities |
| *Functional domain* | |
| Min-org (physical functions) | Neuromuscular functions, sensorial functions |
| Min-psi (psycho-motor functions) | Orientation in space and time, motor development, facial expressions, body perception, look |
| Min-aut (autonomies) | Nutrition, clothing, hygiene, task performance |
| *Socio-environmental domain* | |
| Min-soc (social functions) | Relationships with schoolmates, family relationships, relationships in school and in the social environment |
| Min-aff (ties) | Emotional tie with mother, emotional tie with father, mother, self-awareness, affection |
| Sr | Measures the capacity to share responsibility in respect to the problem of the person and his/her family |
| Lpsvr | Measures the ability of action and collaboration in building the personalised plan |

Going back to Figure 5.4, in respect of the line-group, on average, the grey-group presents a more severe situation because it concentrates towards the centre of the diagram, mainly within the social and environmental domain.

■ grey-group ☐ line-group

**FIGURE 5.4 Average comparison among two groups of children**

Along with the scores obtained using the nine scales, other variables were considered in relation to demographic characteristics, interventions (for example, the quantity of help, costs and the organisation of interventions) and expected and obtained results. This generates a list of variables to be controlled that are more than those usually recommended in traditionally designed studies.

This study involves 120 children and their families (60 in the control group and 60 in the experimental group). As suggested in Table 5.1, the results could be ranked as a 2+ that would lead to a grade of recommendations 'C'.

The analysis of data relating to the first measurement (time $T_0$) highlights a positive consistency between the capacity of the pre-assessment grid to select cases to be included in the study and the results of a more detailed needs assessment. The higher risk is concentrated in the socio-environmental domain, in particular on the rays *sr* and *lpsv* (Canali and Vecchiato 2010; Vecchiato *et al.* 2009; Zeira *et al.* 2008). The polar scheme obtained as a multidimensional index represents the severity profile: such a profile represents the risk for each group at one time (in this case $T_0$), before developing an individualised care plan.

The diagram generated with the polar scheme facilitates a multidimensional perspective. The priorities and risks that need to be contrasted can be better identified. Also, it is possible to think about the results that could be obtained through an individualised care plan, that combines the assessment of needs and the decisions related to expected and obtained results. The outcome measurement can be represented in two ways: (1) in terms of different measures on polar schemes in different times, and (2) comparing the expected and obtained results after implementing the individualised care plan.

The scores related to need and outcome evaluation deriving from the comparison of polar schemes facilitate a comprehensive evaluation of changes over time.

In our study we are now associating the level of evidence, the related strength of the recommendation and also the number of variables to be considered (Figure 5.5). The aim is to explore the likelihood of the experimental findings having a positive impact on the target population – in this study that is around the 1 per cent of the children.

Findings from similar research (Vecchiato, Canali and Innocenti 2009; Vecchiato and Mazzini 2008) highlight that the experimental design is not difficult to manage although the number of variables to control is quite high. The key element is represented by the collaboration between professionals and researchers who share responsibilities and solutions oriented to reach the expected outcomes in real life. Also, the strength of recommendations can be defined from grade 'C' as in the traditional paradigm and as $f[x,y,z]$, that is as a function of the three proposed axes as suggested in this section.

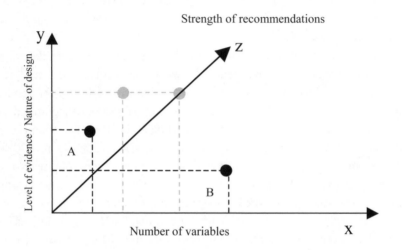

**FIGURE 5.5 Level of evidence, strength of recommendations and number of variables**

Children at risk of being removed from their families represent a specific population with multiple needs. The more effective solutions that are outcome-based we find, the better we can reduce their sufferings and improve their well-being.

# Chapter 6

# Understanding the Nature, Structure and Context of Services in Family Support Centers

Marianne Berry and Colleen Reed

Family support centers, also called community centers, are increasing in number around the world, as a means of providing preventive and supportive services to individuals, children and families in their own localities (or neighborhoods or environments). National policies in many countries are moving away from formalized services provided by large-scale bureaucracies toward social and supportive services provided in more natural settings, influenced and shaped by the members of the communities in which they reside (Manalo and Meezan 2000; Warren-Adamson 2001; Wise 2003). Given this devolution, there is increasing interest in these centers, prompting multiple studies and evaluations with promising results (Gardner 1998; Warren-Adamson 2002a).

In the USA, the development of family support centers is associated with early settlement house work (Warren-Adamson 2001). Community-based family centers emerged as a service and resource aimed at preventing individual and family problems. Their development reflects ties with social work traditions including the emphasis on the context in which individuals and families live, attention to development and the life span, and ongoing efforts to establish and enrich community partnerships (Leon 1999). Internationally, the advent of family support centers coincided with a shift in attention from a strict child and crisis focus to a wider focus on families and community-based supports geared toward strengthening and assisting families (Manalo and Meezan 2000; Warren-Adamson 2002a).

Contemporary descriptions around the world point to family support centers as an exciting service delivery setting where families are often engaged in holistic, strengths-based, empowerment-focused work (Batavick 1997; Warren-Adamson 2001). In these descriptions, the uniqueness of the center as the setting for the delivery of helping services is often highlighted. In particular, family support centers are known for serving a variety of people within a community or neighborhood context and for engaging in service provision with flexibility (Warren-Adamson 2001).

Family support centers provide a multitude of services: financial assistance, educational programs, clinical interventions, and information and referral. These services are aimed at achieving a variety of outcomes: prevention of child abuse and neglect, promotion of community health and mental health, family preservation, positive youth development, academic success and enhancement, vocational enrichment, increased community participation, and enhanced social networks. Clearly, support and promotion of well-being represent a positive addition to the community landscape, giving families access to resources that might have been previously non-existent or more formalized and restrictive. Evaluations and research within these programs have shown them to be effective in preventing child maltreatment, promoting family health and integrity, preventing juvenile delinquency, and providing benefits through other community improvements (Gardner 1998).

A cursory review of these programs illuminates significant differences in ways in which family support centers operate. They serve a variety of populations, focus on distinct problems or service goals, and occupy different spaces in the continuum of service designed to ensure the welfare of children and families. Why might these differences matter? These centers operate in the community context and the culture in which they were built and are based, and which shape the structure and nature of the services delivered as well as the outcomes sought. Therefore, care must be taken to understand these contexts and the structure and nature of services, if one seeks to translate their benefits to other communities or cultures.

Research focusing on family support centers is timely. The dynamic helping processes occurring in these settings and their outcomes has yet to be adequately understood. Much remains to be learned about ways in which individuals and families experience family support center services. Making the research processes more transparent and conducting research with more specific descriptions is a first step to increasing understanding about these centers, particularly in light of the interest in importing center models from one country to another.

Increasingly, scholars are mapping the array of family support centers, their consumers and services (Manalo and Meezan 2000). The developing body of literature on family support centers consists primarily of reports of program evaluations and a growing number of research studies that examine program outcomes (Warren-Adamson 2001). If we are to learn important lessons from research in – and evaluations of – these centers, we need to know that we are comparing similar entities that have similar goals.

Sadly, most of these studies focus on unique, unitary centers in a specific community with particular target populations and goals. Most fail to provide detailed descriptions of theoretical orientations, service consumers, intervention elements, or service delivery methods. These studies are limited in their ability to follow program outcomes over time, use multiple methodologies or samples of participants, and encounter other threats to research rigor. These research gaps largely prohibit the application of knowledge about a particular center to other center settings, and particularly in regard to other countries. The benefits and pitfalls of family support center services may be overlooked if not described accurately and evaluated clearly (Manalo and Meezan 2000).

In this chapter we present an organizational scheme to guide the conceptualization and operationalization of family support center research, aiming to increase awareness of the multiple and critical layers and connections regarding the centers and the services they provide. We focus on three layers of the essential elements of family support centers: their nature, their structure, and their contexts. By examining and explicating these essential elements, we can help develop outcome research in this field and provide cross-national comparisons that are much more meaningful and useful to program development and understanding across national boundaries.

## Nature, structure, and context

The organizational scheme is represented as a set of nested constructs (Figure 6.1). The core concept is the *nature* of family support in a family support center, which is comprised of the underlying philosophies, values, theory and orientation to social problems and service delivery that come together to form the ideological/philosophical foundation of a center. The *structure* of a family support center refers to the means and methods by which services are delivered. Surrounding these, the delivery of services occurs in multiple *contexts* including the agency, community, and national and political contexts (Warren-Adamson 2001). These three layers of a family support center, which are interdependent, together define and illuminate the identity and purpose of the center.

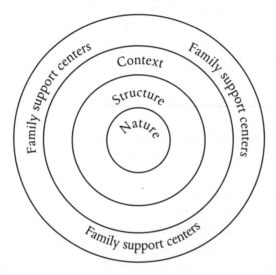

FIGURE 6.1 Nested constructs of nature, structure, and context of family support centers

## *The nature of a family support center*

The work of family support centers varies, reflecting differing undergirding philosophies, values, program missions, and theoretical orientations – essential elements of the *nature* of family support center services (Berry, Bussey and Cash 2001). As explained by Manalo and Meezan (2000) and Wise (2003), attention to these elements contributes information relevant to better understanding the following:

- One center in light of others or distinguishing between types of centers.

- The fidelity with which a center's services reflect its philosophy, mission, and theoretical orientation.

- The match between the undergirding nature of a center, its services, and outcomes.

Similarly, philosophy, mission, values, and theory influence the research itself, and are reflected in methodological choices and execution techniques. In essence, the lens with which researchers approach family support centers is influenced by philosophy and values. For example, adherents of a constructivist perspective may approach their research with attention to narratives and thick descriptions, perhaps using ethnography as their research method. Furthermore, values may guide the inclusion or exclusion of particular constituent voices. The nature of family support center research may be revealed, for example, in decisions about who helps formulate important definitions, such as determining the desired outcomes (Gardner 1998). Some scholars stress that a family support center value is enacted with the inclusion of multiple voices and the participation of consumers, asserting that they enliven research (Eayrs and Jones 1992; Fernandez 2004).

In the same way that the program mission informs a family support center's approaches to services, the mission or objective of inquiry guides study design. Researchers may seek to provide in-depth descriptions of center processes, identify factors associated with family well-being, test theory-based hypotheses, and examine consumer satisfaction (De'Ath 1989). The aims of evaluation research include tests of intervention efficacy, between-center comparisons, and examinations of service outcomes.

Greater transparency, moreover, can be achieved in the evaluation of outcomes. This can be accomplished with greater clarity about the extent to which desired outcomes have been specified in service provision, and through detailed reporting of unanticipated or unintended outcomes linked with interventions (Berry, Bussey and Cash 2001; Fernandez 2004). Kamerman and Kahn (1995) suggest that research both defines and measures the quality of services. Some scholars suggest that the complex nature of family support services may be best examined with the use of mixed-methods research (Batavick 1997; Batchelor, Gould and Wright 1999; Fernandez 2004). Indeed, the ways in which interventions are determined to be effective (e.g. observable changes in behaviour and/or demonstrated mastery of skills) and the selected measurement frame (e.g. point in time, stage of intervention process, product or process outcome) are critical aspects of the nature of family support center research (Berry *et al.* 2001; Dawson and Berry 2002; Gardner 1998; Lightburn and Warren-Adamson, Chapter 4). Table 6.1 identifies the key research approaches and questions yet to be explicated in studies of family support centers, which will elucidate the *nature* of the work.

TABLE 6.1 Researching the nature of family support centers

| ESSENTIAL ELEMENTS | RESEARCH BEST PRACTICES | QUESTIONS FOR THE RESEARCHER |
|---|---|---|
| Undergirding program philosophy, its origin, and influence<br><br>Theoretical orientation | Examining the extent to which the philosophy and theoretical orientation drive interventions and the identification of outcomes | What is the focus of the work of the family support center? How do program outcomes tie back to program goals? |
| Program mission, goals, and objectives<br><br>Identification of the service need or social problem | Conducting investigations of intervention efficacy grounded in theory and testing theoretical assumptions<br><br>Matching research methodology with philosophy and values | What values are apparent in the organization/ interventions/outcomes?<br><br>What philosophical stances and values inform the research inquiry? How do they relate to the program values? |

## *The structure of a family support center*

Guided by axiological and epistemological underpinnings, interventions, resources, and helping approaches comprise the *structure* of family support center services. Given the multiplicity of center aims, it is not surprising that the actual services and the methods of delivery vary widely. Still, services that mirror a holistic view of individuals and families are a hallmark of family support centers. Examinations of service delivery methods and processes complement research focused on service components and represent efforts to better understand consumers' experiences of engaging in center services (Gardner 1998). Attention to the structure of family support center services will increase understanding about:

- the units of attention of interventions and types of services
- service delivery approaches (e.g. intervention models, treatment formats)

- service delivery pathways, including patterns of service use and providers of center service.

Family support center staff members, diverse themselves, provide an array of services that include resource brokering, therapeutic interventions, family supports, and community education. Lightburn and Kemp (1994) specify that services available in – and pertaining to – the center are distinct from those that are oriented toward enhancing the lives of consumers in their natural contexts. Services can be categorized into two streams: those focused on the individual and those with a wider aim – for example, family, group, neighbourhood, or community (Gardner 1998; Warren 1997). These services are formulated to best meet the needs of numerous consumer constituencies, including children, adults, individuals, families, groups, neighbourhoods, and communities (Chow 1999).

Driven by professional commitment to service and professional curiosity about 'what works,' service outcomes are often the focus of family support centre structure research. Research on family support centre structure also has great relevance for examining the fit among theory, specific service elements, and the methods of inquiry employed in the research itself (Berry *et al.* 2001; DeVoe and Kantor 2002). Such structure-focused research can heighten our understanding about the change processes associated with work in these unique settings by attending not only to service elements and grand outcomes but also to sensitive outcomes. Seeking understanding of both process and product outcomes ensures concordance among the scope of research, measurements, and methods with the service consumer/participant(s) (DeVoe and Kantor 2002). For example, an inquiry solely examining adults' parenting behaviours will not best explain the efficacy of a community-focused intervention aimed at improving family safety. Explicitly including attention to both the grand and sensitive outcomes in the scope of research facilitates this examination, as emphasized by Lightburn and Warren-Adamson (Chapter 4).

The selection of appropriate research approaches and techniques relates directly to the specificity and accuracy of the findings. When employing quantitative methods, the quality of research is influenced by the use of reliable and valid measures and the observation of the conventions of statistical testing procedures. In qualitative studies, the demonstration of trustworthiness and credibility of findings and the maintenance of a detailed research audit trail are approaches that contribute to the quality of the research (Batavick 1997; Berry *et al.* 2001; DeVoe and Kantor 2002). Examples of this include selecting statistical tests that fit the data elements and for which assumptions can be met and/or choosing a fitting qualitative approach (e.g. focus groups, semi-structured interviews, in-depth participation/observations, or case-study).

Employing appropriate types of measurement bolsters research on community service structure. This includes the use of measures with the highest level of precision possible and which best represent the operationalization of center program objectives (Berry *et al.* 2001; DeVoe and Kantor 2002). Similar specificity about service delivery and its links with research inquiries is necessary to understand better the structure of center services, service use patterns, and service-related changes that take place over time. For example, initiating research at the outset of service engagement is critical for outcomes evaluation (Berry *et al.* 2001). Periodic research assessments can be used to shape service-planning decisions (Fernandez 2004). Service-use patterns can be explicated in terms of amounts, frequency, and duration of services (Berry *et al.* 2001; DeVoe and Kantor 2002). Without this information, practitioners may be quick to adopt strategies reported to be successful without understanding that the successful outcomes could have been tied to a specific pattern of application.

Inadequate descriptions of interventions contribute to muddled findings and hamper learning lessons from other centers' successes or challenges (Gardner 1998). Providing clear descriptions of the processes by which methodological and technical choices are made can contribute to greater transparency in center research. Further explication of the structure of community services and research is detailed in Table 6.2.

TABLE 6.2 Researching the structure of family support centers

| ESSENTIAL ELEMENTS | RESEARCH BEST PRACTICES | QUESTIONS FOR THE RESEARCHER |
|---|---|---|
| Types of family support center services | Situate the research within the larger body of literature | What is the concordance between the nature and structure of services (e.g. do the interventions match the identified theoretical orientation)? |
| The locus of services (center, partner agency, external agency) | Use measurements with the highest degree of specificity, validity, and reliability | |
| Referral and/or enrollment processes | Take multiple measurements | How does staff training relate to the agency mission and the service? |
| Intervention methods | Include multiple voices | Are the types of services and methods of delivery known as 'best practices' in the field? |
| Service providers | Pursue rigorous methods to ensure that the data are credible and trustworthy | |
| Patterns of service use | | |
| | Identify and report 'sensitive' or 'process outcomes' in addition to ultimate outcomes | What kinds of error pose threats to this research? |

## *The context of a family support center*

To this point, we have examined the nature and structure of family support center services. Both exist within a dynamic set of contexts that range from the individual or personal to the larger political arena. Better understanding of these contexts sheds light on the workings of a particular family support center in a particular community (Munford, Sanders and Maden, Chapter 14). Beyond that, however, knowledge of the contextual systems in and around which a family support center operates can help facilitate cross-national discussions about the workings of these unique service settings. The inclusion of such contexts may expand understanding about:

- consumers' life experiences (separate from their family support center participation)
- the workings of the family support center as a social service agency
- the interface between the center and the neighbourhood in which it is located

- the ways in which centre operations reflect the larger national and political environment.

Attending to *context* in family support center research includes considering spheres of influence that have bearing on service delivery, consumer engagement, center structures, service outcomes, and more. Examining the contexts of consumers is necessarily part of providing a detailed description of the sample (Berry *et al.* 2001). Culturally responsive research reflects attention to consumers' cultural backgrounds. It employs linguistically appropriate research tools and culturally sensitive approaches with research participants; in addition, it cultivates the consideration of culturally specific strengths and coping strategies used by consumers.

At a time when family support centers proliferate, and emerging center service research points to their potential for helping individuals and families, a greater understanding of centres as a unique family service setting is also needed. Kamerman and Kahn (1995) suggest that an opportunity exists to understand further how quality services come together, by examining the center's staffing, total service population, workload, and salaries. The scope of research into the agency context includes examining the center as an entity itself; agency policies, programming, and services offered; and administration and funding structures (Batavick 1997; Batchelor *et al.* 1999).

Family support centers and consumers who engage in their services are commonly situated in a neighbourhood context, so that services are indeed community-based (Leon 1999). Research about the neighbourhood context can provide important information regarding ways the centers partner with other agencies, the extent to which they are embedded in the community social service arena, and the fit between a center's presence and community culture. For example, research on the neighbourhood context may identify the extent to which consumers are representative of the community population in an effort to reach adequately vulnerable community members (Batchelor *et al.* 1999).

On a larger contextual level, research into the funding streams of family support centers parallels concomitant inquiries into the cost and affordability of center services and into the fee and financing structures as a whole (Kamerman and Kahn 1995). Research on family support center context can be influenced by service and research funders that may, for example, request the use of specific research techniques or particular kinds of data. Alternately, research may wield influence itself in that the identification of successful interventive strategies may support requests for future program funding (Batavick 1997).

Contextual influences, moreover, can range from narrow to broad in scope. Although impossible to achieve fully, family support center research could ideally account for environmental influences (DeVoe and Kantor 2002). National forecasts such as mortality rates, employment trends, or an upcoming surge in the elder population all have bearing on family support centers and their consumer constituencies. Awareness of these potential contextual influences can help researchers to use tools from demography, sociology, and political science, thus monitoring social changes to plan better for future services (Leon 1999).

Understanding social values as they shape relevant definitions also is critical to engaging in – and interpreting – family support center research. In particular, social norms, expectations, and definitions regarding family life, childhood, the seeking and provision of help, and the role of community all play an important role in the way the environmental context interfaces with center dynamics. This issue is especially relevant in cross-national research. For example, in a particular country cultural norms regarding childbirth and infant care may be operationalized in one setting as the responsibility of the whole of society. In that country, policies and services may reflect this value with widely available, low-cost, non-stigmatizing publicly funded infant and child care. Another country, however, may place social value on parent/family-based child care and an overarching social expectation of personal responsibility. In the latter case, it is likely that there would be fewer child care options available – their use may be attached to some stigma – and publicly funded child care settings would likely have low status as compared to those paid for privately. Similarly, societal values can be powerfully enacted in times of economic stress and determine the nexus of helping services (Wise 2003).

Perhaps more broadly, or at least beyond national entities, the *environmental context* of human services shapes family support center research (see Figure 6.4). The dearth of studies that employ experimental or quasi-experimental designs to examine center outcomes may reflect a position that children and families in need should not wait for available services. Perhaps it even portends the use of current, more holistic methodologies and the development of new ones. In sum, in the environmental context of family support center research itself, the network of consumers, providers researchers, and other stakeholders, there is a call to carry research findings to the implications level and to disseminate findings in ways that enliven these centers (Gardner 1998). Table 6.3 points to critical features of this very process.

TABLE 6.3 **Researching the context of family support centers**

| ESSENTIAL ELEMENTS | RESEARCH BEST PRACTICES | QUESTIONS FOR THE RESEARCHER |
|---|---|---|
| Consumer identity, memberships, and affiliations | Using culturally responsive research tools and techniques | In what ways do the identity, memberships, and affiliations of the research influence the research? |
| Organizational structure of the agency including staffing (training, work patterns, and supervision) and governance | Formulating inquiries that extend beyond singular narrow foci | What is the role of supervision in the center? |
| Natural environment and physical plant | Privileging multiple ways of knowing | How might the multiple relevant systems and the research itself be impacted by institutionalized oppression? |
| Funding sources and processes | Conducting research at multiple system levels and examining the interplay of elements at varied levels | In what ways might context explain or confound the research findings? |
| Center auspices and collaborations | Examining the relationships with collaborating agencies (division of labour, shared goals, funding) | How might the use of different research methodologies change the texture of the inquiry? |
| Neighborhood and community characteristics and interactions | Disseminating research findings and seeking feedback from the wider community of scholars | How will the research findings be made available and relevant to policy makers? |
| Influential national, state, and local policies | | |

# Conclusion

The variations in approaches to family support center research point to a need for sophisticated holistic methodologies and multidimensional techniques, so as to capture the complex nature of services in such a dynamic context (DeVoe and Kantor 2002). With much to be gained from comparisons among family support centers, no single research approach emerges as the singular most efficacious strategy with which to guide inquiry. In-depth ethnographic and qualitative methods can yield rich descriptions of the nature, structure, and contexts of a particular center. Still, that approach is best suited for a stand-alone description rather than for use in cross-national comparisons. Conversely, effect sizes of rigorous intervention outcomes may be compared across centers to determine the most efficacious practices. This approach, too, falls short, with frequent insufficient detail about the nature, structure, and contexts of the centers. In those cases, even attempts to control for program and research differences with nested statistical models will be insufficient.

With the proposed multidimensional methodologies, expanded scope of outcomes, technological and travel advances, and increasingly global economies, the time is right to embark on cross-national inquiries into the workings of family support centers. Cross-national research elevates the potential to improve family support centers. Generally, it facilitates investigation of the influences that shape practice across vastly different settings and provides opportunities to learn from successful centers (Hetherington and Piquardt 2001). Specifically, cross-national research can illuminate previously overlooked relationships or shake free conventional thinking toward new creative possibilities. As such, the benefits of cross-national research will likely be realized in the planning and development of family support center services as well as in the further development of human services providers and researchers in this time of growing global connectedness. Social work is well positioned to step forward in this realm (Caragata and Sanchez 2002).

# Chapter 7

# In Their Own Words
## Alumni of Foster Care Talk about Preparation for Independent Living

Anne Nicoll, Kate Holmes Thompson, Peter J. Pecora,
Catherine Roller White, Kirk O'Brien and Arron K. Fain

## Foster care in the United States

Current foster care practices and programs in the United States are governed by an intricate set of policies and laws at the federal, state, and local levels (Curtis, Grady and Kendall 1999; Lindsey 2004; Pew Commission on Children in Foster Care 2004). According to federal standards, public child welfare agencies need to achieve a small but critical set of outcomes in three broad outcome domains: child safety, child permanence, and child and family well-being (American Humane Association *et al.* 1998; Pecora *et al.* 2010; US Department of Health and Human Services 2003).

Unless a state implements the provisions of the Fostering Connections federal law, foster youth are supported by state or private foster care agencies typically until they are 18 years of age. At this point, foster youth are expected to be able to live on their own, independent from state or private funding. In federal fiscal year (FFY) 2008, over 29,000 older youth emancipated to adulthood from a foster care setting

(US Department of Health and Human Services 2009b; US Department of Health and Human Services 2009c).

Increasingly, youth perspectives on the services they received while in out-of-home care are being addressed (Bernstein 2000; Curran and Pecora 1999; Hormuth 2001). This chapter summarizes qualitative data collected from interviews with foster care alumni about their preparation for independent living. The data collected from these alumni were part of two studies of these alumni (Casey Family Programs and Foster Care Alumni of America 2008; Foster Care Alumni of America 2009).

## Transition of youth from foster care to independent living

In FFY 2008, 29,000 older youth emancipated to adulthood from a foster care setting (US Department of Health and Human Services 2009a; US Department of Health and Human Services 2009b).

The transition to independent living is a challenging time; youth leave a structured living situation, lose the financial support of an overseeing agency, and must begin to create a life of self-sufficiency. The time, preceding this decidedly significant life change, is a crucial opportunity for independent living skills development as well as maturation of self-confidence and decision-making competencies. Providing the necessary independent living skills services is vital to youth's success in independent living. Service providers can improve service delivery by careful early life skills assessment (Nollan *et al.* 2000) and incorporating youth perspectives and recommendations regarding transition services.

## Youth needs

According to the US Department of Health and Human Services (DHHS), positive youth development requires that adolescents are provided services and opportunities to develop 'a sense of competence, usefulness, belonging, and empowerment.'[1] For older youth (and especially for children who have survived child abuse and neglect and who have been placed in foster care), necessary supports include stable living situations; healthy friends of a similar age; stable school enrollment and attendance; educational skills remediation; dental, medical, and vision care; mental health services; adults who provide a consistent positive force in their lives; and networks of social support (Casey Family Programs 2001, 2003).[2]

Life skills preparation is also very important, covering such areas as daily living tasks, self-care, social development, career development, work and study skills, money management, self-determination, and self-advocacy. Housing and community resources are also necessary. One alumna of foster care summarized the key factors very succinctly:

> Outcomes for emancipated youth are mixed at best. While many emancipated youth succeed at living independently, earn post-secondary degrees, and find employment, others experience homelessness, educational and financial difficulties (resulting in the need for public assistance), and difficulty adjusting to living on their own. (Courtney *et al.* 2007; Pecora *et al.* 2010)

Youth transitioning from foster care to independent living often lack these tangible and intangible personal development resources that lead to successful independent living (Kerman, Wildfire and Barth 2002).[3] In a recent study of alumni of foster care, less than half reported having $250 in cash when they left care and less than a quarter had dishes and utensils; these items can be a proxy for independent living preparedness and have been found to be associated with positive adult outcomes (Pecora *et al.* 2005; Pecora *et al.* 2010). A study of Wisconsin youth transitioning from out-of-home care revealed that less than three in four had received training in financial management, parenting, or use of community resources (Courtney, Piliavin and Grogan-Kaylor 1995). Some youth who have left care resort to illegal activities in order to earn money, including selling drugs or exchanging sex for money (Reilly 2003).

## Transition services

Transition services help youth develop the competencies necessary to manage the day-to-day details of their lives. Youth who participate in structured independent living services are more likely to be employed for over a year and to be more satisfied with life than youth who are not involved in these services (Cook, Fleishman and Grimes 1991; Cook 1994). Youth who participate in transition services report that personal financial management – for example, understanding how credit can be built and abused, developing personal budgets, and evaluating purchase decisions – was extremely valuable as were specific skill classes – for example, looking for housing, comparison shopping, and self-care skills development (McMillen *et al.* 1997). Furthermore, one recent study found that broad life skills preparation and provision of concrete resources for transition to adulthood are linked with positive adult functioning (Pecora *et al.* 2005; Pecora *et al.* 2010).

The stress of transitioning from foster care to independent living may be mitigated by the presence of social support (Cheever and Hardin 1999; Dubow and Tisak 1989). However, research on social support experienced by transitioning youth indicates that some youth do not have anyone in their lives to turn to for positive social support (Barth 1990; Cook *et al.* 1991). Positive supportive relationships from foster families, birth families, adults, and peers can provide a stable foundation for emancipating youth during challenging and uncertain periods of transition. Adolescents who perceive family support may be more likely to utilize this support in dealing with stressful events rather than resort to avoidance strategies – that is, behavioural efforts to avoid dealing or confronting a stressful situation (Bal *et al.* 2003).

## Method

Two linked studies of foster care alumni provided information about youth's experience with transition services. For both studies, interviews were conducted between September 2000 and January 2002.

The Casey National Foster Care Alumni Study focused on the nature of services and outcomes of alumni served by Casey Family Programs offices from 1966 to 1998. All 1087 alumni in this sample were between the ages of 20 and 51 at the time of the interview. The Northwest Foster Care Alumni Study evaluated the intermediate and long-term effects of family foster care on adult outcomes. The investigation focused on adults maltreated as children who were served by Casey Family Programs; Washington Department of Social and Health Services, Children's Administration, Division of Children and Family Services (CA/DCFS); or Oregon Department of Human Services; Children, Adults and Families, Community Human Services (Oregon DHS, CAF, and CHS) between 1988 and 1998. Within this sample, 479 were interviewed. They ranged in age between 20 and 33 years. Participants from both studies had been placed with a foster family from that agency for at least 12 months, and had been discharged from foster care for at least 12 months prior to the interview.

Each study had a high response rate; response rates for the National and Northwest studies were 73.2 percent (refusal rate: 3.8%) and

75.7 percent (refusal rate: 5.5%), respectively. Additional information is available on the Casey Family Programs website (www.casey.org).

Due to a small overlap among the samples, interviews were conducted with the 1455 alumni in person or on the phone by professionally trained interviewers from the University of Michigan Survey Research Center (SRC). The interview protocol contained several standardized scales and covered a variety of relevant outcome areas. Open-ended questions focused on perceptions of agency services, helpfulness of foster parents, suggested improvements for the transition to independent living, and assistance from people or services.

The data reported here are from questions related to alumni's preparation for transition to independent living. Themes and findings are summarized from two open-ended questions: (1) Could anything have been done to improve the move from foster care to independent living? (2) If you could tell children coming into the foster care agency anything right now, what would you tell them?

## Data analysis approach

An independent evaluator (the primacy author of this chapter) conducted the initial qualitative analysis on the open-ended questions. Microsoft Excel 2000 (© Microsoft Corporation) was used to review, sort, and develop preliminary categories used in the qualitative analysis. NUD*IST software provided a structure by which the initial descriptive data were coded, indexed, and grouped. Alumni quotes included here were selected by the independent evaluator. They are illustrative of the themes that were identified and represent the range of experiences (both positive and negative) that alumni chose to reflect on in answering these two questions.

## Results

### Experiences with transitioning to independent living

Alumni reports of the transition to independent living were various and often quite disparate. Responses ranged from descriptions of a smooth transition with generous support, to transitions that were completely unexpected or without any preparation. Responses were categorized into three primary types: (1) abrupt transitions, (2) poorly prepared transitions, and (3) smooth transitions. Reports of abrupt transitions sometimes also included examples of the lack of skills or resources to make the transition to independent living successfully.

### ABRUPT TRANSITIONS

Abrupt transitions were identified by their unexpected, unforeseen, or sudden nature.

> I graduated one day and my graduation present was a pair of boots and backpack. I took that as a message to leave.

> The day I turned 18, my foster parents packed my bags and put me out. I didn't know what to do or where to go. As a result, I never finished high school. I only had three months left, but I couldn't do it.

> It was so abrupt when they kicked me out. I was 19 and I had been through alcohol treatment twice and they kicked me out when I was in the hospital for a suicide attempt. I got kicked out of the house when they found out I was going to be a daddy.

### POORLY PREPARED TRANSITIONS

Alumni reported a wide range of levels of preparedness in making their transition. They described lacking the necessary skills to cope with independent life. Some alumni noted that they had poorly developed skills in decision-making processes, did not have basic living resources, or were unfamiliar with how to rent apartments or manage their financial situations.

> I probably wasn't ready for the world and not knowing resources. I didn't feel comfortable making my own decision[s] as I had always discussed everything with my foster mother or social worker.

> They could have prepared me a heck of a lot better, make sure I had what I needed – bed, clothes, dishes, make sure I knew how to handle my finances, make sure I had the right skills to get a job, and given me a better chance to continue my education as well.

> She could have taught me how to save money, to rent a house. It would have been helpful if she taught me basic things like how to unplug a toilet or buy and prepare food.

SMOOTH TRANSITIONS

In contrast, other alumni had distinctly different and decidedly more positive experiences in transitioning to independent living. These alumni recounted that they did not feel rushed to leave their families and were well equipped with the skills and resources they needed to begin their independent life. Alumni who indicated they were prepared to live on their own said they had skills and knowledge in managing money and keeping a home, had gained information from independent living skills classes, and had been provided basic items necessary to live independently. Some of these alumni also felt they embarked on living independently with the support of their birth or foster family.

> I think the way [my foster parents] transitioned me was great – it was a really smooth transition. In the months before I moved out, [my foster mother] taught me things about money, housework, and independent living skills – they still supported me for months. I wasn't ready to move out when I was 18 and they let me live there for a little while longer.

> Casey [Family Programs] makes sure they give you living support classes before they let you go. They take you grocery shopping and do all that.

> I was fortunate enough to be with my aunt and uncle to make that transition much easier. I think in a sense that I always had their support. I could call them. I knew they were my connection, once I moved into a dorm on my own. It was nice for me.

### Non-utilization of transition services

Not all of the alumni who were interviewed were able to utilize transition services. Some had exited foster care at an early age; others ran away before they could take advantage of the services; and some alumni went straight from foster care to correctional facilities. An additional group of alumni said they simply chose not to use the services that were available to them.

> The programs were available to me. I just didn't take advantage of it. I was too stubborn and thick-headed. Now I ask why I didn't do it. Most of my motivation was to get out in any way, shape, or form.

I was nine when I started. Job Corps gave me a way out… You feel you are big enough to be on your own.

They had all those resources, but I didn't use them or need them because I joined the military but I knew people who did use the resources and I heard nothing but good things about it.

I just left. I didn't give them a chance to help me.

I went straight from a foster home to jail.

## Alumni recommendations for improving transition services

*Create a longer timeline for transitioning*

One theme from alumni responses was a suggestion to increase the period of time youth are involved in transition services. Alumni noted that offering independent living skills development programs during a person's eighteenth year does not provide enough time to facilitate full maturation of these skills or development of the self-confidence necessary for successful transition. Many alumni observed that it is important to provide a strong foundation for each of the many dimensions to independent living, such as financial management, securing housing, and self-care skills.

[Provide] classes from the agency, beginning when I'm 16 or 17, until you move out, actually classes until maybe 21. Still have a social worker until age 21.

You need to prepare better. Casey [Family Programs] should start at 15 toward 18 moving you to independence. Explain to me how to fill applications, deal with situations, regular life, medical doctors, money, pay bills, and manage money.

Kids really need courses early on, much earlier counseling on the resources available and how to manage your life. Why do parents not tell kids about living until they're 17? It's criminal! Teach a person at 14 how to manage money, legal things, contracts, insurance, interest rates, credit, consequences, pre-credit counseling.

They had the idea of a 'transition week' intended as a middle step of transition, but one week is not enough to smooth out going to big university from a little school and when you're the first in your family to go to college. It was a drastic change from home and a little school and friends to NOTHING.

### Increase opportunities to practice living independently

Another theme that emerged was related to increased opportunity to practice living independently in an environment that promotes independent decision-making, but also provides resources for youth to draw upon when needed. Many alumni said they exited foster care and were left to fend completely for themselves without a safety net, social support, or an opportunity to safely make the mistakes associated with personal development.

> Make transitions to independent living an experiential process where youth are living independently with a safety net of support.

> I was somewhat prepared, but there was no safety net. They said they'd tried to help and then it was up to me, which was the hard way. I wish there was a safety net; most families have that. They need to have better support.

> It would be good to have transition apartments to work with independent living, like a practice run. Have mentoring on living – especially after Casey just takes care of everything. And kids getting to interact together often – they share a lot of issues they can't talk to anybody about.

### Utilize transitional housing

The option to utilize transitional housing was identified as a potential bridge to successful independent living transition. Alumni pointed out that it is a momentous life change to move from living in a home with adults to being completely self-sufficient. Safe, supportive, and temporary living arrangements would provide the structure necessary for emancipating youth to progress away from restrictive living environments.

> It would be good to have transition apartments to work with independent living, like a practice run – mentoring on living.

> Maybe make a program during junior year, like during the summer when kids aren't in school, and make them live on their own. Have orientations with college students.

> There should have been a half-way house where you could get prepared for living on your own. For example, buy groceries and doing some living on your own.

### Provide more information about the 'real world'

Another theme that emerged addressed their limited understanding about what they could expect when living in the 'real world' of independent living. Alumni wanted to be told how much money they should expect to budget for living expenses and that the process for renting an apartment involved more than signing a few papers.

> I wish we were forewarned about the cost of living and rent. Have us put money to the side for maybe two years.

> I think if they set up a way to teach you how to deal with the real world, if you took someone and said, 'This is what a rental agreement looks like and this is what these things mean.' Or, 'This is how you save' and went through entire stuff. It would be boring but later you'd realize, 'Gosh that helped' – to be able to call up the electric company, the telephone company – calling these people isn't easy if you've not done it before, or only a couple of times.

### Learning from older youth and alumni

A final theme suggested the value of learning from those who had previously exited foster care. Several alumni suggested that youth currently in foster care would benefit from being able to talk to emancipated youth about their experiences with transition.

> Maybe if some other Casey kids came back and talked to us. But they should have more training and teen nights when foster kids get together and there are guest speakers who can teach them about what's going to be happening after foster care.

## Advice to youth currently in foster care

Alumni were asked to provide advice they might have for youth who are currently in foster care. Primary themes found in the interviews addressed educational skill development, a focus on the future after emancipating from foster care, and taking advantage of available resources while still in foster care.

### Education-related

Alumni encouraged youth in care to complete their education and to use the resources offered to them. The context of these suggestions indicates that many alumni believe that higher education is key to providing a better life to alumni.

> Accept all help they can get to further their education. It's too big of a decision to have to make right at 18, especially when Casey will fund it, and I thought I was beyond help, couldn't do it. The older you get, the more you realize what you missed. Remember that whatever you do now, you will grow up and become part of society and what you do determines how you'll come out of it.

> Get an education. Strive for what you want in life. Don't give up because of your childhood situation.

> No matter how hard it is, try to finish college because later on you'll wish you had.

### Future-oriented

Alumni reminded foster care youth to think about the future and stay focused on where they are headed when they emancipate from foster care.

> Prepare for the future. It's not all always going to be like this. You have to think about tomorrow. Otherwise you'll be stuck in this cycle. There are better things out there but you have to prepare for tomorrow. And be a little selfish to survive. It's too bad you don't learn to be a little selfish before you move around a few times. There is nobody there to support you when you are going through this. Deal with one day at a time.

Think about your future. Look at the picture. Try to find a picture in your life – meaning the things that you want to do or want to have, no matter how crazy it might seem. Just look at the picture and start taking a little piece to get there.

### *Take full advantage of the available resources*
Finally, some alumni addressed a better understanding they had of the resources that had been available to them and the importance of taking advantage of those resources in a timely manner.

> Do any extra programs that they can get their hands on. Utilize all resources the foster agency has.

> Kids coming into Casey: it's okay to take advantage of Casey because that's what it's for.

> Utilize the resources available, it can give you a head start when it's time to do something for yourself.

## Implications for practice
The use of qualitative methods provides agencies with the opportunity to hear from the perspective of the clients, in their own words, what worked and did not work about their transition to adulthood and independent living. These questions allow us to better understand what the discrepancies were that existed between the services that youth received and what they reported they needed to support themselves once they left care.

Alumni were able to articulate that the duration of independent living skills development is a concern; many did not feel they have enough time to practice and gain proficiency in personal financial management, securing housing, utilizing resources at their disposal, and developing robust self-care skills.

In addition, a gap in services was identified for those alumni exiting from foster care prematurely due to incarceration or running away. These youth are missing critical skill development opportunities and will experience more challenges in independent living than those who remain in care and participate in independent living skills development.

As such, collaboration with service providers (e.g. homeless shelters, juvenile justice agencies, and child welfare agencies) is one possible strategy to ensure youth have an opportunity to utilize independent living skills services.

For those who opt not to participate in transition services at the time the resources were offered (reporting being too stubborn or not ready), these responses support a case for providing multiple opportunities for youth to participate in transition services, even after they have aged out of foster care. The use of alumni as resources themselves for helping foster care youth transition into independent living also emerged as a potentially valuable asset for services providers.

The use of a personal interview methodology that allows us to hear from clients, in their own words, the experiences they've had with the independent living services allows agencies the opportunity to listen and adapt those services to better meet the needs of future clients.

Finally, the use of the research literature can also help us identify areas that were not mentioned frequently enough by participants to have warranted a separate theme, but are critical to include as a part of service delivery. These include access to medical and mental health treatment for the mental health disorders with which many alumni are struggling – disorders such as post-traumatic stress, depression, social phobia, and generalized anxiety (Pecora *et al.* 2005).

The transition to independent living is a challenging time for most people, whether the transition is from the home of a birth family or the child welfare system. The experience can be even more stressful and difficult when a youth lacks self-care skills, independent living competencies, or a safety net of people and resources to turn to for assistance. Providing independent living skills development opportunities to youth emancipating from foster care is a vital service which can prepare youth to live independently. As indicated by alumni's experiences with transition and suggestions for improvement, the timing of transition services, content of classes, opportunity to practice skills, and availability of a support network are critically important.

## Notes

1.  See the 'Positive Youth Development' fact sheet on the US Department of Health and Human Services, Administration for Children and Families website at www.ncfy.com/pyd/factsheet.htm.

2.  For more information on youth development see the Search Institute website at www.search-institute.org.

3.  For more information about training materials that case workers and foster parents are using to teach life skills, see www.caseylifeskills.org.

# Chapter 8

# The Challenge of Using Administrative Data in Cross-National Evaluations of Services for Children in Out-of-Home Care

June Thoburn

The global transfer of social science knowledge is having an impact on child welfare policies as well as related areas such as anti-poverty strategies. This chapter arises from a strand of work undertaken at the University of East Anglia's Centre for Research on the Child and Family (Dickens *et al.* 2007; Schofield *et al.* 2007; Thoburn 2007). It explores the potential use of data that are routinely collected for administrative purposes to provide context for cross-national learning and practice developments. In earlier publications the complexities of cross-national comparisons of child welfare outcomes have been explored using the example of adoption as a route out of care (Thoburn 2002, 2003). The chapter looks more broadly at administrative data on general populations of children in out-of-home care.

The chapter begins with a summary of lessons learned from earlier work using administrative data on a large population of children in out-of-home care in England, to illustrate how such data can provide the necessary context for policy makers looking at initiatives in other states or countries in order to improve outcomes for their vulnerable children (Dickens *et al.* 2007). It goes on to use administrative data from 28 jurisdictions in 14 countries to identify what can be learned from cross-national comparisons of administrative statistics, and also to identify the potential pitfalls of making inappropriate comparisons (Thoburn 2007, 2010).

## Re-working administrative data to assist service planning in England

On 31 March 2001, there were 58,900 children looked after in out-of-home care by the 150 councils with social services responsibilities in England (an average rate of 53 per 10,000 children). The number and rate has since risen to just under 60,000 in 2008 (54 per 10,000), despite the efforts of central government and local authorities to reduce them through better targeted preventative services, improved assessment and decision-making processes, and a drive to get more looked after children adopted (Department of Health 1998b, 1999, 2000a). There was, however, a reduction in the number of children who *started* to be looked after away from home each year, down from 32,500 in 1994–95 (23 per 10,000 children) to 23,000 in 2001–02 (21 per 10,000 children) (National Statistics and Department of Health 2003; National Statistics and Department for Children Schools and Families 2009). This indicates, over the period studies, that the increase in the *in-care* population was in large part explained by children staying longer in care rather than by increased need for the service.

A research study undertaken by the author and colleagues (Dickens *et al.* 2007) was commissioned by senior managers in 24 English local authorities who were concerned to understand the reasons why authorities with similar populations had very different rates of children coming into public care, and why children in care experienced different patterns of placement and lengths of stay. It was based on a study of the 11,630 children looked after on 31 March 2001 by these 24 authorities (20% of the children in care in England on that date). There were three parts to the study.

The first part consisted of a secondary statistical analysis of the key publicly available data about looked-after children throughout England, including variations in performance on key indicators and government performance targets. The second part involved a more detailed analysis of a data set known as the SSDA903 made available by central government for the 24 participating authorities (National Statistics and Department of Health 2002, 2003; National Statistics and Department for Children, Schools and Families 2009). This annually-produced data set provides fairly basic (anonymised) data at the level of the individual child, for a one-third sample of all the children in public care at any time since 1998, and all children starting to be looked after and ceasing to be looked after each year (after 2004 data have been collected on the full sample of care entrants). Data are available on age, sex and ethnicity of the children; date and age of each episode of out-of-home care; broad reason for coming into care; legal status; placement and any change of placement, including length of time in each placement and frequency of moves.

The third part of the study comprised two questionnaire surveys seeking more detailed information from the social workers of two sub-groups of children: those who entered care between October 2000 and March 2001 and those who had been continuously in care for four years or more as of 31 March 2001. The questionnaires enabled the research team to complement the information in the SSDA903 return with additional 'softer' information – for example, fuller details on the child's needs and the care plan and the various factors affecting the implementation or change of the original care plan. As well as being a significant proportion of the 150 councils, the 24 authorities were considered a representative sample because they included a wide range of organisational and demographic features. The group ranged from densely populated urban areas, some with substantial ethnic minority populations, to geographically large, rural authorities with very heavily white British populations. There were some very deprived areas and others that were much more affluent, although even the more affluent ones had pockets of deprivation.

The national data sets and the reworking of data from the one-third sample pointed up the extent of local variation and some possible reasons for it. Just over 25,100 children started a period in care in England during the year ending March 2001 (National Statistics and Department of Health 2003) with a national average rate of 23 starts per 10,000 English children aged 0–18. However, the national average disguised substantial variations between authorities, with a range of 9 to 78 per 10,000. Amongst the 24 authorities there were just over 5000 starts during the 2000–01 year, and the rate per 10,000 children ranged from 11 to 41.

Interviews with senior managers and data from the survey of recent entrants and those placed for four or more years indicated that various factors accounted for these differences. In other words, start rates and in-care rates are the result of a complex interaction of a wide range of factors, important amongst which is the organisational and professional culture within local departments (Dickens *et al.* 2007; Schofield *et al.* 2007).

## Underlying need as an explanatory variable

As anticipated, differences in levels of need and deprivation in the authorities played the biggest part in explaining differences. We used the government's Standard Spending Assessment (SSA) for children's social services for 2000–01 as a measure of relative need in the 24 local authorities. By dividing each authority's SSA for children's services for 2000–01 by the size of its child population, we arrived at a figure for SSA per head for our study year. Though not without its faults, this approach provided a workable tool for comparing the deprivation factors among the 24 authorities.

The two authorities with the lowest levels of need also had the lowest rate of starts, confirming that underlying levels of need are an important factor (Bebbington and Miles 1989). However, need is not the only factor since both of these authorities are admitting even fewer children than need alone would predict. The two authorities with the highest start rates do not have the highest levels of need. The analysis indicated that relative need only accounted for 40 per cent of the variation in start rates. When the same exercise was done for the rate of children actually in care on 31 March 2001, relative need accounted for 52 per cent of the variation. In other words, the study confirmed the Department of Health's conclusion that relative need is a better predictor of how many children remain in care for longer periods of time, whilst other factors have more of an influence on start rates (Department of Health 2000b).

## Local authority policies on the use of out-of-home care as a component of family support and child protection services

In order to understand the impact of local authority policy and procedures, we explored start rates alongside the length of time that children remained in care. It is clear from other research studies that some authorities view short periods in out-of-home care as part of their family support services for families under stress, whilst others view it as something to be avoided if at all possible (Department of Health 2001b; Packman and Hall 1998). These different perspectives show up in the variations in the proportion of children coming into care at the request of parents rather then via a court order. Nationally, the average proportion of children who entered care following a court order or police intervention was 22 per cent, but amongst our 24 authorities this varied between 10 per cent and 53 per cent.

Other differences also show up in the reasons for entering care. Nationally, 62 per cent of children started on a period of public care mainly because of concerns about abuse or neglect, but on this variable, the 24 authorities in the study ranged between 37 per cent and 90 per cent. A lower threshold for the provision of an out-of-home care service (that is, a greater willingness to see a period in care as a part of the family support service for a wider range of need) might be expected to be associated with a shorter stay away from home. Therefore, the trend for higher start rates might be expected to correspond with higher turnover and lower start rates with lower turnover was expected. However, in the study, 'high start rate, high turnover' did not hold invariably. For example, the authority with the third highest start rate had a below-average proportion of children leaving care within eight weeks.

Thresholds for entry into care and turnover rates are also likely to reflect the availability of other services, notably those that support children and families in the community. Some of these will be provided by the local authority children's social care or education departments, but some by other agencies, such as health or youth justice services. The data from the surveys and interviews with managers support the conclusion that agency policies on thresholds and variation in rates of children in care are influenced by the availability of support services and the effectiveness of inter-agency collaboration as well as by the general approach to the provision of out-of-home care in a particular local authority.

It is important to state here that, from this study, it could not be concluded that 'high start rate, high turnover' was necessarily good or, for that matter, bad. It could have been an indicator of poorer preventive services, lower thresholds of entry, better reunification services or a particular departmental culture around the appropriate use of out-of-home care (or any combination of these). By looking at the questionnaires from the authorities with the highest and lowest start rates, it was not possible to conclude that the high-rate authorities were admitting children who should not have been admitted or that the corollary was the case: they were all children who, from the data provided, appeared to need out-of-home placement. It is equally impossible to say that 'low start rate' was automatically either good or bad. It might have been a sign of good support services or of very high thresholds for entry and a negative view of the potential of care to be of benefit to improve the life chances of vulnerable children.

In summary, high or low thresholds for entry into care and rates of turnover make a contribution to variance but do not entirely explain differences between authorities with similar levels of need.

## Management systems and control mechanisms

The third area for more detailed exploration in the survey schedules was the extent of management control of the decisions of frontline professionals as to whether an out-of-home care service should be provided to a particular child and whether this should be accomplished via the 'voluntary' route or through the courts. The findings showed that there was a notable difference in organisational decision-making between authorities with the highest and lowest start rates. In the high-start authority, the decisions tended to be made at a relatively low level, by district or team managers. By contrast, in the authority with the lowest start rate, decisions tended to be made at a high level by senior managers at headquarters or by a panel of professionals acting as 'gatekeepers' to the service. However, the questionnaires from other authorities showed that in two authorities, decision-making was primarily undertaken at district or team manager level in 2000–01, but they still reduced their start rates during that year.

To summarise, this work based on routinely collected administrative data in England attempts to explain the variation between local authorities in their rates of children in care at any one time (the stock rate) and of children entering care in a given year (the flow rate) and has highlighted a number of possible factors. These include the impact of underlying need and deprivation in each local area; departmental policies and operational processes such as the availability of family support services and decision-making procedures; resource and staffing levels; and the wider culture of the department, including the beliefs of individual workers and managers about the benefits or harmful effects for children of coming into public care.

## The potential for cross-national comparisons of administrative data to point towards promising interventions for children in out-of-home care

Workshops at which the findings of the research on the 24 authorities have been presented have provided opportunities for politicians, planners, managers and practitioners to debate the potential of new practice interventions, as well as policy changes to improve services to children who may need out-of-home care or are currently in care. However, the data and the discussions point to the conclusion that simply bringing in a ready-made initiative that appears to have worked in another authority is not to be recommended.

A glance at the international child welfare journals shows that state governments are more frequently importing what appear to be promising interventions in another country or state into their own services, but it is not always clear that this is preceded by an analysis of any differences in context. Because there may be important differences in the composition of the in-care populations, it may be entirely inappropriate to assume that an intervention that is associated with positive outcomes for children in out-of-home care in one country will benefit children in care in another country. It is the author's contention that, alongside peer-reviewed research, routinely-collected administrative data can help to provide the necessary context for these cross-national debates and initiatives. Even with these large data sets, inappropriate comparisons between apparently successful outcomes in different countries can be made and can lead to misleading conclusions and inappropriate policy changes.

To give some examples of important policy differences that impact on the profile of children in care as shown up by administrative data sets, in the USA children are often adopted by relatives and therefore no longer appear in the in care statistics, whilst in other countries it is rare for relatives to adopt their kin and so they remain in the in care statistics. In New Zealand, for example, around 60 per cent of children in out-of-home care are in kinship placements (Thoburn 2010), and the proportion in Spain is similarly high (Del Valle *et al.* 2009). In other countries many of these children would be financed and supported through the general family support and welfare benefit systems and would not appear in the in care statistics. In Sweden and Scotland, almost all young offenders are included amongst the statistics for children in care, whilst in other countries, such as England, more young offenders are in custody and included in separate data sets. In the USA, a higher proportion of adolescents than in most other countries is cared for away from their families in group care facilities provided by mental health services and these do not appear in the in-care statistics.

## Mapping the availability and comparability of data sources across state and national boundaries

Following in the tradition of this England study, a similar methodology was used to understand similarities and differences between in-care populations in 14 countries with reasonably well-developed child welfare systems (Thoburn 2007, 2009). The objectives were as follows:

- With respect to participating countries (or states within countries with a federal system of government), to research and make available a list of administrative data sources providing routinely collected information on children in out-of-home care.

- To work with research colleagues, policy makers and statisticians in these countries to produce a glossary of terms that may have different meanings in different countries, and thus provide guidance on how routinely produced statistics can be understood and used cross-nationally, whilst taking into account differences in demography, society and political systems.

- To work through international networks of academics, researchers, statisticians and policy makers to make this information available so that children in care gain the benefits from international collaboration whilst avoiding the pitfalls inherent in too crude an interpretation of comparative data.

Table 8.1 illustrates differences between rates entering care and rates for 'snapshot' populations of children in care for four of the countries.

Available administrative data, research interviews with statisticians and policy makers and discussions with international collaborators in the cross-national study (Thoburn 2007, 2010) indicate that the variables used to understand in-country differences in placement patterns and service level outcomes in the England study are relevant to international comparisons.

The different characteristics of children coming into care in different countries, including their pre-care experiences and relationships, will impact on the challenges presented to those caring for them and the likelihood of more or less positive outcomes:

TABLE 8.1 Rates entering care and rates in care in four countries, 2004–05 (numbers in care and entering care in brackets)

| RATES | ENGLAND | AUSTRALIA (ESTIMATE) | SWEDEN | USA (ESTIMATE) |
|---|---|---|---|---|
| Rate in care per 10,000 0–17 years | 55 per 10,000 (n=60,900) | 49 per 10,000 (n=23,695) | 63 per 10,000 (n=12,161) | 66 per 10,000 (n=589,003) |
| Rates entering care per 10,000 0–17 years | 23 per 10,000 (n=24,500) | 26 per 10,000 (n=12,531) | 32 per 10,000 (n=6,115) | 42 per 10,000 (n=311,000) |

*Source:* Data adapted from AFCARS 2005; Australian Institute for Health and Welfare 2005; Department for Education and Skills 2005; Socialstyrelsen 2004. (Federal data for Australia and USA are compiled from data supplied by States in aggregated form.)

- Most studies have found an association between age on coming into care and outcomes and routes out of care. A great deal of research (see, for example, Bullock *et al.* 2006) supports the conclusion that children placed as infants are more likely to grow up in stable placements and have good outcomes. Children coming into care when older, especially those exposed to maltreatment, are less likely to have good outcomes. If we allow for the fact that 73 per cent of those who came into care in Sweden in 2003–04 were aged ten or over, we might anticipate different outcomes than for Australia, UK and USA, where over a third came into care when under the age of five and fewer than half when aged ten or over. To counterbalance the above figures, those countries that do not use adoption as a route out of care will have a larger proportion of their long-stay group who came into care as infants and had stable placements. Consequently (and depending on the proportion who come into care when young), one would expect the outcomes for their in-care populations to look more positive than for those countries, mainly Canada, the USA and the UK, which place the youngest (easiest to parent) children for adoption and are left with long-term care populations made up of the most challenging children.

- The welfare and support provisions available to all families and the services provided to children and families identified as vulnerable also impact on those entering care and potentially on outcomes. Such provisions and services depend on the wealth of the particular country and also on policy decisions regarding the proportion of national wealth to be devoted to child and family support services. High-wealth and high-tax countries with a high expenditure per child on family support services are likely to have in care a larger proportion of children from families with very serious and complex problems. Irrespective of the resources they put into their in-care services, it might be expected that more of the children coming into care in these countries will have poorer outcomes than in countries where some children come into care at a younger age in order to meet material needs. On the other hand, some countries with well-funded child and family welfare systems use long-term care (including boarding education) as part of their support services to vulnerable families. Lower thresholds for entry in care (in Denmark, for example) result in high rates in long-term care, continuing parental support for the children whilst in placement and support for their carers, and higher rates of placement stability.

A more technical problem in comparing data from different countries is to understand which children living away from home for welfare, protection or community safety reasons are included in the child in care statistics. Again, this will impact on the *difficulty* of the in-care populations of a country and the likelihood of successful outcomes. The main variables identified in regard to this problem are the following:

- The interaction with health services, especially disability and mental health services. In countries such as France, there are separate systems for providing out-of-home care for disabled children (including those with mental health problems), whereas in Sweden and the UK nations, similar children are likely to be included in the in-care data.

- The interaction with youth justice services. The proportion of young offenders in the in-care statistics will have an impact on the proportion of those achieving successful outcomes. Sweden's policy of keeping most young offenders within the child welfare system explains in large part the high proportion of young people who are aged ten or over when coming into care.

- Whether children in out-of-home care at the request of their parents rather than on court orders are included in the in-care statistics.

- What proportion of those in kinship placements are included in the in-care statistics and data bases.

- Whether, as in Scotland and to a lesser extent in other parts of the UK, children in need of protective services but living at home under supervision are included as being in care.

## Conclusion

The overall aim of this cross-national project was to take a modest step towards improving the well-being of children in care by providing improved access for policy makers and their academic advisers to data on children in out-of-home care in other countries. The project also provided contextual information that may account for different outcomes in different countries. These, it is argued, are necessary steps before moving on to a consideration of *what works* across national boundaries, for different types of children, in different contexts and at different stages in the placement process.

The central objectives of these linked studies has been to help increase the appropriateness of comparisons of available data, within and between jurisdictions; to guide the improvement of information systems; and to alert policy, practice and research communities to meaningful comparisons that can guide their work. The hypotheses underlying this work are that high-quality administrative data sets have an important contribution to make to the evaluation of outcomes for children in care. Their strength is that they provide data on whole cohorts and large numbers of children. They are particularly useful if they report longitudinal data on the care and post-care careers of groups entering care in a particular year (sometimes referred to as a flow sample) as well as on children in care at any one time (a stock sample). See especially Wulczyn, Kogan and Jones Harden 2003 and Vinnerljung, Oman and Gunnarson 2005, for examples of this.

The weakness of such administrative data sets is that they rarely provide robust details on the children beyond demographic characteristics, and almost nothing on the methods of intervention. Most provide information on placement type; some provide limited data on reasons for entering care, movements within the system (including disruptions), frequency of moves and the circumstances of leaving care. The data sets, therefore, need to be complemented by more detailed quantitative and qualitative research.

In their search for evidence of what works at lowest cost, governments are increasingly looking across national boundaries. This is to be welcomed, provided that due care is taken to understand the similarities and differences between the in-care populations and systems in the country where a particular innovation has been developed and the one into which it is being imported. A failure to understand differences among children entering the system, different approaches to placement, and different organisational and professional cultures and services for young people leaving care can lead to failed policy initiatives, poor use of resources and further harm to individual children, their parents and carers.

# Part III
## Evaluating Outcomes in the Real World

### International Evidence from Community-Based Practice

# Chapter 9

# Taking Standardised Programmes to Different Cultural Contexts
## An Example from Scotland

Jane Aldgate and Wendy Rose

This chapter describes how a standardised programme of group work intervention with parents and children was applied in the context of three centre-based projects established by a national voluntary children's organisation in Scotland, with government funding, to work with primary-aged children displaying challenging and antisocial behaviour.

## The background to the projects

The Directions Projects were set up by a large Scottish voluntary agency, Children 1st, in 2003 as the result of a successful proposal submitted to the Scottish Executive's Youth Crime Prevention Fund, in partnership with three local councils. The proposed projects were designed to fill a gap for primary-aged children who were exhibiting antisocial, aggressive or acting-out behaviours. The proposals were influenced by findings from research on interventions aimed at reducing or preventing the precursors to offending behaviour (Zigler, Taussig and Black 1992) and the value of concurrent child and parent training (Richardson and Joughin 2002).

The main aims of the projects at the point of start-up were:

- To provide individual and group work for children aged 7–12 years who had challenging antisocial behaviour. The aim was to help them address difficulties, which might undermine their ability to achieve their personal or educational potential and to maintain them in their own family, school and community.

- To support, assist and advise parents who had difficulty in providing appropriate parental care and control.

An integral part of the funding was to commission external evaluation from the authors, working closely with the projects from the beginning and provide a final report at the end of three years (Aldgate *et al.* 2007).

## Putting standardised measures of change in a local context

Central to the evaluation was a core standardised groupwork programme which had a built-in self-evaluation for those taking part. Standardised tests were also included to permit comparison with other studies and to measure change over time, as well as data on both the circumstances of children and their families and the ethos of the centres. In recognition of the challenge of evaluating complex family support projects, a broad definition of evidence was taken and an iterative approach. In addition to measuring change at the beginning and end of specific interventions in a more traditional way, the evaluation also included other dimensions related to how the services were offered and the relationship between these processes and outcomes (Wigfall and Moss 2001).

A central part of the evaluation was to include the views of children and parents. Seaman *et al.* (2005, p.11) support the exploration of children's and families' experiences as part of the process and argue that evaluation should 'draw on participants' own definitions and priorities', recognising the plurality of their experiences (see also Lurie and Clifford 2005).

## The whole is greater than the sum of the parts

The evaluation team also regarded as important current thinking that evaluation of centre-based intervention should strive to capture the idea that 'there is "something" in centre practice which is greater than the sum of the parts' (Warren 1997) and which may facilitate energy between the parts 'to interconnect creatively' (Warren-Adamson 2006, p.178; Lightburn and Warren-Adamson, Chapter 4). The team's challenge was to find sensitive ways of capturing that synergy if found in the projects' work.

## Developing a mixed approach to evaluation

Everitt and Hardiker (1996) suggest there are two approaches to evaluation: 'formative', looking at processes, and 'summative', focusing on outcomes.

Both approaches were incorporated into the multi-method design of this evaluation. Although some summative outcome measures were deployed in relation to some of the first groups of children who went through the Webster-Stratton programme, the evaluation has also included qualitative data from individuals. As Lurie and Clifford (2005, p.31) suggest, the main limitation of dealing with quantitative methods alone is 'that the impact of treatment upon families, from their own perspective, is not particularly well understood'. It was also important to seek an understanding of the development of the projects in order to help others who were setting up similar projects. Thus, the evaluation provided 'a more rounded understanding of service effectiveness than would be the case with a single methodology' (Sanders and Roach 2007, p.162). This broad-based approach reflects the methods employed by other evaluators in Scotland (see Stradling and MacNeil 2007). As the chapter will show, this mixed-methods approach provided a rich pattern of dimensions to bring together in measuring change.

## The core intervention – the Webster-Stratton programme

The projects chose as their core intervention the well-tested Webster-Stratton training programme, The Incredible Years, lasting 14–17 weeks, with parallel programmes for children and their parents.

The Incredible Years is a video-based social learning parenting programme, developed in Seattle in the USA over 25 years by Carolyn Webster-Stratton and positively evaluated in other countries (Webster-Stratton 1992; Webster-Stratton and Taylor 1998). The approach is described by Utting *et al.* (2007) as 'based on "videotape modelling" where parents discuss video clips that show parents using a range of strategies to deal with everyday situations with their child' (p.32). In 12–14-week programmes, parents are enabled to become familiar with parenting skills 'known to promote children's social competence and reduce behaviour problems, including effective non-violent strategies for managing negative behaviour' (p.32). Parents are then encouraged to try out these strategies at home as 'homework' and to discuss their experiences within the group. In parallel, there is a child training programme, called the Dinosaur School, based on the use of life-size dinosaur puppets and video clips, purpose-designed for children aged 2–7 but also appropriate with further programmes for school children aged 5–12, which teaches children about becoming sensitive to others, developing empathy, managing conflict and learning friendship skills.

The Incredible Years programme is seen as a collaborative process taking place between trained group leaders and parents (and similarly with children), addressing both behaviour and relationships. It requires sensitivity to families' circumstances and attention to their recruitment and retention in the programmes.

Although the programme is aimed to be multicultural, the evaluation suggested that contextualising began because there was a need to adapt some of the language which was creating a sense of cultural dissonance for some families in the Directions Projects. As one service manager commented, 'the programme has a very middle class view of what is and is not acceptable family behaviour', whereas another drew attention to the barriers presented by multiple problems families were facing (Aldgate *et al.* 2007, p.31).

The Incredible Years parents' programme makes considerable demands on parents over and above the commitment to attend the group sessions, getting them to try out new parenting strategies as homework. It requires a degree of literacy and emotional literacy. Another area for contextualising emerged when project staff found there were very mixed levels of literacy among parents, and groups included parents who could neither read nor write. Staff responded with a number of measures: for example, providing additional home support, and using different coloured paper and bigger print in group sessions. The core programme also requires role-play activities which some parents found uncomfortable, particularly if the situation did not reflect their own. As a result, staff sometimes added activities and changed the pace of sessions to give parents time to relate the activities to their family circumstances (Aldgate *et al.* 2007).

Some parents told the evaluation team that they experienced the video vignettes as false, dated and 'not real life'. They were mainly aimed at families with two children whereas many parents had three or four or more. The programmes were not really related to the complexity or the severity of what they were experiencing, such as living in stepfamilies, the effect of older teenagers in the household, not addressing 'bad behaviour' outside the home, their children getting into gangs and parents having to compete with other influences.

One major problem was that the programme was designed with an upper age in mind. Some of the children exceeded this age and found the puppets and interactions too babyish. The response of the projects was to keep faithful to the content and purpose of the programme but devise a means of communication that was appropriate to the local group of older children in the projects, including the use of interactive computer programmes. The innovation was greatly successful in engaging this group of children. It may be that, when using standardised programmes, there will always be the need to adapt them to local context and take account of the fact that, over time, cultural expectations of children's age-related behaviour may change. Having said this, what the evaluation did show was that Webster-Stratton retains its validity even over two decades.

Although there were limitations to the Webster-Stratton programme, parents commented on positive attributes of the programmes and distinguished the parts they found helpful from those they did not. This self-evaluation was an additional component of the programme and helped understand parents' responses to it, as well as giving feedback on the efficacy of the programme itself.

## Contextualising parental drop-out

In traditional evaluations of standardised programmes, there is often little discussion about drop-out rates other than to record their frequency. Contextualising measuring the outcome of the intervention meant adding in some understanding of the reason behind drop-out rates. It took into account the measures the project staff adopted to respond to this problem.

Parental drop-out on a standardised programme has implications for the adults concerned, but, even more importantly, it has direct consequences for the children. The Webster-Stratton programmes are predicated on parental involvement. This also raises a practical and ethical dilemma of whether children can continue in the Dinosaur School programme if their parents are no longer participating. These issues were discussed long and hard in the Directions Projects, and staff carefully analysed information about children and parents who dropped out.

Staff commented on the influences of what was happening in families' lives: of relationships with other services and the inevitable unexpected incidents that occur in families' lives. However, the pattern was of increasing and sustained parental involvement in the programmes since they began, supported by a dedicated worker in the project and alternative strategies being tried.

It was agreed that dropping out should not always be seen as entirely negative – some parents were able to get 'something' or 'enough' from their participation, and for other parents their lives were too full, chaotic and problematic for them to be able to sustain attendance (Manby 2005). Several parents expressed a desire to return when they were in a better state or their life circumstances had improved sufficiently to recommit. Indeed, some returned to repeat the programme, others were re-referred, and some went through the programme more than once with younger siblings of the first child, which allowed reinforcement of learning at the parent's pace. Without understanding this context, the evaluation of the success of the intervention might have been misleading (see Aldgate *et al.* 2007 for more detail).

There was also the ethical dilemma of whether a child should remain in the programme if a parent had withdrawn, for whatever reason, since that was a usual condition of the Webster-Stratton programme. The staff were very concerned that this rule might have a negative effect on already vulnerable children. It was decided that, generally, it would be inappropriate for a child to continue if their parents did not attend as well, but there were always exceptions. Because of the vulnerability of many of these children, removing them from the programme was handled with great sensitivity, and children were offered a period of alternative activity with the project through short programmes or individual work on issues such as self-esteem and anger management, while work to re-engage parents continued. Simply recording that a child has withdrawn would not have captured any of this context.

### Standardised tests

To attempt to measure the complexity of children's and families' circumstances and to ensure that the evaluation had a degree of objectivity, at the point children and families were accepted for intervention, several standardised tests were administered by project staff on behalf of the evaluation team during the assessment process as well as at the end of the group work programme. These scales were selected because they were standardised assessment tools which staff could use to assist in gathering information and in reviewing progress, which could also double as evaluation tools.

The tests used were:

- *The Strengths and Difficulties Questionnaire.* This test is designed to assess children's emotional and behavioural problems (outlined in a research note by Goodman 1997). It includes hyperactivity, pro-social behaviour, conduct problems and peer relations.

- *The Parenting Daily Hassles Scale.* This scale (developed by Crnic and Greenberg 1990) aims to assess the frequency and intensity/impact of 20 potential parenting hassles experienced by adults caring for children. It has been used in a wide variety of research studies concerned with children and families.

The importance of using standardised tests is that they had been validated by research and therefore would give reliable data. Additionally, 'the respondent does not have to interact directly with the assessor while they are completing the questionnaire and can, therefore, concentrate on voicing their needs and concerns unimpeded' (Department of Health, Cox and Bentovim 2000, p.3). All of the tests used were chosen because they were reliable, short and easy to administer. It was acknowledged that it was unlikely the tests would show major shifts over a short period of time but, given the length of the evaluation period, it was hoped that it would be possible to assess change for individual children and their parents over several months, if not over one year.

It was suggested by the authors of the tests (Department of Health *et al.* 2000) that it was usually best if the child or parent completed the scale in the presence of a project worker. What the manual does not say is what to do if a parent has literacy problems. Without help, answers could be incomplete. Sensitivity to this issue was developed in the projects with staff administering the scales verbally. It was also recognised that there was potential for a crossover between research and practice on occasions. Completing the scale might be an important point of entry for discussion with the worker about family and other issues affecting the parents or child.

## The outcomes from the scales

The evaluation of the Directions Projects took place over a relatively short time. On a quantitative basis, the results of the evaluation were 'promising' and reflected those of other UK evaluations of early intervention programmes (Smith 2006, p.57). They showed that specific interventions could be employed to achieve positive outcomes for children and families.

The standardised tests employed at the beginning and end of the programme suggested many children and families had a low starting point for success with around two thirds of children showing a high level of behavioural and emotional problems, a much larger proportion than would be expected in the general population. Although some children still had serious problems at the end of the programme, there were indications of positive movement at the second point of testing after the programme ended on all the dimensions of the Strengths and Difficulties Questionnaire, though some dimensions indicated more change than others.

There was a clear improvement on the Conduct Problems Scale and also considerable improvement on the Hyperactivity Scale. Least change occurred in the Pro-social Scale and the Peer Relations Scale but, even here, there was some minor movement for the better. Although these gains seemed modest and certainly did not represent wholesale changes for every child, given the very low base from which children and parents began, the results are very credible. They showed that, even in children with serious behaviour problems, change can occur in the short term with the right kind of intensive support. (See Aldgate *et al.* 2007 for a full description of the findings.)

The Parenting Daily Hassles Scales showed that around one third were experiencing serious frequency and intensity of hassles at the beginning of the programme. There was some reduction in this level by the end of the programme (Aldgate *et al.* 2007).

There was no doubt that many children felt the intervention had given them strategies for managing their behaviour, were enjoying being praised and had more self-esteem. Parents and schools reported they had observed improvements on a range of dimensions, with most progress being made in conduct, concentration in class and children's ability to make friends at school. It was not within the scope of the evaluation to undertake a rigorous follow-up over time, but feedback from staff indicated that, for many of the children and their families, the time with Directions had been a significant turning point.

Most parents who were able to complete the group work programmes reported improvements. There were indications that parents felt more in control of their children and their homes, a finding shared with Manby (2005). They were feeling better about themselves, less alone in their difficulties and more confident. One or two were beginning to look for opportunities for training and employment outside the family.

What the changes did not show was the relationship between the effort and imagination that had been put in by the projects to provide supporting services for children and families to give them the opportunity to complete the core intervention programme. It was only by looking at the wider context of the projects that some insight was gained into factors that had contributed to the changes.

## Measuring the processes that surrounded the core intervention

To look at the wider picture, alongside measuring outcomes and understanding their context, the evaluation took into account the multiple variables and interactions involved in the families' engagement with the projects. Therefore, looking at the process of the projects was relevant in understanding the outcomes.

The parts of the mixed evaluation methods to explore the issues of process included participant observation, children's views, interviews with staff, focus groups with parents and feedback from schools.

## Accounting for the context in which the outcomes occurred – factoring in children's and families' histories and lifestyles

There has already been some discussion of the cultural and social context in which the group work took place and parents' reactions to a 'standardised package'. The evaluation included information gained from staff about the context in which families had come to the project. This was an important part of contextualising the use of standardised programmes because it helped to show the context in which families were operating and showed how the responsiveness of staff to family needs and capacities was an essential part of creating an environment for change. A flavour of these issues illustrates the approach. The lifestyles of many of the children and families who came to the project were characterised by multiple problems over long periods of time. Following the experience of running the initial Webster-Stratton programme, the staff came to the view that it was not possible to recruit parents and children to a group work programme without first winning their trust. Many of the families referred to the projects had complex histories of involvement with agencies. Some found it difficult to engage with any professionals, or their earlier experiences had left them suspicious of agencies; some children were not emotionally ready to participate in a group programme; some parents similarly were not ready or they had difficulty making the practical arrangements necessary to attend regularly. It became apparent that home-visiting was a valuable support before, during and after the group work programmes to encourage and retain some families' participation, as well as maintaining contact by telephone. For others, some preparatory induction work, either on an individual basis or using a short group work programme, assisted parents and children to commit themselves to a longer period of engagement. The family's dedicated worker was a critical ingredient in gaining families' trust and being the person regularly in direct contact and accessible for the families.

For some children, their behaviour was so challenging when they joined the project that skilled individual work was necessary to win their confidence, to introduce them to concepts that were alien to their current perceptions of behaviour towards others and help them manage themselves in group situations. Although this was very time-consuming, the results suggested that it paid dividends in terms of children's engagement with the Webster-Stratton programme. Consequently, it became a standard part of the intervention to include preparation for the Webster-Stratton programme for those who needed it, and as follow-up to some aspects of the programme.

Building into the evaluation evidence of the starting point of families in relation to being able to engage with services was therefore very useful in contextualising their responses and evaluating change over time.

### Providing a nurturing environment

This emerged as a key factor in evaluating the readiness of children and families for change. Sensitivity and flexibility to the different needs and circumstances of family members was a key feature of the way in which the parent training and Dinosaur School programmes have been offered by the projects. Two critical practical needs for parents were carefully addressed: how to reach the projects on a regular basis and how to organise the care of other, younger children in the household. Transport to and from the centres for parents and children, including picking up children from school to come to the groups, was provided and also, where possible, crèche facilities. Attention was paid to the timing of programmes and to accommodating school term and holiday arrangements as far as possible to fit in with families' pressures. In other words, the evaluation attempted to record as part of the context the values of the project that parents need nurturing. It was important to record that parents needed to feel valued and respected, they needed to be able to relax as well as to work together, and they needed to have fun and enjoyment in what were often stressful lives.

## Evaluating parents' perspectives

The focus groups were illuminating in showing how important it was to take into account the context in which parents were living, both the drudgery of their day-to-day living circumstances and the importance of the attitude and ethos provided by the project.

Parents told the evaluation team how much they enjoyed the tea and food provided on arrival at the projects, the comfortable surroundings, the welcome they received and the fact that 'workers make you feel at the same level'. Coming to the projects helped 'to raise your spirits'. 'It's like a wee family place,' said one mother. They enjoyed being with other adults who were found to share similar difficulties, so their sense of isolation decreased. A rare treat for many parents was having time to themselves without their children – 'no wee hands tugging, shouting at you all the time'. Furthermore, parents trusted the staff with their children without feeling disempowered: 'the workers are awfully good with the bairns'.

The context of nurture and fun was also important for the children. Understanding this would have been missed if only the standardised test and interventions had been used. Staff empowered children attending the projects to comment on their enjoyment of coming to the projects, the welcome received, games and having fun, having something to eat and drink, and participating in cooking and preparing food (although clearing up at the end was rated less highly). However, when children are referred to services, knowing what is going to happen to them is important and such information is all too often not available (Rose 2006). Among a range of imaginative activities with them, the projects involved children in preparing appropriate information for other children who would be attending the projects. The evaluation team felt that the values and attitude of staff towards children could be captured through the feedback of the children.

## Creating and sustaining a learning organisation

One question to ask in undertaking a contextualised evaluation of a standardised programme is: To what extent is the project able to provide a positive and developing environment for its staff? A significant factor in the overall development and success of the Directions Projects was the creation of the culture of a learning organisation. It is difficult to capture completely the creativity and responsiveness of staff to the needs of the children and families. Providing a dedicated worker for each family, adapting the programmes to older and younger children, developing wraparound services to support parents to attend and the quality of interactions with staff reported by children and families, along with the evaluation team's observations of the interactions, ethos and outcomes of the Directions Projects are all evidence of the dynamic nature of the projects. The staff's ability to adapt and grow in confidence was underpinned by training and being open to new information. This they then used to enhance participation and partnership with the families.

## The role of managers

Linked to the development of a learning organisation was the role of the projects' managers, who played a fundamental role both in setting up and leading the projects. The management was characterised by a transformational leadership approach (Pine and Healy 2007), which allowed staff to participate in the development of the projects. Managers shared a common vision about the overall aims of the projects. They worked together to bring staff on board, convert them to the common aims and processes, thus building confidence but not stifling creativity. The participatory approach of the service managers, who were operationally involved in delivering the services, gained the respect of staff. Equally, the service managers' ability to manage the boundaries with other agencies and negotiate a respected place for Directions Projects within local communities contributed to the development of the projects. It is noteworthy that there was a low turnover of staff in the first four years. These factors were a significant context for creating the opportunity for children and families to change.

## Establishing the projects within their communities

The context of the community also contributed to the outcome. The effectiveness of the projects was dependent on how they had been perceived by agencies in the community. Local agencies respected the projects because they knew what the projects were offering and who they could help.

It was evident that, where the Directions Projects were located in areas that had a strategic approach to the planning and provision of family support services, the projects were able to flourish. It was more difficult for the projects to be located in areas where there was a limited range of family support services either in the statutory or voluntary sectors or where other key agencies were in a state of constant reorganisation and upheaval. Another contributory factor to embedding the projects in the community was the active links that were made with local services such as the Fire Service and Police to increase the community awareness of older children, which increased the public services' understanding of the work of the project.

## Understanding the synergy in the Directions Projects

As this chapter has shown, in measuring outcomes, the context contributed to and supported the core intervention of the Directions Projects. How the projects developed and were organised and the standard of practice all played their part in supporting changes. What became evident was that the projects were complex systems of 'contingencies and connections' between the various parts (Agar 2004, p.414).

In this respect, complexity theory may have something to offer in understanding the processes and outcomes of the projects (see Lightburn and Warren-Adamson, Chapter 4). There is evidence that the projects were able to develop and build on themselves and that changes could happen with surprising speed, given the right conditions. They demonstrated that 'a small input can bring about a large output, if the input occurs at the right time and the right place' (Warren, Franklin and Streeter 1998, p.364). In a relatively short time, the Directions Projects established themselves and had a clear impact on the lives of the children and families who crossed their thresholds. They also had an impact on the communities they were serving.

The projects grew out of the initial aims and achieved the desired outcomes of helping children with challenging behaviour and their families. The way they developed allowed for changes and innovations along the way. The manner in which they reached their achievements reflects that outlined by Loeb, quoted in Lightburn and Sessions (2006, p.542):

> A patchwork, partially constructed vision may strike exactly the balance between humility and boldness that's needed in these unpredictable times...we may proceed best, as Mary Catherine Bateson writes, 'by improvisation, discovering the shape of our creation along the way rather than pursuing a vision defined'. So long as we stay open to new information, learning as we go, not allowing ourselves to be distracted by the search for absolute certainty, we can continue to work towards goals we can feel proud of.

Understanding the significance of this synergy between a coalition of forces and factors that create a context for change may be the most critical dimension in bringing about and providing the means of measuring change in community centre-based services for children and families. What the Directions Projects showed was that, even with very vulnerable children and families, adopting a contextualised approach was successful in setting the children and families along the road to changing their lives.

# Chapter 10

# Child Physical Abuse and Neglect
## Risk Assessment and Evaluation of Early Prevention Programmes

### Hans Grietens

Child maltreatment (physical, emotional or sexual abuse, neglect, witnessing domestic violence) is a serious problem in our Western society, which brings much suffering and significant costs. For years now, policy makers have tried to cope with this problem by stimulating agencies, practitioners and researchers to cooperate and develop preventive initiatives. However, child maltreatment remains widespread. Recently, researchers showed that in industrialised countries the incidence of all forms of child maltreatment is much higher than would be expected (Gilbert *et al.* 2008). This sometimes makes us doubt the effectiveness of prevention programmes, and some people may be skeptical when they read about high incidence rates and the cost of prevention campaigns. However, we all agree that, in the best interests of children and their families, prevention efforts need to be continued. In order to do this in an effective way, we need to know what good prevention of child maltreatment is, and what ingredients a prevention programme should have in order to work. This chapter aims to contribute to the debate and to provide some answers to these difficult questions by presenting the research on the early prevention of child physical abuse and neglect from Belgium.

This research programme started in 1997, when Belgium was recovering from the shocking Dutroux affair, a case of severe extrafamilial child sexual abuse. The programme was developed in close cooperation with Kind & Gezin (Child & Family), a statutory agency that is commissioned by law to promote of health care and well-being of families with children from birth to three years old in the Flemish community of Belgium. The programme has three interrelated objectives. The first research objective was to develop a screening instrument for nurses who do home visits (social nurses). They are employed by the agency to identify early risks for child physical abuse and neglect during home visits to families with a newborn child. Gradually, the researchers also became interested in the issue of evaluation of early prevention programmes. The agency considered the screening instrument as a first step towards the implementation of a child maltreatment prevention plan. For this reason, it was decided to review what works in early prevention programmes, particularly in programmes including home visits. The researchers reviewed the literature on the effects of early prevention programmes and conducted a statistical meta-analysis on 40 evaluation studies in order to estimate overall effects (reduction of child abuse and neglect, risk reduction) of early preventive measures. Next, the researchers performed an in-depth multiple case study to find out how social nurses actually dealt with families where children were at risk of child physical abuse and neglect. The researchers followed the interventions the nurses made during the counselling process and asked the parents about their satisfaction at the end of the process. This information was considered necessary to optimise the quality of care provided to families at risk of child abuse and neglect.

This chapter will first explain how preventive care for young children in Flanders is organised and what is meant by prevention of child maltreatment. Then, there will be an outline of the theoretical framework underlying the research programme. In the third part, the main findings of the study will be presented. Finally, there will be some concluding remarks.

## Preventive care for young children in Flanders (Belgium)

Preventive care for families with a newborn child is organised by Child & Family. The agency employs about 600 social nurses to follow up families with a newborn child through home visits and consultations. Usually, after an initial visit in the hospital, about three home visits are planned within three months of the birth in the case of a first child; two home visits within this period are planned in case of a subsequent child. Within the first three months, there are two agency-based consultations. The agency reaches more than 95 percent of all families with a newborn infant (Child & Family 2008), including children born in refugee families.

For decades, the nurses have focused only on medical issues – for instance the child's and the mother's health, or the child's physical development. For 15 years, the nurses have also focused on parenting and psychosocial issues. At this moment, the latter issues take a very prominent place in the agency's vision and many efforts are undertaken to translate the vision into practice. One central topic is the prevention of different forms of child maltreatment. Although the prevention of child maltreatment has been a major theme for Child & Family for quite a long time, a strong impetus to undertake visible actions was given by the political context in Belgium following cases of missed and murdered children at the end of the twentieth century (Dutroux affair).

It is in this context that the researchers' work on the prevention of intrafamilial child maltreatment began. In order to reduce the number of cases of intrafamilial child abuse in Flanders, the agency requested the development of a screening instrument that could be used by the social nurses during home visits and consultations; its purpose was to identify early signs of disturbed parent–child interactions which could end up in child physical abuse and neglect. During a four-year project, a screening instrument was developed, tested and implemented in the organisation. Meanwhile, research was begun on the outcomes of early prevention programmes in families at risk of child physical abuse and neglect. Most of the research activities were conducted in close cooperation with the agency, following implementation of the above-noted changes within the agency.

According to MacMillan *et al.* (2009) prevention of child maltreatment can take different forms and serve several aims. It can focus on prevention before maltreatment has taken place, either in a universal way (focused on the whole population) or in a targeted way (focused on at-risk groups or vulnerable families and children). Further, actions can be aimed at preventing recurrence of maltreatment or to prevent impairment.

Our meta-analysis of early prevention programmes, as well as the in-depth multiple case studies, were on 'targeted' prevention in at risk groups (selective or secondary prevention).

## Theoretical framework

Underlying the research is an interactional view of child maltreatment. This view is based on ecological models on the determinants of parenting (Belsky 1997) and on psychological (Cerezo 1997) and pedagogical (Baartman 1996) theories of child maltreatment. One core element is that child physical abuse and neglect are considered as extreme manifestations of parenting problems, reflecting severe problems in the relationship between parent and child. Other core elements are the cumulative effects that longstanding negative interactions with parents may have for the child and the mediating or buffering role that the parents themselves may play against outer stressors (e.g. unemployment) or predisposing child factors (e.g. difficult temperament).

There is ample empirical evidence that early signs of inadequate parenting and disturbed parent–child relationships are precursors to child physical abuse and neglect (Ammerman 1990; Becker-Lausen and Mallon-Kraft 1997; Milner 2000; Rogosch *et al.* 1995). Central to the interactional view on child maltreatment is the concept of parental awareness. Baartman (1996) reviewed the literature on parenting and child maltreatment and reintroduced this concept (for reviews of parental awareness in English see Bouwmeester-Landweer 2006 and Grietens, Geeraert and Hellinckx 2004), which was first used by Newberger (1983, p.512) and defined as 'an organized knowledge system with which the parent makes sense out of the child's responses and behavior and formulates policies to guide parental action'. According to Baartman (1996), the dynamics underlying parental awareness are the parent's capacity to take the child's position and the parent's willingness to serve the child's needs and claims.

Parents whose children are at risk of child physical abuse and neglect may be characterised by a lack of perspective-taking abilities and a decreased willingness to serve the child's needs and demands. This is manifested by inappropriate or forced expectations in the parents with regard to the meaning the child can have for their own well-being; or they have negative emotions towards the child, regardless of the child's characteristics or actual behaviour and they have a lack of sensitivity and responsiveness towards the child's needs for care and safety.

Other risk factors taking a prominent place in the interactional view on child physical abuse and neglect are a history of maltreatment in one or both parents, a lack of social support, and parental personality problems such as depression (Baartman 1996; Coohey and Braun 1997; Kolko 1996; Rogosch *et al.* 1995). There is empirical evidence that these risk factors intercorrelate. Grietens and Hellinckx (2003), for instance, demonstrated in a non-clinical sample of mothers with a birth-to-one-year-old baby that disturbed parental awareness was significantly predicted by a parent's negative childhood experiences, low levels of social support and negative maternal characteristics (e.g. inability to cope with stress).

## Summary of the main findings

### 1. A risk-screening instrument to prevent child physical abuse and neglect

The risk-screening instrument was developed in two stages. In the first stage, a set of items was selected. Each item represented a single risk factor for intrafamilial child physical abuse and neglect. The selection of items was based on the literature on child maltreatment. Only items measuring risks and significantly predicting child physical abuse and neglect were selected. In order to apply risk factors in practice and to embed the instrument into the social nurses' context of home visits and consultations, group interviews with social nurses (focus groups) were organised. The group interviews also helped us to formulate items on a topic related to risks of child maltreatment which was not covered by the available literature, namely the relationship between the parent and the nurse.

The total set of items contained 71 items, covering four topics:

1. Interaction between parent and nurse.

2. Parent–child interactions, with items on inappropriate expectations, negative emotions, and lack of sensitivity and responsiveness.

3. Parental and family characteristics, with items on history, social support and non-child-related parental personality characteristics.

4. Child characteristics.

In the second stage, the set of items pool was collapsed. To realise this goal, 40 randomly selected social nurses were trained to score the items during a three-month registration period. The items had to be scored at the end of the regular home visits, namely after three visits in case of a first child and after two visits in case of a next child. The nurses also collected information on medical (e.g. weight) and social issues (e.g. social deprivation). At the end of the registration period, they had obtained information from 391 mothers. Within this sample of births for which regular home visits ended within the registration period, a sub-sample of abusive/neglectful mothers (n=18) could be identified. These mothers were diagnosed as abusive or neglectful by multidisciplinary Confidential Doctors' teams working under the auspices of Child & Family. Confidential Doctors' teams register reports of child maltreatment, examine reported cases and provide treatment. They consist of a child psychiatrist or pediatrician, a child psychologist or pedagogue, and social workers. Diagnoses were only based on the general procedures used by the teams (Child & Family 2003). General procedures did not include scores on the risk scale. The social nurses involved in the study were blind to the diagnoses. These were only known by the agency's officials responsible for coordinating the data collection.

The set of items was reduced according to two criteria: the prevalence of items (risks) in the sample and the discriminatory power of the items. Items with a prevalence rate below 5 percent were omitted, as were items which could not significantly distinguish maltreating (n=18) from non-maltreating mothers (n=373).

Using these criteria, a scale containing 31 items was developed. Factor analysis yielded a three-factor solution:

- Disturbed parent–child relationship (13 items, e.g. 'Mother expects the baby to give abundant love').

- Communication problems (7 items, e.g. 'Mother does not keep to the appointments regarding home visits and consultations').

- Psychological problems (11 items, e.g. 'Mother is not able to adequately seek help or support').

Scores on all three sub-scales (factors) significantly predicted scores on a social deprivation scale, which in turn significantly distinguished maltreating from non-maltreating mothers. Mothers scoring high on the risk sub-scales obtained higher scores for social deprivation than low-scoring mothers. The 31-item version of the scale has been implemented in the agency and is now used by the social nurses (see Hellinckx *et al.* 2001; Grietens *et al.* 2004).

## 2. A statistical meta-analysis on the effects of early prevention programmes

During the last four decades, many secondary or selective prevention programmes for intrafamilial child physical abuse and neglect have emerged. These programmes focus on families whose children have been identified as being at risk for maltreatment and attempt to decrease the influence of risk factors (e.g. poor parenting, social isolation). Many programmes have been evaluated, using randomised or (mostly) non-randomised designs. Outcomes of these studies differ and show small, moderate or strong effects. Some programmes have even produced negative effects. Furthermore, often large within-programme differences were found, with some outcome indicators producing strong effects and others producing small effects. High variability between and within programmes makes it difficult to draw conclusions about the elements necessary to produce positive change. To find out what were the overall effects of secondary prevention programmes and to examine the impact of programmes on different outcome indicators, the researchers conducted a statistical meta-analysis (Geeraert *et al.* 2004). The research questions were:

- Is there an overall positive effect of early prevention programmes for families with young children (birth to three years) at risk of child physical abuse and neglect?

- Do these programmes decrease the manifestation of abusive and neglectful acts, as measured by direct (criteria) or indirect criteria (e.g. hospital admissions, out-of-home placements)?

- Do these programmes have a positive effect on the child's functioning, the parent–child interaction, including the atmosphere and parental management, the parent's functioning including physical, psychosocial/behavioural and functioning as a parent, the family functioning and the family context, including the socioeconomic situation and the social network?

- Are studies/programmes equally effective?

As a first step in the meta-analysis, we produced an inventory of studies. We consulted multiple international databases (PsycLit, MedLine and so forth). We included studies in the meta-analysis using six criteria (see Table 10.1).

TABLE 10.1 Selection criteria for studies on outcomes of prevention programmes

| |
|---|
| • The study takes place between 1975 and September 2002. |
| • The programme focuses on the prevention of child abuse and neglect in at-risk families. |
| • The programme is an early prevention programme starting before birth or in the first three years after birth. |
| • The programme focuses on physical abuse and neglect, not on sexual abuse. |
| • The intervention takes place before any physical abuse or neglect had been identified or substantiated. |
| • The impact of the intervention is examined by means of a randomised control design, or at least a pre-test/post-test design. |

Forty evaluation studies met the criteria. Only in a few studies were randomised control designs used. If only these studies had been included, it would have been impossible to perform a statistical meta-analysis. For this reason, non-randomised studies, in particular studies with a pre-test/post-test design were included. According to Veerman and Van Yperen (2007), these type of studies shows the indicative evidence of interventions. This is the second highest level of evidence, next to the randomised control design by which causal evidence can be demonstrated. Although the number of intervention studies using randomised control designs has been increasing during the last decade, many researchers still include studies showing indicative evidence of interventions in meta-analyses (for a recent example, see MacMillan *et al.* 2009).

Most studies were conducted in North America. In each study, results were converted to the standardised mean difference *d*, a common measure in the meta-analytic literature (Rosenthal 1984). As most studies used more than one indicator to evaluate the effect of the intervention, a large number of *d*s had to be computed (n=587). Figure 10.1 visualises the reported effects. The figure reveals that effect sizes vary considerably, with some studies even producing negative effects. The variation between reported effect sizes can be situated on three levels. A first source of variation is sampling variance: if in a study a different sample of study participants had been taken, the results would probably have been somewhat different. A second explanation is that studies often use various criteria (e.g. number of reported cases of child abuse or improvements in parent–child interaction) to evaluate the programmes. Effect sizes therefore differ according to the criteria they refer to. Finally, studies differ in the characteristics of the programme that is evaluated, or in other study characteristics (e.g. the location, the point in time or the target population). It is plausible that for this reason results differ from study to study, resulting in a third source of variation.

The analysis was refined in order to estimate the overall effect size, as well as the between-study and within-study variance. The estimate of the overall effect size equals 0.29 (standard error of estimation=0.044). This overall effect size differs highly significantly from zero (z=6.59, p<0.001). This means that there is strong evidence that the programmes for prevention of child abuse and neglect in general have a positive effect. Translating this result using the formulas proposed by Rosenthal (1984), this means an average reduction in abuse or risk of about 14 percent.

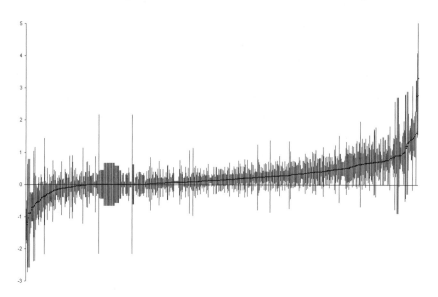

FIGURE 10.1 The reported effect sizes
*Source:* Geeraert 2004

Besides the differences between studies, the researchers investigated within-study differences. As discussed before, there are two kinds of criteria that are used in the studies to evaluate prevention programmes for child abuse and neglect: indication of child abuse or neglect and indication of risk. Both groups can be further divided in different categories. The researchers estimated the overall effect in each of the groups and in each of the 11 categories. Results are presented in Figure 10.2.

A first conclusion is that the effect on the different categories of effect criteria is rather similar. There is a tendency that the effects on the risk indications are somewhat larger (a difference of 0.038), but this difference is not significant. Similarly, there is a tendency that the programmes seem to have a larger effect on some categories of criteria, but differences between categories are again statistically not significant. Note that in each of the categories, the effect is statistically significant on an alpha level of 0.05. This is also true for the first category (number of reports; $z=2.33$, $p=0.02$), although in this category the effect size estimate is the lowest and the uncertainty (indicated by the standard error) about the estimate the highest. This means that for each of the 11 categories of effect criteria, there is relatively strong evidence that the programmes have an effect. Finally, we note that by taking the nature of the criterion into account, the between-study and the within-study variance hardly change: distinguishing between the two groups (reduction of child abuse and neglect, and risk reduction) or between the 11 categories of effect criteria results in between-study variance estimates of 0.65 and 0.61 respectively, and in within-study variance estimates of 0.047 and 0.047. That there are two groups or 11 categories of criteria thus cannot explain the differences between effect sizes from different studies or between effect sizes from the same study.

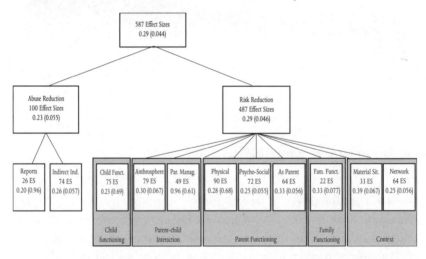

FIGURE 10.2 Number of effect sizes, the mean effect size and (in brackets) the standard error of estimation for the whole data set, the two subgroups, and the 11 categories of criteria

In addition to the statistical meta-analysis which was published in 2004, an interesting review on interventions to prevent child maltreatment has recently been published (MacMillan *et al.* 2009). The authors concluded that 'home visiting programmes are not uniformly effective in reducing child physical abuse, neglect, and outcomes such as injuries' (p.250). Using rigorous scientific standards, including the use of repeated randomised control trial studies, two programmes were found to have to have 'good to best' evidence: the Nurse-Family Partnership by Olds *et al.* (1997) in the United States (the researchers included this programme under different names in the meta-analysis) and the Early Start programme by Fergusson *et al.* (2005) in New Zealand. Parent-support and parent-training programmes such as Sanders' Positive Parenting Programme (Triple P) (Sanders *et al.* 2004) showed promising evidence to reduce child physical abuse and neglect, as did abusive head trauma education programmes in hospitals (to prevent the shaken impact syndrome) and programmes enhancing paediatric care for families at risk. The Nurse-Family Partnership and Early Start are both intensive home-visiting programmes. What they have in common (MacMillan *et al.* 2009) is that they (1) have been developed as research programmes rather than as service provision methods, (2) use highly qualified workers, and (3) make substantial efforts in ensuring treatment fidelity.

## 3. Multiple case studies on interventions by social nurses in at-risk families

Meta-analytic studies do have much to offer practitioners as well as policy makers, but one of their main limitations is the de-contextualisation of practice (Eysenck 1995; see also Biehal, Chapter 2; Thoburn, Chapter 9). It is good to know that there are programmes in North America, Australia and Europe which reduce actual abuse and risks of abuse and identify what makes these programmes work. But what about the practice in preventive care settings in Flanders?

As far as we know, there are no evaluation studies on early prevention programmes for child maltreatment in Flanders. Child & Family coordinates preventive care for children between birth and three years old, but little is known about the services they provide. What do the nurses actually do in the families where there are children considered to be at risk of child physical abuse and neglect? Which interventions work in the setting and which do not? In cooperation with the agency, the researchers conducted a study on these issues, electing to use a multiple case study and to collect data by means of semi-structured interviews with a small sample of nurses. During one year, we closely followed up the nurses' work in the families that they considered as being at risk for child physical abuse and neglect. After each intervention in the family, nurses were interviewed and asked to describe what type of action they had undertaken and what the consequences of these actions were for the parent–child relationship. They were also interviewed about the relationship they had with the parent(s). Much attention was given to processes of change within the one-year period. At the end of the follow-up, parents were interviewed about their perceptions of the nurses' interventions and about their level of satisfaction (Geeraert 2004).

In-depth interviews were carried out with twelve nurses. The interviews were tape-recorded and stocked by means of NVIVO. They were analysed using qualitative data analysis techniques (cross-site as well as within-site analyses) (Miles and Huberman 1994). The interviews offered the research team a wealth of information on the interventions of social nurses in at-risk families.

Different types of interventions could be distinguished throughout the counselling process. The most basic and predominant type was the analysis and follow-up of the family's situation. With nearly half of all interventions focused on analysis and follow-up. Focus of the intervention was the baby, the parent, the material conditions the family was living in and, less often, the parent–child interaction. In addition, nurses sought to present themselves to the parents as support figures. The support they provided varied from giving information or advice to giving emotional support and initiating behavioural changes (e.g. by modelling with regard to feeding, care, safety and social interactions). In general, nurses wanted to present themselves as support figures rather than as therapists. Their work with families can best be characterised as driven by a generalist approach (and less by a specialist approach). Often, the objectives they formulated were general and unspecified (e.g. 'building up a trustful relationship with the mother'). When they referred the family to another professional, they seldom played the role of coordinator. Instead, they considered giving useful information to other professionals as one of their core tasks. One very important factor facilitating (or, reversely, hampering) their work in at-risk families was the work setting in the agency. Cohesive and dynamic teams with opportunities for supervision clearly facilitated the work with these families.

## Some concluding remarks

Does targeted prevention of child physical abuse and neglect make sense? Taking into account the findings from the author's research programme and the literature on this subject, the answer to this question seems to be obvious. It makes sense. The question may even become somewhat rhetorical. We clearly know what to prevent: injuries, omissions of care and parent–child relationships that become disturbed by conflicting claims, distorted parental expectations and inadequate parental beliefs and practices. We now have insight in the mechanisms that underlie intrafamilial abuse and neglect; we are aware that the cycle of family violence is an intergenerational issue. Further, we know that it is much more difficult to prevent child physical abuse and neglect once it has occurred. Recurrence rates are high and preventive efforts provide little benefits compared to efforts taking place before occurrence (MacMillan *et al.* 2009).

Why should we hesitate to implement early prevention programmes showing good evidence? Well, before doing this, at least a few comments have to be made. First, do we know well enough which families to target? How do we identify those families most in need of early prevention, without stigmatising, over-identifying certain groups (e.g. underprivileged families), or under-identifying other groups (e.g. middle- or upper-class families)? Screening devices like the one we have developed for the social nurses of Child & Family may be of good help, but the implementation of such instruments is of vital importance and not without problems. Second, one could argue that universal prevention may be a good alternative. It may be less stigmatising than targeted prevention and reach all families. The former indeed is an advantage; the latter, however, may be problematic too. Do universal prevention programmes, like some of the modules in Triple P, really reach everybody, and do they reach early enough those families most in need? And what is the long-term cost-effectiveness of such programmes?

Finally, child maltreatment is a political problem, as it touches the heart of our societies (Baartman 2005), and the children who are hurt today will be tomorrow's parents. The efforts societies undertake to prevent child maltreatment depend upon the views they have about which of both parties should be cared for most: children first or families first. These views change over time, due to, among other factors, the revelation of cases of fatal child abuse and neglect. Our thinking about child maltreatment and our actions towards it will never be fully rational.

Krugman (1999) discerned waves of thinking and acting, as is made operational in the control–compassion model. Nowadays, the issue of control (safeguarding children's lives, well-being and development) seems again to prevail over the issue of compassion (preserving families, giving second chances to parents). This implies that early prevention may become too easily and too quickly 'early control' – for instance by placing children out-of-home without doing sufficient efforts to keep families together. We should all be aware of these movements and reflect upon them continuously, as they create the political, financial, judicial and organisational contexts within which our actions towards children and families will take place.

Chapter 11

# Identifying Outcomes at the Sunshine Family Centre in Outer London

### Marian Brandon

This chapter considers what we can learn from a pilot case study that sought to use collaborative enquiry to offer a more nuanced understanding of why family centres are so successful. Alongside researchers from other countries, we set out to discover whether and how the emotional and practical support offered to families helps to reduce risks of harm to children and reduce parental stress to 'free up carers to be more responsive and available to their children' (Howe 1995, p.279).

The study took place at the Sunshine Family Centre[1] in England. A key finding was the way in which the centre appeared to extend emotional and practical support not only to families but also to social workers within and outside the centre. The centre seemed to have a significant role in propping up ailing parts of its own local social services agency.

## Policy context and review of outcomes of similar services

Family centres provide 'protection, nurturance and avenues for development for parents and their children' (Warren-Adamson and Lightburn 2006, p.270). The outcomes of this type of family support generally include 'alleviated stress, increased self esteem, promoted parental/carer/family competence and behaviour and increased parental capacity to nurture and protect children' (Hearn 1995, p.3).

Family support services in the UK, as elsewhere, encompass protection against neglect and maltreatment as well as prevention: 'Child protection cannot be separated from policies to improve children's lives as a whole' (Department for Education and Skills 2003a, p.5). Family centres have developed to fit this shifting continuum, either as voluntary services at one end or as more coercive, legally mandated aspects of provision at the other end. Tunstill (2003, p.33) points out that the UK's vision of a span of universal and selective services creates problems in researching outcomes of family centre work. There is a problem in locating boundaries between different types of services, which may co-exist within the same centre. For example, services which involve the assessment of parental competence, services which remedy identified deficits, and services which build on existing levels of parental competence where no deficit has been identified may not all produce the same outcomes.

Gauging outcomes is always problematic and much depends on the definition and timing of the outcome measured (Hill 1999). There is, however, evidence that intensive family support programmes produce stronger outcomes of success than more didactic and periodic interventions (Hess, McGowan and Botsko 2000; Nelson, Landsman and Deutalbaum 1990). Much of this work takes place in integrated centres. There is also a small body of evidence that points to successful outcomes from more specialist family centres operating primarily in the sphere of child protection and serious family dysfunction (Pithouse, Lindsell and Cheung 1998). Families in this study said it was the centre that helped them to change, and spoke of their changed attitude, behaviour, self-esteem and self-confidence as well as improved relationships with children and partners. They suggested that change had been a gradual process rather than a single event (Pithouse *et al.* 1998, p.75).

Specialist centres focusing on serious family dysfunction and child protection, as in the case of the Sunshine Family Centre studied here, tend to have restricted access via professional referral only. Attendance can be part of a court-ordered treatment plan, court-ordered assessment of parenting, or court-ordered parental control of children's behaviour. Because of its intrusion into the private sphere of family life, family support in this guise can be seen as an arm of state power and authority in its efforts to promote parental capacity and responsibility (Pinkerton and Katz 2003, p.4).

## Policy and structure of centre studies

*Centre policy*

The Sunshine Family Centre is part of one local authority's state-funded social work service for children and families, and is accessed by families referred to children's social care who meet the high threshold for a service. The centre works with families with children aged 5–18 years who are experiencing trauma or stress. The centre is required to meet targets for different aspects of the service which are set by the employing local authority. This then helps the local authority to meet performance indicators which provide cash for outcomes (Department of Health 1998a). This target-driven system produces particular points of pressure, such as avoiding a backlog with the increasing number of public child welfare cases in court proceedings (Department for Education and Skills 2003b). For the year of the study (2003–04), a policy directive was issued requiring family centres to organise their services so that 70 percent of capacity was set aside for court assessments. The remaining 30 per cent of time was left for preventive family support, which could be carried out only if the core business of court work was fulfilled. Over the year April 2003–March 2004, the centre worked with a total of 75 cases (126 families and 211 children) carrying out court-commissioned assessments of parenting capacity and parenting orders and offering other group and individual sessions for children, parents and carers.

*Funding*

In spite of the tight boundaries, the centre tries to find creative ways of providing and resourcing preventative services. For example, it was successful in its application to government funding aimed at children aged 5–13 to combat social exclusion, and used the additional funding to employ a part-time counsellor. Berry and Reed (Chapter 6) have pointed out that funding streams have powerful effects on family centre services. In this instance, additional money gave the centre some autonomy and the ability to offer a non-mandated support service which would not otherwise exist. The counsellor is the only member of staff who does not keep family notes and does not report back to the referring agency.

In spite of individual successes in meeting targets and securing additional funding, core funding for family centres cannot be guaranteed within local authority services. Cost-effectiveness, added value and ultimately year-on-year savings are increasingly sought by employing bodies and government performance indicators. As such, family centres are a potentially vulnerable stream of service provision, which may be overtaken or replaced by integrated children's centres offering multidisciplinary and inter-agency services, often based in schools (Department for Education and Skills 2003a, 2003b).

## Exploration of sensitive outcomes

The Sunshine Family Centre was purposefully selected as a likely example of good practice. Centre staff members were eager to be involved in the study and the centre manager facilitated negotiations with senior management. The local authority Research Governance Group and the university both gave ethical approval for the study.

### Methods

The primary research question to be addressed is: What are the sensitive indicators, or 'steps along the way' in a community-based centre? The case-study approach adopted incorporates both process and outcome measures. The design for the research is based on collaborative inquiry (Reason and Bradbury 2001); it is participative and allows for learning and growth across the relationships among researcher, practitioner and service user. The researcher joins with the practitioner and both examine the proposed intervention and the desired outcomes. In the dialogue between researcher and practitioner, we delineate intermediary stages, or 'steps along the way' to accepted longer-term outcomes, such as changed behaviour in the child or more confident parenting. In this way we envisaged that some sensitive, mediating or 'containing' outcomes would emerge (Berry, Bussey and Cash 2001).

The case-study method also used secondary sources and structured interviews. To illustrate service use, one family's route through the centre was traced. Standardised measures were administered to provide an additional dimension of outcomes for this family. The data were triangulated so that interviews, case notes, centre records, reports, policy statements and the standardised scales were used to test the findings. The final, international stage of the collaborative enquiry was to compare findings and sensitive outcome indicators with other researchers at an international seminar. Researchers from other countries in the European Union, Australia, Canada, Israel, New Zealand and the United States presented equivalent studies of a community centre. A matrix of common themes was established and the international relevance of the findings from each study was discussed and validated. In this way the validity of the single case-study method was assured international relevance (Berry *et al.* 2006).

To understand how the centre functions and connects with its employing agency, as well as the overall approach to work with individual families and groups, the following activities took place:

- visits to the centre to carry out focus group discussions with the staff and individual interviews with its ten staff members

- tracing one family's route through the centre

- scrutiny of centre workers' case notes and information prepared about the family for the purposes of the study

- interview with a parent and her two children (Mrs Good, Joshua aged 12 and Kelly aged nine)

- administration of standardised scales with this family by the centre workers at the beginning, and by the researcher at end of the intervention

- scrutiny of centre publicity, policy and reports.

## The culture of the Sunshine Family Centre

The findings from this case study reinforced the hypothesis that the concept of containment was important in the success of family centres. This concept, drawn from object relations theory, refers to the process of absorbing and holding the projected anxieties and emotions of vulnerable families. Following such a concept, Warren-Adamson and Lightburn (2004, p.220) describe centres as a 'safe haven, a holding environment that supports and challenges'. Interviews with centre staff helped to shed light on how Sunshine creates a sense of containment, primarily through its culture of care (Lightburn and Warren-Adamson, Chapter 4). A brief description and analysis of the centre and its functioning shows the way in which a number of factors contribute to the culture of care it generates.

### *Location and physical attributes of the centre*

The Sunshine Family Centre is located in a densely populated urban area with high levels of deprivation – in a 'new town' in the outer London suburbs. This and similar towns were built in the 1950s and 1960s to house families moved out (not always willingly) from the slums of the East End of London. The town has experienced growing levels of unemployment and poverty and some estates of public housing have been demolished and rebuilt, using government urban regeneration funding, in an attempt to combat crime and social disorder.

The centre itself is not in an area of high crime but is an ordinary detached house situated in a relatively quiet and peaceable estate of public housing. The centre house looks similar to its neighbouring dwellings and has no sign outside indicating its identity as a family centre but has a car park at the side, next to the garden, which distinguishes it from other houses. Sunshine staff members say that they aim to blend into their surroundings. Inside, the centre is comfortably furnished, well stocked with toys, well maintained and decorated. It has no graffiti or apparent damage and is visibly well cared for. There is little interaction between the centre and its neighbouring community. In this respect it is *in* rather than *of* the community and the services offered are not directly available to the community, although many of the people who use the centre live nearby.

## The staff group

There is a fully staffed group of ten female workers. The centre is led by a social work-qualified manager and there are five other qualified social workers, one unqualified social worker and two support workers. All employees are experienced and well trained, and all of the qualified staff, including the centre manager, were undertaking some form of post-qualifying study. There had been full staff retention (100% over the previous year) in a local social services area which carries a very high vacancy rate among social agencies. The national social work vacancy rate at the time was 11 per cent, rising to 20 per cent in London (Department for Education and Skills 2003b, p.85). Recruitment and retention continue to be a problem in the south-east of England although national vacancy rates have improved slightly in other parts of England (Children's Workforce Development Council 2008). The contrast at Sunshine was illustrated well by one member of staff: 'Staff stay for a reason – people want to work here. You feel you're given time space and flexibility. Caroline [centre manager] is our biggest asset here.'

## The centre's approach to the work

Although each case is individually referred, there is a common approach to cases and the order in which services are offered is important. Parents need to be at the right stage to embark on, for example, a parenting programme. The preferred centre order is for parents to see the counsellor first. This has resonance with the approach advocated by Crittenden (2008) and Howe *et al.* (1999, p.278), who suggests that 'practitioners should manage and plan their interventions in some broad developmental order', beginning with emotionally supportive interventions such as counselling, before considering, for example, behavioural techniques. Centre staff determine how long families stay at Sunshine in conjunction with the area team social worker and the families themselves, although there is pressure from management for short-term work:

> We have to battle really hard for the area team not to close the case too early. If you keep closing the cases too soon they come back as referrals. We prefer to hold them, and see them through to a managed ending. (Caroline, centre manager)

## Staff care

The manager's leadership at the centre was mentioned by most of the workers and it seemed to have an effect in creating a culture of care which started with the staff caring for each other and then permeated to the care that was offered to families. Interviews with members of staff reflected this theme of care strongly:

> You're not put in a position where you feel overwhelmed. Clients are protected as well because that's what our work is about.

> You feel cherished and cared for and protected. People do things to make you feel safe which helps you to cope with losses like bereavement.

> Lots and lots of support – it's a very supportive team... It's a nice place to work if things aren't going right.

The feelings of care and support were contrasted by workers' views of their previous posts as an area team social worker, and of the workers' impressions of the current experiences of area team social workers. For example:

> In the area teams they ricochet from one disaster to another and nothing gets done properly – things do get done properly at Sunshine; people get the sort of service they deserve.

> Before I came here I was grinding my teeth and having palpitations. There was no support at senior management level, no resources and no back-up. People didn't care about children and what was happening to them – they were just numbers and cases.

The effect of working in this apparently low-morale, high-pressure environment was illustrated by the description of the management of the Good family's case before they came to the centre. The mismatch of family views and disagreements was mirrored in social services' ineffectual activity. Decision-making and planning either failed to happen or were not properly thought through and no agreement could be reached. In this context the children were passed around from adult to adult to be cared for.

The culture of care at Sunshine appeared to enable the staff to reflect on the children's often painful experiences rather than to distance themselves:

> You think differently about families here. In the area team you feel shut off from children's emotional damage. Here we work more with the children and think more and discuss more. The impact of the damage and abuse becomes clear.

This experience resonates with Pithouse, Lindsell and Cheung's (1998) study where the centre was less narrowly confined to technical and procedural matters than the area teams and could be therefore be more focused on the inner realm of people's lives. It appeared to be easier to offer therapeutic services in the centre, whereas mainstream area team social workers were more bounded by a preoccupation with 'risk reduction', which did not allow for more therapeutic interventions.

## The Good family

*Family background*

Mrs Good has a history of depression and substance misuse. She is a single parent with two children, Joshua aged 12 (who has Tourette's syndrome and attention deficit disorder) and Kelly aged nine (who has anxiety-related health needs). Mrs Good separated from the children's father six years ago and the children see him and his new partner occasionally on weekends. The family was not previously known to children's social care but both of the children's schools report a history of their being poorly clothed, smelly and suffering repeated bouts of head lice. The high school had made several contacts with children's social care, with concerns about Joshua's behaviour and appearance but received no response.

When the school contacted the family home because of Joshua's absence, they discovered that he and his sister had been left alone overnight and that the house was in a poor state with no food available. When Mrs Good returned home, she asked for her children to be looked after, saying she could not cope. The children stayed with their maternal aunt for six months before returning home in an unplanned way, after a succession of family disagreements. The family was then referred to the Sunshine Family Centre. The children each had a child protection plan, highlighting concerns about the risk of further neglect and about the children's safety at home.

## The family's route through the centre

The Good family engaged quickly with the centre. Such readiness to engage was also found among the most successful families in a UK study of an intensive Family Preservation Service (Brandon and Connolly 2006). Mrs Good chooses the pseudonym 'Good' at a time when her family, and social services, were not seeing her as a 'good' parent. Play-based sessions were held with Joshua and Kelly, to give them the opportunity to speak with someone away from the home and to assess their worries and general well-being. For Mrs Good, counselling and a behaviourally based parenting group (Webster-Stratton 2000, p.7) were provided and also sessions to discuss parental responsibility with the children's father. There were also meetings with extended family, and a final review meeting to conclude the work at the centre. Follow-up services included continuing social work support and continued links with the centre through the offer of a parenting training group for teenagers (Dinkmeyer *et al.* 1998).

## Outcomes

### *Outcomes for parent and children*

Successful family support aims to inculcate in parents the experience of themselves as worthy, and to foster self-esteem, self-confidence and enhanced competence as a parent (Hearn 1995). These self-attributes stem from the emergence of trust through the experience of successful relationships (Crittenden 2008). At Sunshine there is also a clear focus on children having separate needs from their parents; also, similar attributes are hoped for with both children and parents. Six months on there were signs of promising outcomes:

- *Emergence of the self as likeable.* The centre helped Mrs Good to change her social worker and she realised that her new social worker and Sunshine staff now saw her as a 'good' parent and person.

- *Enhanced competence as a parent.* The children continued to be clean and well presented. They are encouraged and supported at home and at school, and behave better and are calmer at home.

- *The removal of the children's names from the child protection register* two months after the family left the centre.

There are still unresolved issues for Mrs Good, including discord with extended family. The standardised scales (Abidin 1995) showed marked improvement over time in her interactions with Joshua, but the overall score gained at the end point of service was still just below the level that would be expected in the general community. The Rutter, Tizard and Whitmore (1970) Malaise Inventory, an indicator of the degree of emotional distress and depression, revealed that Mrs Good's health was poor, and indeed there had been a slight deterioration. These scales perhaps indicate that high-threshold cases with deep-rooted problems will not be 'cured' by short-term services and appear to justify continued involvement with social services. The outcomes for the children included:

- regular attendance at school (Joshua was awarded a prize for good attendance)

- clean clothes, no more head lice and more predictability at home (parent in control)
- the ability to 'have a say' in their lives and ongoing contact with practitioners whom they trust.

Unresolved issues for the children included Joshua's anxiety that things might go wrong again at home. This was demonstrated by his mixed feelings about continuing involvement with social services: 'I'm still here with social services on my back. It's good and bad, a bit of both.'

*Possible outcomes for area team workers*
The experience and outcomes for area team workers, who join with the centre for as long as their referring family receive centre services, seem potentially to follow a process comparable to the one that characterises families, as suggested in Figure 11.1.

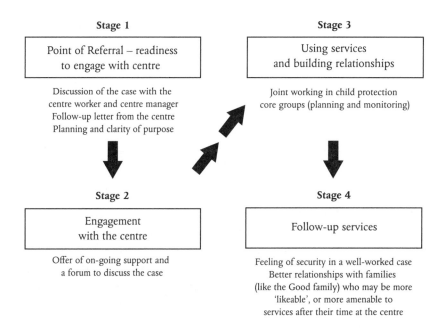

**Stage 1**

Point of Referral – readiness
to engage with centre

Discussion of the case with the
centre worker and centre manager
Follow-up letter from the centre
Planning and clarity of purpose

**Stage 3**

Using services
and building relationships

Joint working in child protection
core groups (planning and monitoring)

**Stage 2**

Engagement
with the centre

Offer of on-going support and
a forum to discuss the case

**Stage 4**

Follow-up services

Feeling of security in a well-worked case
Better relationships with families
(like the Good family) who may be more
'likeable', or more amenable to
services after their time at the centre

FIGURE 11.1 Steps along the way: containment for area team social workers working with the centre

As seen in the experiences of successful groups, centre staff members appear to have various needs: the need to feel connected; the need to believe one is competent or capable; the need to feel valued and that one counts; and the need to overcome fear and face challenges or to have courage (Lew and Bettner 1996). Social workers coming to the centre are also able to take advantage of the culture of care offered and may then take on the above-noted attributes, which are associated with positive psychosocial development and therefore a healthier work force. How the culture of care works is illustrated in Figure 11.2.

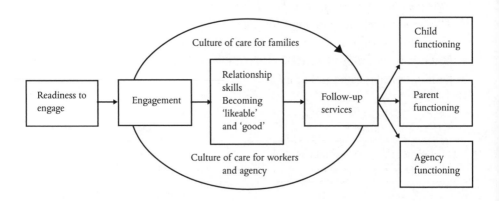

**FIGURE 11.2 The culture of care**
*Source*. Adapted with permission from Chaskin 2004 and Warren-Adamson and Lightburn 2004

## Lessons to be learned
The evidence from this pilot study shows that, as in the other parallel international pilot studies, families were able to benefit from their connections with the centre in a staged process where it was difficult to pinpoint any single turning point. The key learning from the study in relation to sensitive outcomes, however, has come from a deeper understanding of family centre staff from their own perspectives and their contribution to the culture created at the centre. This was most evident in the care that staff members took of each other, as well as care for the families, and indeed anyone who crossed the threshold of the centre. Centre workers were all well trained and well supported and secure in themselves and their roles. The sum total of these attributes

promoted a special sensitivity to the children and the families, as well as an awareness of the impact of this emotionally draining work on themselves.

The containment offered by the group under the steady leadership of the centre manager functioned so that the group was a repository for the emotional states and needs not just of the families but also of the workers who referred the families and other professionals who worked alongside the centre. In this respect, the centre extended and exported its culture to help look after external teams and individuals. The centre apparently was providing a stabilising role to counter dysfunctional parts of the agency exemplified by low morale and high vacancy rates. These findings have implications for the way child and family services are planned and delivered within large organisations in a climate which is starting to challenge defensive, bureaucratic and procedurally led practice. The publication of the Social Work Task Force Report (2009) makes this lesson about how to offer a supportive environment for families and workers very topical.

The enhanced confidence in the centre, particularly evident in the manager, enabled staff to work creatively and constructively and to exercise professional discretion, within tightly prescribed policy guidelines. Difficult professional decisions were made regularly about parenting capacity and the nature of this task forced the centre to be more child-centred than parent-centred. Practitioners were comfortable in this role and did not feel that it compromised their work in supporting parents. For example, preventive services were still offered through the on-site counsellor, at a time when the prevailing policy was dictating a high preponderance of court-based work.

The set of case studies in which this example fits (Berry *et al.* 2006), show that rich detail about practice contributes to a better understanding of how good child outcomes are promoted. For research that seeks to understand the quality of relationships in service delivery, it is important to assess the emotional as well the structural and policy climate (Ezell 2004). Qualitative methods can provide data which offer a good barometer of the health of agencies.

## Notes

1. 'Sunshine' is a pseudonym.

*Chapter 12*

# The Important Place of Professional Relationship
## A Case Study of an Israeli Family

Anat Zeira

Several innovative community-based interventions for children at risk and their families have been employed in Israel during the past decade (Ministry of Labor and Social Affairs 1998). Key components of the interventions include increasing parenting skills and providing safe and enriched environment for the children several hours of the day. Provision of services is based on assessment of the families' needs and capacities and on availability of services. The services are provided and funded by the local welfare agencies and by sub-contractors.

In this chapter we examine through a case-study approach the 'steps on the way' – or treatment activities – of a family that has been in intensive contact with the local welfare agency in a northern neighbourhood of Jerusalem. Our analysis suggests implications for review and evaluation of child and family services in other countries. Looking closely at services from a theoretical–professional perspective and on the basis of their social and political context enables us to identify the 'active ingredients' of interventions that are of a more general character.

## Method

Continuing the line of partnership between academia and field delineated in Zeira (2002, 2010), this case study is a product of collaboration among several partners: a university researcher (the author) and two undergraduate social work students in their third (and last) year of study have joined two social workers, one a family worker and the other a child protection officer, in the local welfare agency. This team has been supported by the agency's director and supervisors in the Municipal Department of Social Services. Together we have outlined and unfolded the process through which placement has been avoided and children have been provided with community-based interventions to ensure their welfare.

The case study is based on partnership between practitioners (insiders) and researchers (outsiders) who represent different perspectives on the object of study (DePoy and Gilson 2003). The outsider is generally free from emotional involvement, whereas the insider has to cope with it. Thus, the outsider can offer another dimension to viewing the process of intervention. Since each side brings into the study a different agenda, such partnership creates a tension between the insider's wish to assure the survival of the intervention and the outsider's commitment to conduct a rigorous inquiry. Therefore, compromise is required on behalf of all partners.

Ethical considerations prevented me from interviewing the family and joining the intervention meetings. The relationship between the agency and the mother was very tense, intense and loaded. The agency's director was afraid that adding researchers to the relationship might destroy the delicate balance of the intervention and harm the process. As the researchers, the students and I agreed with her fully and limited ourselves primarily to in-depth interviews with the social workers involved. With the mother's informed consent, we analyzed the case records and the practitioners' notes. We also conducted two interviews of about one and a half hours each with the practitioners; we employed a semi-structured interview method to ensure covering the various aspects of the case.

Analyzing the case records and social work notes required a decision on the theoretical framework according to which the information should be categorized. In line with the person-in-environment theoretical perspective, it was only natural to choose an ecological systems theory to help organize the process of the case study (Compton and Galaway

2005). This perspective integrates the personal, interpersonal and social factors in a particular case and shows how they interact. Furthermore, it emphasizes the importance of working with systems of different sizes. That is, client problems are not considered at the personal level alone, but at the level of the wider context of both the immediate (e.g. family and community) and the extended (e.g. social and political) environments.

In consultation with agency staff we chose the following case, which is representative of the agency's caseload except for the large number of children in the family. We analyzed the information by means of content analysis, as suggested by Rubin and Babbie (2008), when dealing with questions of 'who did what to whom, why, how, and with what effect?'

## Case example

### History

Mrs. C. is a 35-year-old mother of ten children ranging in age from one to 15. She grew up in a family that was in deep distress. They were poor and as a child she was a victim of abuse and neglect. Despite the ultra-orthodox religious way of living that she led with her husband, which partially explains the number of children and their spacing, she continued to be a victim of domestic violence throughout her marriage. Her 36-year-old ex-husband abandoned her after the ninth child was born. His whereabouts are not clear. During the divorce Mrs. C. had very little emotional and financial support from her extended family.

Soon after the birth of the youngest girl by an unknown father, Mrs. C. moved to the neighbourhood that was the setting of our research. Following her arrival, contact was established with the local welfare agency, because the school reported that the children showed signs of neglect and abuse. The child protection officer who visited the family noted severe poverty, physical violence of mother toward the children, mother's inability to provide basic needs (e.g. clean diapers to babies, food and drink), lack of parental authority, and manifestations of severe behavioural and emotional problems in the children. What she found was a typical picture of a multi-problem family (Gaudin *et al.* 1996), although rather extreme given the young age of the mother and the number of children. After a short but intense legal process, the five older children were placed by court order in residential settings. The remaining five young children were left at home under the supervision of the child protection officer. This is where our analysis of this case begins.

## Problems and treatment plan

Most families in deep distress are poor, and thus dealing with poverty is a primary concern in such cases. But poverty usually does not come alone. The other problems of Mrs. C. and her family can be organized in three domains: cognitive, psychopathology and social relations. Following is a brief description of each domain.

### COGNITIVE

Mrs. C. has a hard time observing herself and, in particular, difficulty in seeing how she contributes to the family situation. She is mostly preoccupied with the extremely difficult financial situation of the family. She has no time for herself whatsoever. Despite her understanding of the impact of her neglect of the children (e.g. not following through with their immunizations), she is not able to take any action to remedy the damage.

### PSYCHOPATHOLOGY

Mrs. C. presently is a single mother who seems to be completely disorganized. She has problems in setting and enforcing rules pertaining to mother–children relationships. For example, there are no rules about bedtime, eating habits, role hierarchy or respect for family members' privacy. The younger children are expected to carry out adult tasks that involve risk, such as cooking. Moreover, she does not seem to care about her older children when they are out of the home. In school, the children suffer numerous difficulties: they are isolated, have no friends, are chronically late, and exhibit inappropriate behaviour, such as taking off some of their clothes during class.

### SOCIAL RELATIONS

Mrs. C. is isolated. She has no friends and rarely sees anyone from her extended family (brothers and sisters). She has not established any contact with neighbours. In addition, she is not able to create a stable relationship with anyone. Reports from the welfare agency in the town where she lived in the past have revealed inconsistent contacts and persistent need for help. The children are isolated as well. Most other kids reject them, in part because they smell badly and behave aggressively.

Based on Rosen's (1993) conceptualization of the intervention process, Figure 12.1 illustrates the treatment plan for the family. The plan is presented in a general format that illustrates the sequence and linkages among the identified problems, the desired outcomes and the interventions. The social worker had to deal with several issues: neglect of the children, care for basic needs, social isolation and unemployment, but first and foremost she needed to help engage the mother in relationships with various practitioners with whom the family was directly or indirectly involved. The social worker hoped that pursuit of the intermediate outcomes would prevent placement of the younger children and eventually lead to the return home of the older children.

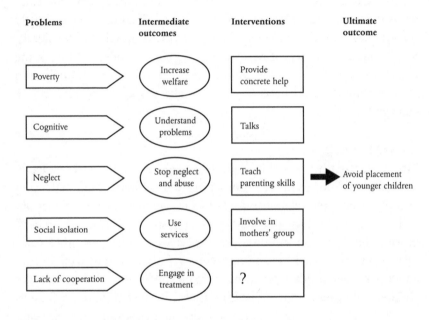

FIGURE 12.1 Treatment plan for the C. family

There was, however, a major obstacle: the mother would not cooperate. She did not show up for most of the meetings that were scheduled at the agency. She did not even go to collect food stamps or other supplies, and donations were sometimes left on her doorstep. Unlike the usual pattern of families in neglect, in which provision of concrete services enhances cooperation (Berry, Charlson and Dawson 2003), Mrs. C. did not enroll in any of the available programs. It should be noted that even though placement of the remaining children seemed unavoidable at this stage, the agency's policy had been to try and prevent it. Such a policy reflected partly a recent directive by the Ministry of Welfare that limits the extent of placement to four years (Zeira 2004), and partly a financial constraint on the number of placements, which are reserved for the most severe cases of abuse and neglect.

## Turning point

As mentioned at the beginning, the challenge to the practitioners in this case was twofold. With very limited community-based resources, the family's social worker wanted to provide the mother with every concrete service possible to help her out of the cycle of poverty. At the same time, the child protection officer summoned the mother to the agency's Decision Committee, which assigns the children to community-based services and, if needed, recommends out-of-home placement. Given the children's ages, and in the absence of immediate family members who could foster the children, the Committee made every effort to assure the children's safety within the community. Three of the children who were in school (ages six, seven, and eight) were referred three times a week to an after-school facility that provides hot meals, an enrichment program and help with homework. The school also provided school supplies and extra assistance to the children during school hours. The younger children (ages one, two, and five) were assigned to a multi-purpose day care centre where they stayed until early evening.

The mother's cooperation was minimal. Mrs. C. used most of the services but would not talk to the workers or attend any of the services that were offered to her (e.g. mothers' group). It seemed that, despite all the efforts and huge costs in both time and money, the services did not fit Mrs. C's needs or expectations. Moreover, there was friction between the mother and the welfare agency, and she even wrote to the Minister of Welfare to complain about the agency. At the same time, workers were not very gentle: hoping to 'shake up' the mother and force her to cooperate, they used their authority and threatened to remove the children and even suggested offering her baby girl for adoption.

At this point, as members of the university team that analyzed the documents, we offered our perspective. As outsiders to the process without the burden of emotional involvement, we could suggest that the social workers take a step back and try to look at the mother alone as a person with her own needs and even dreams. After all, she was a very intelligent young woman immersed in troubles, had no life of her own, had children living in many different places, and in her own way was crying out for help. Threats would not help because she was desperate. At one point Mrs. C. was strong enough to accuse the workers and the entire, woman-only Decision Committee of being judgmental of her. This showed that Mrs. C. had some strengths, and eliciting them was the social workers' responsibility. They had to be on her side. Clearly, the practitioners needed to support the mother and not to oppose her, a function that has been defined as 'containment' (Lightburn and Warren-Adamson, Chapter 4).

Gaining the mother's trust and building a partnership that would promote her empowerment were the first steps in the provision of services. The family worker understood that she needed to accept Mrs. C. and look for ways to attend to her needs, even informally. Such understanding led the practitioners involved in this case to revise their treatment plan and set other priorities for intervention. For example, one change pertained to the role of Mrs. C.'s relatives. Originally, the social worker thought that the extended family would be a positive resource for Mrs. C. Eventually she realized that Mrs. C.'s brothers and their wives were very critical of her; they did not accept her way of living (especially the fact that the father of the baby is unknown), and they did not provide any social, emotional or financial support. As a result, the practitioners eventually gave up on involving the extended family in the treatment process. Before any other resources would be allocated or any decisions made about the mother or the children, the practitioners had to establish an equal and sincere relationship with the mother. This, of course, involved an attempt to accept and listen to her unconditionally and without judgment. It was only then that the mother opened up, went to meetings with the family worker, and expressed some of the pain that she had been carrying for so many years. Because she had some talents and her children were secured in educational and welfare facilities throughout the day, she attended a mothers' group and began looking for a job. She also started to welcome the older children (who were out of home) to spend weekends with her – a necessary step to their return home.

## Summary

The social workers of the local welfare agency could not implement the initial treatment plan because they claimed – as we too often hear – that Mrs. C. was not cooperative. From an insider's point of view this was true. The social workers felt that they offered the mother and her children all possible resources. Given the circumstances in which they work, their efforts to provide one family with services to such an extent should not be underestimated. Yet, the mother did not know that, nor did she care about it. This interaction illustrates a possible reason for a rift between the practitioners and the client. As described below, the former were also in distress and were unable to see beyond the here and now. Thus, the collaboration that eventually developed between the outsiders who monitor the process and the insiders who are involved in the case clearly contributed to the process and led to positive outcomes.

## Discussion

### Interventions employed

Examination of the interventions employed with Mrs. C. using an eco-systems perspective demonstrates that the family worker had contacts with service providers on various levels: starting with the mother and her children (micro level); moving to the extended family and neighbours through the welfare, health and educational services in the immediate community (meso level); and going up as far as the legal system and the social security institute (macro level). However, having contacts with systems at the various levels does not mean that action was taken with all of them, or that they were all a target for change on the part of the staff.

The practitioners expected that change would take place only with the mother. Child welfare services sometimes focus on the children and tend to overlook the parents' needs (Jergeby and Soydan 2002). The reason may be the limited availability of resources (e.g. time, caseload) or the fact that their primary concern and legal responsibilities are to the children. But the picture of a family in deep distress is complicated and, in order to achieve change in such a family, a more comprehensive approach should be taken (Berry, Charlson and Dawson 2003). The eco-map that the author prepared of Mrs. C. and her family revealed a long list of services provided and of systems with which the family was involved. Starting with the extended family and neighbours, continuing with the welfare, health and educational services in the immediate community, and going as far as the legal and social security services, the family extracted almost every possible level of help that is available in Israel. The case shows that, before engaging so many systems with one family, practitioners should set better priorities to meet the family's needs and use available resources.

Looking as outsiders at the intervention with Mrs. C., the researcher had the impression that the workers are like firefighters in a burning field. It is not that there was no treatment planning. We even found evidence of systematic thinking, reflecting a linkage among problems, outcomes and intervention. What impressed the author was the fact that, despite all the investment of the practitioners involved, they reached a point where they were stuck and unable to help; they reached a dead end. The outsider's involvement and perspective eventually enabled progress in this case. There could have been even more – and quicker – improvement if there had been sufficient resources for the agency to provide supervision and guidance to the practitioners on a regular basis.

## Constrains and issues

Achieving positive outcomes with families, as the case presented in this chapter illustrates, is very costly to the Israeli taxpayer. The economic reality of Israel is harsh for people from low income groups. Resource allocation to welfare shrinks almost on a monthly basis; unemployment rates are high (close to 11%) and there is no clear political or social agenda for the near future. This reality poses a true challenge to social workers in local authorities. They are forced to respond to a growing number of clients whose major problem involves limited financial resources. When one of every three children in Israel is under the poverty line, social workers are looking for innovative ways to help clients. Yet other problems that concern the family (e.g. domestic violence) and the children (e.g. neglect) are often evident. Practitioners are called to be creative, engage the clients and empower them to take an active part in the process of change. An example of such active participation comes from the neighbourhood summer camps that are operated by unemployed parents in order to help working parents to keep their jobs during the summer.

The case of Mrs. C. demonstrates the constraints and issues inherent in social work with children at risk and their families in Israel. It shows that evaluation of the outcome of intervention must bring into account the cultural and societal circumstances in which the practitioners function. The latter too often report that they cannot provide their clients with the resources that are most appropriate to their needs, because these are not available. This is true both for community-based programs and for out-of-home placement services.

Social workers nevertheless must respect and follow the values that are the basis of the profession, even in hard times. Inappropriate use of authority, for example, brings nothing but antagonism on behalf of clients, as could be seen in the case that we have presented. In cases of abuse and of severe neglect, out-of-home placements may be unavoidable. But in cases where neglect is a by-product of poverty and distress, focusing on the ultimate outcome of child safety is not enough. At times it may even worsen the family's overall situation. These cases, whose number is growing in Israel as elsewhere, require different intervention strategies towards different intermediate outcomes. Clearly, the success of these intermediate interventions will be measured by other indicators than a child's placement, such as improvement in parental functioning.

It is evident, as the case presented in this chapter illustrates, that families in deep distress, typically characterized by multiple problems such as severe poverty, unemployment and neglect, present a challenge to Israeli social workers. In many cases there is no clear evidence for abuse, and neglect is suspected. Even with clear evidence of neglect, removing the children will not necessarily improve the family's situation, but it is more likely their situation will become worse. Social workers, therefore, are required to attend simultaneously to both the family's needs and the safety of the children.

Limited community-based resources for dealing with poverty and unemployment create a tendency to place children who suffer neglect in residential settings (Dolev, Benbenishty and Timar 2001). There are similar trends in the USA (Berry *et al.* 2003). In Israel the vast majority of school-aged placements are in residential settings, whereas most of the younger children (five and under) are placed in kinship or 'regular' foster care (Ben-Arieh, Zionit and Berman 2008). There are no satisfactory national statistics on this issue in Israel, but practitioners in local welfare agencies feel that in many cases where placement is considered, they are able to keep families together. In a country that allocates only 30 percent of its annual welfare budget for children at risk to community-based services (Zeira 2004), such efforts should be encouraged and supported.

## Cross-national perspectives

Most of the outcome-based evaluation literature in child welfare comes from the USA and other English-speaking countries. However, cultural differences as well as variations in political climate and social agenda suggest the advantage of cross-national collaboration in implementing and evaluating social services. Even among Western countries, programs and services that are grounded in similar theoretical approaches may be implemented differently. In addition, funding is yet another critical issue everywhere and much can be learned from sharing cross-national experiences. For example, limiting the extent of care on the grounds of cost is not unique to Israel, and policy makers could benefit from comparing experiences on the resulting costs and benefits.

Jergeby and Soydan (2002) suggest that understanding practitioners' work processes in different countries may contribute to developing new perspectives. Practice procedures in the area of child welfare may differ in their explicit and implicit cross-national agendas, but they have fundamental similarities as well. The differences may be related to cultural, legal and institutional factors. The terminology used in different countries and the definition of children at risk, abuse and neglect may differ. For example, in Israel the definition pertains to three levels of children at risk:

1.  Children at imminent risk, such as children who are in direct and immediate danger because of abuse and neglect.

2.  Children who live in an endangering environment or children who are exposed to indirect danger, such as those witnessing violence or living in poor communities.

3.  Children who live in circumstances that bear risk, such as children from families in divorced, single-parent families or families experiencing unemployment (Ministry of Labor and Social Affairs 1998).

Because the consequences to the child are different at each of the above levels, it follows that the desired outcomes (both in terms of the long run and the short run) are different and require different intervention approaches. Cross-national variations in such definitions and consequent variations in laws and practice may shed light and improve our understanding of processes and outcome. Practice lessons can be generalized to other countries and constitute equally important contributions in cross-national comparisons. For example, Lau (2003) raises the issue of single-parent families in Hong Kong, where cultural values are very dominant and shape policy and social services for families.

## Conclusion

In many countries the extended family plays a major role when families are in crisis, as it is often required to assume child care responsibilities. In other countries the extended family is a weaker resource and other solutions must be sought. In this chapter we have presented a case that demonstrates some similarities and differences across countries and cultures. The similarities are obvious, as poor families with single parents and many children are classic clients of child welfare services. Similarities in the methods of treatment by social workers are also evident. But in this case some of the problems faced by the family are specific to the community from which they come – an ultra-orthodox Jewish community – as well as to the segregation between religious groups in Israel, both in living areas and in school systems.

The particular values of this community explain the mother's need to leave her town and move to a new neighbourhood when she stops being 'religious'. Also explained are the ability of her ex-husband to escape supporting the family and the unwillingness of the extended family system to support Mrs. C. in a country where family support typically plays an important role. But these specific aspects of the case do not shroud the deeper meaning of its story: respecting the humanity of people in need can go a long way toward helping them to overcome their problems. Furthermore, analyzing a range of typical cases can contribute to the measurement of success in child and family services.

# Chapter 13

# Evaluation of Sensitised Practice in a Community Centre in Aotearoa, New Zealand

Robyn Munford, Jackie Sanders and Bruce Maden

In this chapter, evaluation is explored in the context of sensitised practice in a community centre. The chapter is based on findings from an ongoing study of the interaction between a *whanau* (family) and a community centre in Aotearoa, New Zealand. The focus in particularly on evaluation findings from the process of early engagement with a *whanau* because it allowed the research team to explore more fully the ways in which sensitised practice unfolds and to consider the particular benefits in terms of outcomes for children and their families. When talking about sensitised practice, the authors refer to work with families that is based in the communities in which families live and involves practitioners in responding to the needs they present to agencies across a range of service domains. This work provides a foundation for assisting families to engage in positive change processes. Such practice is fundamentally multidisciplinary in nature. It avoids confining families to particular service lines such as counselling, early childhood, family preservation. Rather, sensitised practice seeks to fit interventions around families, drawing from a broad spectrum of professional expertise in a tailored fashion. It requires culturally competent practice which understands in depth the ways in which culture shapes understanding. Finally, it actively promotes high levels of user involvement in determining the nature of the helping relationship and in organisational decision making (Hess *et al.* 2003).

The chapter begins with a brief overview of the evaluation design; then Te Aroha Noa is introduced, the organisation that was the focus of the evaluation and the case study *whanau*. Attention then turns to several of the key findings from the evaluation. The chapter concludes with reflection on the evaluation process. This discussion illustrates the complex and subtle ways in which the initial phase of the intervention created a framework within which long-term family development and change became possible.

## The evaluation design – collaborative inquiry

Collaborative inquiry (Handley *et al.* 2009) was chosen as an evaluation design because of its emphasis upon collaboration and active engagement of client and community members. Collaborative inquiry provides a framework for active engagement between evaluators, service providers and families as the evaluation proceeds. It requires that evaluators be prepared to invest time in building relationships with all key parties and that they maintain open communication with practitioners, service managers and client families throughout. Te Aroha Noa Community Services is a 'learning organisation'; it has made a commitment to ongoing development and growth and has a long-term vision of families becoming partners in the management of the organisation and the delivery of services. The evaluation methodology needed to work with this overriding organisational mission and to be flexible enough to adapt to organisational change over time.

The evaluation utilised a range of methods including individual semi-structured interviews, focus groups, observations and reviews of organisational documents. Individual interviews were completed with service users and with staff. Four focus groups were completed with vertical and horizontal slices of stakeholders – including governance group members, community members, users and staff. In addition to these activities, 14 in-depth guided reflection sessions were held with key agency personnel to articulate and then test out their theory of change. A number of evaluation documents were produced that included a formal report (Handley *et al.* 2009) and a number of internal documents. Finally, observations were conducted in the public areas of the centre which included the early learning centre, group rooms, and reception and meeting areas.

## The agency and its practices

Te Aroha Noa operates in a community that is often described as having high social and economic deprivation. Issues of culture have also been prominent as local people have worked to find ways to encourage young people to find positive cultural role models that counterbalance the attraction of harmful activities, such as gang life and substance abuse. Connecting with cultural heritage is seen as a critical intervention strategy because of its role in building a positive sense of belonging. Many parents identify risks to their children in this community and face real challenges in trying to keep them safe.

The works of Friere (1985) and the focus on education and development inform engagement with families. Te Aroha Noa uses strengths-based principles and builds interventions around an understanding of how culture and context inform practice. Staff members are clear that they are not *the* solution to family issues, but rather they provide opportunities and support for people to find their own pathways through the challenges they face. In a community that has few material resources, finding novel ways of solving resource issues is a focus of the work, as is working extensively with other agencies to help families to meet their own needs. A broad spectrum of services is available to families at the centre. These include early childhood education, adult education, counselling, preparation for school (HIPPY), intensive family development and community development activities that support families to become engaged with community resources and opportunities.

## The case study *whanau*

This chapter focuses on the story of one family that participated in this evaluation to allow the research team to elaborate upon the ways that sensitised practice contributed to good outcomes for children. This family is an extended network, centred on the relationship between three sisters (see Figure 13.1). The sisters have shared the raising of their children, including providing *whangai* care (culturally based kinship care) when needed. They have a strong sense of internal integrity and have always cared for each other, done whatever was necessary and solved their problems internally. The oldest sister made a promise prior to her mother's death that, as the oldest sister, she would take care of everybody. Keeping this promise has presented her with many challenges, and she has made sacrifices in order to honour it. These women have a very strong attachment to each other, and what troubles one generally troubles all. Moreover, spirituality is particularly important to the sisters.

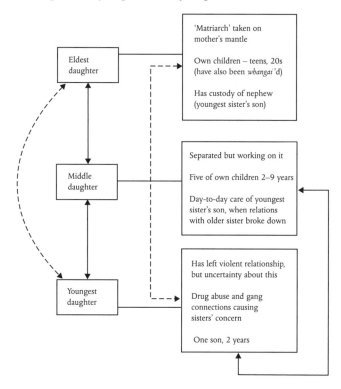

FIGURE 13.1 The case study *whanau*

Six children under ten years were the immediate focus of the work undertaken. Five were the biological children of the middle sister; one was the child of the youngest sister. The older sister had children who were older and who were *whangai'd* by her mother, and so they were both nephews and brothers to the middle and younger sisters. The two older sisters provided most of the care for these children. The children appeared very comfortable with their aunts, receiving much unconditional and very open love.

Being able to appreciate, respect and work with this complexity and to understand that ultimately the whole family comes first in this unit is critical. Although there was substantial conflict between the oldest and youngest sisters that resulted in their seeking support from Te Aroha Noa, it was equally apparent that the preservation of the unit was critical to the well-being of all its members. Simply agreeing to disagree or walking away, although talked about by the sisters, was not an option that would bring positive benefits for these women and their children.

In order to try to protect the youngest child (the youngest sister's son) from a very violent and unstable father, the oldest sister, acting in her role as matriarch and with the mother's (youngest sister's) agreement, took shared custody and guardianship. The two older sisters expressed an ongoing concern that the younger sister was not attentive to the safety issues that her lifestyle created for their nephew, and so the custody arrangements provided a legal framework by which they could act to protect him. Until recently, the youngest sister had accepted this and had also agreed to have the oldest sister provide day-to-day care for the child. These actions meant that the statutory child protection agency did not need to become involved with the family.

The youngest sister visited her son daily at Te Aroha Noa's early childhood facility and came to the point where she was ready to have full care of him. However, after finding her sisters unwilling to step back and allow this, she instituted legal proceedings to remove her sister's legal status in relation to the chid. This was the issue that prompted the *whanau* to seek Te Aroha Noa's help. Lying behind this issue were tangled and painful experiences, losses and grief and sometimes a sense of overpowering fear and hopelessness.

The sisters came to the agency because it was willing to work with them in diverse and flexible ways, helping when they asked and stepping back when required. They recognised that the agency was a mainstream organisation (i.e. it was not provided by a tribal authority or other cultural organisation). However, they found it to be very responsive to their needs as Maori, particularly in terms of recognising spiritual matters, respecting and using family protocol as part of the helping process, and working with them as a complex whole. For their part, the agency exercised great care in acknowledging these matters.

## Findings from the evaluation – learning about sensitised practice at Te Aroha Noa

The following discussion maps out the process of early engagement between centre staff and *whanau* and in so doing highlights several components of sensitised practice, drawing particular attention to the subtle ways in which the community centre created an environment within which small steps on the way to change became possible.

## 1. Early work as scaffolding

During the evaluation the authors observed the early processes of engagement by a number of workers from different disciplines with this *whanau*. This early process was like scaffolding, creating structural pieces of relationships around which specific interventions, or focused pieces of support, would later be built. This way of thinking about the early process has important implications:

1. Time must be allowed to get the scaffolding right. Too much involvement might mean that the *whanau* loses its integrity, as good supportive relationships can risk supplanting *whanau* relationships that are under stress. Too little involvement could mean that the *whanau* is left without adequate support. Community centre receptivity is a critical aspect of scaffolding construction in the early period of support.

2. Workers understood that the scaffolding is temporary; it can later be dismantled and the *whanau* can carry on without it.

3. As is the case with all scaffolding, the work takes place with care and attention to detail to ensure it can carry the weight it needs to bear. This implies sufficient resources and capacity to do the work required.

The scaffolding metaphor appeared to come closest to describing the early months of the service. This gentle process of unfolding support can often be missed in evaluations; indeed, it is often largely undocumented and certainly would not be 'counted' for funding purposes. A lot of this early relationship-building took place in the car park when the key worker and a sister met as he was coming back to the office and she was leaving the early childhood centre. These chance conversations enabled the passing on of much information in an unthreatening way, the testing out of responsiveness and trustworthiness, and ultimately the development of a very important helping relationship. The scaffolding helped to make the environment safe with the result that later formal or therapeutic activities could be very focused and effective.

## 2. Early childhood as the spine

In addition to providing a valued local resource for a community's children, early childhood has been described as the 'spine of the resource' in community centres (Warren-Adamson 2001, p.12). In the evaluation the researchers learned that this *whanau* first used the early childhood services, and later, as a crisis arose, family members were confident enough to seek social work and more intensive support services. They explained that they were more confident in doing this because they had watched how centre staff worked with others when in crisis. The early childhood service enables local families to seek support with easily nameable matters (such as time-out, training or employment) while they build confidence to be able to share painful and more challenging troubles (Sanders and Munford 2010).

### 3. Community centres as providers of containment
Warren-Adamson (2001) and Lightburn and Warren-Adamson (2006) have described social work in community centres as offering a sense of containment or holding, linking this to a view of parenting as containment. This sense of containment, they argue, allows for both rational and irrational behaviour to be productively managed in what may appear from the outside to be a chaotic process. The notion of containment provides a framework for social workers to manage their own responses to irrational behaviour and also to offer a sense of refuge to families whose lives are affected by such matters.

The sense of safety and being contained within a secure process was critical to this *whanau*. We noted above that the sisters in our case-study family had a very strong sense of themselves as a coherent and self-contained unit, and the idea of seeking outside help was difficult for these strong women. Finding a place that could contain the emotional and physical pain that had pushed them to the point of seeking help was a matter that the sisters raised frequently in the evaluation.

The agency provided them with numerous workers and different settings where they could attend collectively and individually to different matters, and they had a very strong sense that it would not let them down in this delicate process. They talked of feeling safe and sensing that the workers attached to them had an intuitive sense of what was right at the time. So the sense of safety was not only about security around the implications of their troubles and the protection of their information; it was also a deeper sense of connection to the people who were working with them and who profoundly understood what was happening, even if they did not always know the details.

## 4. Multiple modalities

As implied in the preceding discussion, the agency was able to work in a wide range of ways with the *whanau*, as a unit and also individually. Over the first six months of the service the following resources were provided:

- early childhood care to three preschoolers on a weekly basis
- four *whanau* meetings
- clothing from the community shop
- support to attend lawyer meetings and two court hearings
- personal support and counselling to the three sisters by different members of staff
- care for the school-age children after school so mother could attend classes
- individual counselling to one of the children
- after-school intense interpersonal support to oldest child twice weekly
- advocacy and support in the sisters' interactions with the school.

Staff members were highly inventive about finding routes to engagement, supporting Warren-Adamson's (2001, p.7) reference to community centres as *beacons*. Community centres can provide a variety of 'acceptable' routes for accessing a wide range of services. The multidisciplinary nature of the support provided meant that varying combinations of adults and children could be worked with and individual support could also be provided. The *whanau* found it particularly valuable that they did not have to move among a number of agencies to have their needs met.

Being local was also an important component of effectiveness. The sense of being seen as wanting, or not adequate, was keenly felt by local residents. This undermined confidence when seeking support outside the physical boundaries of the suburb. Understanding the struggles faced by families, who often could not afford to live elsewhere, but equally knowing about the strengths and positive dimensions of life in this community, was important to families. It enabled staff members to target their support knowledgeably. The sisters talked of feeling very warmly welcomed to the centre and that, because staff 'knew how it was', they were able to be themselves.

## 5. Only families can create change

The sisters' narratives highlighted the reciprocal nature of their interactions with the centre. This disrupted the notion of experts telling families how to change and the sense that families are objects of intervention. On numerous occasions the sisters talked to the research team of the contributions they made to the centre and the sense of belonging they had in relation to it. Staff members also reinforced this sense of reciprocity, referring to the cultural expertise the sisters brought to the centre and its importance in deepening their capacity to work with others. The reserchers also observed these reciprocal relationships when they visited the centre, noting staff members seeking guidance from the sisters about cultural protocols, for instance.

Empowerment is a key concept for social work; however, it is not without its challenges when it is packaged with personal support. As Scott and O'Neil (1996) have argued, suggesting that a social worker can empower a client implies a power imbalance that contradicts the very notion of empowerment. Strengths approaches (Sanders and Munford 2010) allow support to be seen as reciprocal rather than one-way processes, and this provides a useful way of thinking about empowerment within an intervention context. Thinking about families as competent and able to give as well as receive support and resources is an important orientation because it is the family that will create and sustain the change (Handley *et al.* 2009). The sisters spoke of a deep respect for the expertise of the social workers. They had checked them out and decided that this centre would be able to meet their needs. This was very significant because there are a number of traditional, *iwi* (tribal) providers in their local community, and the researchers would have expected that, given the significance of their cultural roots to their lives, they might have chosen one of these providers. They noted the respect and recognition that the agency accorded their cultural practices. One sister, in particular, highlighted the care with which workers prepared for the support they gave, making sure that they were well briefed on the most appropriate protocols for different circumstances.

## 6. Patience and care over the process

The evaluation demonstrated that at Te Aroha Noa, individual and family work was only one dimension of practice; staff members also harnessed capacity and drew the community into its work. Work grew out of relationship-building, and normalising the development of helping relationships was an essential characteristic of this work. Support was located on a relational continuum and 'clients' could locate themselves at different points on this continuum over time, giving as well as receiving.

The sisters talked of the patience of staff and a sense that they would not give up, but equally that the centre would not allow them or others to be placed at risk. Although the promise was of unconditional support, it was also of *informed* support, where careful decisions were made about what was and was not acceptable. This was important to the sisters, who talked about the impact on their community of gang life, drug abuse and child neglect. There was a sense that support and resources were available and that acceptance involved understanding the reality of these risks. The sisters also appreciated that paperwork and bureaucratic processes did not drive the support. Their narratives described a menu of resources that they could access as their needs dictated. In this sense the intervention fitted around their lives – not the other way around. They were in control of their own change process (Gilligan 2004), something that was very important, given their desire to resolve issues internally. They talked of acquiring tools that they could then use in other situations. Repeatedly the sisters stated that staff members did not tell them what to do, that they were in control and that the support enabled them to work out what needed to happen. For their part, workers talked about this initial phase as a very uncertain one, where they were working out how far they could go, wanting to contribute to significant changes, but equally not wanting to step in front, rather trying to enable things to happen without pushing too hard.

## Outcomes for children

Work with the sisters and their children continued beyond our project. By the end of the evaluation some interesting changes had been noted in the children's behaviours. Educators who had been working with the children at school, in after-school activities and at the early learning centre noted that incident reports relating to these children had substantially reduced. For the oldest son, who was rapidly becoming labelled as a 'difficult' student, these changes were very important. The balance in his school experience had gradually begun to shift from primarily negative to being increasingly positive. In particular, it seemed that the individualised after-school support he had received from the centre gave him a safe adult to whom he could take his frustrations and worries and with whom he could develop strategies for trying to do things differently at school and home. Behind the scenes, his key worker had met with school staff and also worked with his mother and aunts to encourage them to be ready to respond positively to him when they saw him implementing these strategies, and in this way to help create spaces for him to be recognised for what he did well rather than what he did poorly.

Direct work also occurred with the youngest child in the early learning centre, particularly around behavioural problems he presented with, which involved disruptive and angry outbursts. The centre had a very strong, positive behaviour management plan which was implemented carefully with this young child and which was also used as a framework with the sisters to help identify ways in which they could reorient their parenting strategies with him so that there was consistency between home and centre. Gradually, this little boy's behaviour began to indicate less stress, and staff in the centre began to witness more frequently a delightful child emerge from the angry shell.

Considerable effort was expended with the sisters in supporting them to develop positive child behaviour management approaches that were non-violent. Creating good outcomes for children requires more than strong parenting support and the development of consistent management plans around children's behaviour. The struggles around parenting and the angry and challenging behaviour of children often references back to serious unmet emotional needs in their parents. Building parent capacity and skill alone does not address these issues. Thus, work also focused directly upon the emotional needs of the three mothers in this *whanau*, and it was this deeper set of interventions that created the emotional context within which the sisters could become 'available to parent' and apply the parenting skills they were learning (Sanders and Munford 2010). At the end of the evaluation, the sisters reported increased numbers of positive encounters with their children and reductions in the use of physical punishment, and they relayed stories of happy family outings in public and more settled family times. The reports from school and the community centre indicated that all the children were more settled and were observed to be happier, more content and more confident. Incident reports from both places did not feature their names, as they had prior to the intervention. (Similar responses were found by Aldgate and Rose in a Scottish project described in Chapter 13 of this volume.) The prospects for these children had improved as a result of the multifaceted support they had received from the agency and from their own networks.

## Reflecting on the evaluation processes

The action evaluation developed a 'recursive' character beginning with a fairly standard framework which was based around programme logic and a commitment to produce programme learning for staff throughout. Four key questions structured the evaluation overall; these were negotiated with staff and they were used to shape the questions that were asked in the interviews and focus groups and to structure observation:

1. Who are the people we serve and how do we do this?

2. What values, principles, skills and knowledge do we use to do this work?

3. What difference do we want to make with these people and how do we think that we can best contribute to this?

4. How do we know when we have been successful and when we haven't?

The recursive character developed as evaluation learning fed into service delivery and the development of new initiatives. For instance, once the early focus groups had been completed, staff indicated an interest in pursuing guided-action reflections on a more regular basis with the research team to articulate more fully the theoretical underpinnings of their work as a multidisciplinary team. This work enabled staff to understand more fully how positive change can be achieved and sustained at the micro level in their direct work with families, but also at a wider organisational and community level. Their guided-action reflections developed into a more extensive research programme (Handley *et al.* 2009) which then formed part of the framework for the subsequent development of an innovative community development anti-violence programme, which itself was the subject of a new evaluation and which in turn fed into new programme developments.

In this way, the evaluation produced localised findings that were useful in the immediate context of the family support and early childhood services. It also generated activity and reflection in a more generalised way that led to staff and family interest in ongoing evaluation of activities and the development of new initiatives. Fundamental to all of this activity were the strong relationships and trust established between the evaluation team and staff. As outsiders, evaluators constitute an intrusion into the daily life of workers and families who use community centres. However, they bring useful skills and have the potential to make a valuable contribution to how centres operate, leading potentially to improvements in life circumstances for families. Working carefully to build trusting relationships with staff and with clients who use services is an important part of the evaluation task. This leads to better quality information and it also helps to reduce any negative impacts on the daily work of the organisation. Building strong relationships provided us with a framework within which we could test out our emerging findings and it also provided us with opportunities to undertake peer analysis of data with practitioners. This significantly enhanced the quality of the evaluation and it also meant that staff were enthusiastic about using the findings immediately to build their practice and to innovate in the longer term.

## Conclusion

The data from this evaluation resonates with material generated internationally about community centres. Discussions with agency staff have suggested that members of a complex *whanau,* such as the one discussed here, are frequent participants at the centre, and so we would expect that the flexible and responsive capacity demonstrated here has relevance beyond this single *whanau.* The multidisciplinary capacity of the centre and its ability to be highly flexible and responsive are particularly salient characteristics. Te Aroha Noa has been particularly successful in blending components of cultural practice into their work with family and *whanau* support. This was seen, for instance, in their willingness to intuitively build significant cultural protocols into their practice.

As with many agencies in Aotearoa, New Zealand, the centre operates from a strengths base. What is unusual about it, however, is that it takes this focus on strengths and capacities further, arguing that the *whanau* that come within its orbit contribute to its daily operation and its long-term future. The development of community leaders as part of the process of giving support is a novel approach that, as noted above, is now providing some momentum for wider community-level change around violence.

The focus on individual, *whanau* and community change is complex and presents some significant challenges for the centre as it works to balance all of these different dynamics constructively. In particular, it is clear that the focus on capacity and skill of user-families is a valuable strategy for creating personal change momentum. It encourages the development of outward-looking parents who develop a strong sense of self-worth and efficacy by making contributions to the functioning of the centre and the well-being of others in the wider community.

# Chapter 14

# Assessing Practice in a Child and Family Centre in Australia

Patricia M. McNamara

The primary aim of the study described in this chapter has been to identify the 'sensitive' indicators of change. Sensitive indicators are sometimes defined as 'steps along the way' to long-term outcomes in community-based child and family interventions. In the past we have understood something of these long-term or distal outcomes of interventions but have not identified these sensitive or proximal indicators of change. An example of a long-term outcome of intervention is school retention; a sensitive indicator of change leading to this outcome might be an adolescent's active engagement in a literacy support program. These sensitive indicators are the vital 'steps along the way' to major change; such 'steps' often go unnoticed. These indicators of change are also described as 'mediating outcomes' (Berry, Bussey and Cash 2001; Berry *et al.* 2006; McNamara 2006).

In reporting the findings of this study, the role of the community centre as *container* is considered, in the tradition of object relations theory; the centre almost always offers nurture, support and guidance which can be highly protective of families facing serious social and emotional challenges in their lives (Lightburn and Warren-Adamson 2006). The family–practitioner relationship within the context of broader ecological systems is also explored. In so doing, principles of grounded theory (Glaser and Strauss 1967; Charmaz 2005) and participant action research strategies have been applied (Wadsworth 1999; Hill 2004).

## The research setting

I have joined with a manager, a practitioner and a family using services at a community-based family centre in Melbourne, Australia, to conduct this study. The research setting is Berry Street, one of the largest and longest-established non-government organizations in Australia. This organization began as a foundling hospital over a century ago; it is now perceived as a key Australian provider of child and family programs. The family recruited for the study has been receiving services from the Matters program, based in a suburban regional office of Berry Street. This program offers an extensive range of services to adolescents and their families.

## Research question and framework

The primary research question developed for this study appears disarmingly simple, but is of course, quite ambitious. We ask: What are the sensitive indicators of long-term outcomes in community-based programs?

Ecological systems theory is the overarching framework influencing the focus of this study and the choice of research methods (Maluccio and Whittaker 1997). This flexible and inclusive framework has facilitated the exploration of the unchartered territory of sensitive outcomes. Developmental concepts are also a useful framework, particularly those derived from object relations theory (Mahler, Bergman and Pine 1975). In this regard, an understanding of the community-based centre as 'container' has been important to the research design (Lightburn and Warren-Adamson 2006).

This research focuses in on change and on difference. In systems terms we have been asking: 'What is the difference that makes the difference?' in successful intervention programs. From a narrative-constructivist perspective, the family and professionals have worked with the researcher to form a team of investigators who co-evolve a shared 'reality'. Collaborative exploration of this nature reflects an empowering, strengths-based approach to child and family practice and research. As reflective investigators we have also tried to turn the lens on ourselves and on the narrative as it has unfolded; in so doing we have attempted to apply our collective emotional intelligence to the challenges presenting (Fook 1996; Morrison 2007; Schon 1983).

# Research design

The research design for this investigation is an intensive case study based on collaborative or cooperative inquiry, a participative, user-empowering approach to research (McNamara 2009; McNamara and Neve 2009; Reason and Bradbury 2001). One family was recruited for the study, with the aim of conducting an in-depth single case study over a one year. Together, we have been keen to identify the sensitive outcomes of intervention as these are the previously mentioned 'steps along the way' that contributes to longer-term outcomes.

The practitioner and the family described the desired outcome at the outset of the intervention program as strengthened family relationships. The primary intervention targeted for exploration by this group of collaborators was that of family therapy. Close tracking of that intervention facilitated the monitoring of both sensitive indicators and the long-term outcome goal of strengthened family relationships.

## *Methodology*

Munford and Sanders' (2003) methodological template, a 'Three Stage Model' for conducting qualitative research in community-based centres, has proved well suited to this study. I have also tested many branches of Wolcott's (2001) 'qualitative research tree'. The methods employed have elicited impressively 'thick descriptions' of key phenomena. I also feel able to write and speak about my own experience of our project in the first person rather than cower behind the 'blank wall' of the ethnographer. This has given me permission to experiment with auto-ethnography, exploring the lived experience of the *research for the researcher* (Wolcott 2001). I have invited the family, the worker and manager to join with me both in designing the study and in choosing appropriate research strategies along the way. I have felt able to seek and take direction from these key players; we have gradually come to feel like a 'research team' rather than the 'researched' being directed by me. I have also tried to let the voices of all participants speak freely in reporting the findings.

At Stage One the researcher addresses participant (collaborator) recruitment; once that had been completed the family members and professionals worked with the researcher to provide background information and develop a contemporary status report; Stage Two data collection occurred six months later and Stage Three at a 12-month follow-up (McNamara 2006). At both of the latter Stages there was a primary focus on identifying change and difference. At Stage One, data was collected through conversations between the manager, the worker, the family and the researcher and by direct observation; similar strategies were employed at Stages Two and Three, but with the practitioner, family members and researcher only as reported elsewhere (McNamara 2006). Rigorous application of the principles of participant action research described by Munford and Sanders (2003) and Wadsworth (1998) has been attempted throughout. Curtin and Fossey's (2007) advice was influential in ensuring trustworthiness; trustworthiness of this research was defended through background briefing, an audit trail, direct observation, in-depth interviews, rigorous video and audio recording and transcription, participant checking of transcripts and thick descriptions. O'Neil (2001) and Bessell (2006) were consulted to ensure that ethically defensible empowerment strategies were in place, especially in relation to working with young people, and Wolcott in relation to writing up and dissemination (2001). This has resulted in a minor departure from some more traditional ways of collecting and analyzing data and of disseminating knowledge (McNamara and Neve 2009).

Qualitative research strategies included history-taking, participant observation, action research, application of grounded theory, micro-ethnography, collaborative data collection and reflection. Video recording and observation of a family therapy session took place at Stages One and Two; later, there was a home-based video recording of the final Stage Three case review meeting. The outdoor video production, filmed in the family's much loved garden, was initiated and managed by two of the adolescent children, Sally and Nigel. For the first time in some years their mother, Marjorie, baked the family's favourite cake. The conclusion of this study was clearly also a celebration of the family's resilience. All of this activity seemed to manifest the family's growing interest in directing the research process and their enthusiasm to infuse that process with ritual and even some drama.[1] This was one of many occasions when the mode of data collection spontaneously changed direction from the initial plan.

## Data analysis

The data from the observations and interviews was coded, cross-filed and analyzed thematically; it is reported here as a modified ethno-narrative (Denzin and Lincoln 2005). The participants' voices speak for themselves, in an attempt to achieve an authentic identification of even the smallest steps along the way to larger change. This strategy is consistent with empowerment and feminist methods in social research; these approaches needed to be carefully embedded in a study which took place in the aftermath of serious family violence (McNamara 2008a, 2008b, 2009; Naples 2003).

## Findings

The family and the practitioner were provided with a record of their involvement in the study in the form of videotaped recordings of family sessions and research interviews (O'Neil 2001). The centre as context, the process of intervention and the resulting changes are presented here, primarily through the voices of the collaborative investigators engaged in the study: the centre manager, the practitioner, the family and my own voice, as researcher.

### The centre manager's voice

The voice of the centre manager was heard in several conversations at Stage One as she was engaged in a semi-structured briefing to facilitate collection of agency data. Data collection strategies of investigative journalism and ethnographic exploration were employed. It should be noted that the centre manager was not directly involved with the family in this study. Her engagement in the study was confined to organizational critique and clinical consultation (especially in relation to case selection and recruitment), consistent with her role in the centre. As manager, she referred to the centre's mission statement; the logo derived from this statement is 'Berry Street believes all children should have a good childhood.'

The manager described the centre's demographic make-up as mixed. 'It includes service users living in public housing, working and non-working families on lower incomes, and middle and upper middle class families.' The conceptual orientation of the centre would appear to combine ecological and developmental frames of reference (Bronfenbrenner 1979). Sue presented her agency as also having 'A strong commitment to empowerment and to responsive and creative practice.'

Gender-sensitive family systems practice from the micro- to the macro-systems level is clearly emphasized, especially in the area of domestic violence. The Centre also has a focus on substance abuse and is a statutorily accredited setting for regulation of parent–child access.

Homelessness is addressed through provision of emergency housing, individual and family counselling and referral and liaison services, as noted by the manager: 'Many of our service users are living with a diagnosed mental illness. Some of them, though by no means all, are receiving psychiatric services from other agencies.' Liaison with other services in the ecological niche is an important aspect of the centre's role. The manager remarked that 'we are not a 'one stop shop' but we like to think we can respond to a wide range of needs'.

Foster care and a range of group programs are offered by the centre. Self-referral to the music program for parent and child survivors of domestic violence was the initial point of agency entry for the family engaged in this study. The centre is part of a community service organization largely dependent upon state and federal government funding. The manager made it clear that this centre, like most of its kind in Australia, operates in a context of stringent accountability and funding uncertainties.

### The practitioner's voice

The voice of Tho, the practitioner, an experienced and well-qualified family therapist, was heard in a range of data gathering situations. He was engaged in a preliminary research briefing involving an exploration of organizational culture; later, he was involved in history-taking, a phenomenological file review, and a number of unstructured telephone discussions as well as the researcher's observation and videotaping of two family therapy sessions led by Tho.

At Stage One, Tho met with the researcher to review the family's file and address the points listed on the checklist (Munford and Sanders 2003). The recruited family had presented itself to Berry Street some four months prior to the research. The picture at that time was one of a family in the early stages of recovery from years of trauma. The 20-year parental marriage had ended, with the father moving out of the marital home. This was a union characterized by very serious domestic violence. Both parents had experienced depression for many years and were currently receiving psychiatric treatment. The mother was also struggling to overcome an alcohol addiction; this had recently resulted in a two-week residential treatment program. Tho described Marjorie as extremely fragile. At the first meeting 'she was pale and shaking and even mumbling'. He opined that her alcohol addiction was possibly a form of self-medication resulting from the intense stress she was experiencing as a victim of long-term domestic violence.

Tho also thought that Marjorie was overwhelmed by and sometimes avoidant of the challenging responsibilities of being a primary caregiver of three seriously troubled adolescent children. Each of the three children of this marriage was living with serious social and emotional difficulties. The identified problem at the time Marjorie referred the family to the centre related to Nigel, who is 13. His disruptive behaviour had resulted in his being removed from the local high school. Marjorie found Nigel's hyperactivity and intrusiveness incredibly demanding; he had recently been diagnosed with attention deficit hyperactivity disorder. Nigel's provocation of his sister, Sally, resulted in continuous conflict, which overwhelmed the mother's fragile parenting capacity. Tho described Nigel as 'developmentally rather immature'. He thought that this 'probably related to the trauma he experienced throughout his life'.

Sally, aged 16, had also recently missed several months of school attendance, after a close friend had committed suicide by throwing herself in front of a train. Sally was the last person to speak with her. Following this tragedy, Sally had apparently not been welcome to return to the school she and her friend attended. The event resulted in enormous anxiety and guilt for Sally; she continued to have weekly sessions with a child psychiatrist at the local child and adolescent mental health service. Like Nigel, Sally had just transferred to a new school when this study began; these school transfers appear to have been positive moves in each instance.

The eldest child in the family is Lucy. She is 19 years of age and, although technically still living at home, spends almost no time there. The family rarely knows Lucy's whereabouts. They believe she is staying with various friends and suspect she may have a new partner. Lucy attempted to take her life two years ago. She was treated briefly for depression then but, at the time of data collection, was no longer receiving personal help. Tho described a single session with Lucy and her mother as 'very powerful and moving, as Lucy was supported to drop her rather fragile intellectual defenses momentarily; she was put in touch with the love and loyalty of her mother'. That has been the centre's only direct contact with Lucy to date. The researcher met Lucy incidentally on one occasion, but she chose not to be involved in this study. Tho described the family members as being 'people scattered around, not joining together'.

Tho stressed to the researcher that he focused his work with those family members currently living in the household. The father in the family, Jeff, who has regular access to Nigel and considerably less contact with his daughters, may be invited to join some aspect of the family work at a later stage. Tho's clinical decision appears to have been influenced by the severity of domestic violence in this case, reflected in the local magistrate's court recently initiating a restraining order in an attempt to contain risk to the mother (McNamara 2007, 2008a, 2008b).

During data collection, Tho, who impressed as a creative, compassionate and spiritual professional, stressed repeatedly that 'it is my great privilege to work with such an extraordinary family whose love for each other is a hidden treasure… I am having great enjoyment working this family.'

## The family's voices

The family's voices were heard and recorded during three home visits, several telephone conversations with the mother, an observed family therapy session, a brief but important waiting-area conversation and a chance meeting with several family members in the local shopping mall. For all family members, their experience of help-seeking at this centre has, in itself, been an important step on the way toward improved functioning. The family described the centre as warm, caring and supportive. The children and Marjorie were warm in their praise for Tho as the most important element in this. Marjorie explained, 'I resent being robbed of happiness in my family life…the wheels came off for me a decade ago; only since receiving this help through family therapy do I feel that the happiness is coming back.'

Family members also presented strong positive contrasts between this centre and other services they had experienced, especially mental health services. Marjorie said that the best thing about this help was that 'You are not judged. We are most blessed to have been referred to Tho, he has a lot of insight and he is someone who understands the strengths in our family. You leave there feeling that we are good people who can do things, not just sick little people with problems.' The family liked the warm atmosphere of the waiting area and described the reception staff as welcoming. As Marjorie and Nigel stated, 'They are always smiling! …you feel good just going in there!' Marjorie felt other service users were also affirming and normalizing of the family's help-seeking: 'Even the other people we met in the waiting area seemed very nice.'

Family members were aware of other services offered by the centre should they need them. The children mentioned that school friends had accessed 'youth services' and Marjorie welcomed service information in the centre's waiting area. Marjorie, in particular, seemed to experience a strong sense of containment in the object relations sense. She believed that the centre would be able to refer the family on to appropriate services should the need arise. Marjorie felt that the staff would also be committed to ensuring that such a referral would be closely monitored and she would not be 'left up in the air'. Feeling affirmed and validated by the centre was clearly an important step along the way to larger change for Marjorie and her children.

### The researcher's voice

From tentative beginnings, when the children especially were uncertain whether they wanted to be part of the research, their voices and that of their mother have gradually become more than eloquent. The family and the practitioner have been well able to relate to the aims of this research from its outset. Trust in the collaborative relationship with the researcher grew rapidly. Marjorie shared with me increasingly detailed accounts of the trauma she had experienced within her marriage, including descriptions of multiple serious physical injuries. There was clearly a duty of care incumbent upon me to ensure that she and her children remained safe during this study.

## Sensitive outcomes

There are clearly always going to be areas of commonality and areas of difference amongst participants in identifying steps on the way to crude outcomes. This case study was no exception. One difference observed was the humility of the practitioner in relation to his clinical skills. The sophistication of his interventions was noted repeatedly by both the family and by me. Not surprisingly, Tho did not appear to see himself in the same light as the rest of us – that is, as a powerful agent for change. Overall, however, common perceptions of change amongst the participants far outweighed differences. These common perceptions are those highlighted here. The following appear to be the generally acknowledged steps on the way to the outcome of strengthened family relationships, as identified by the family, the practitioner and the researcher:

- The family beginning to plan outings and activities together, learning to be more sensitive to one another's preferences.

- The mother assuming greater responsibility for family management and parenting, having courageously addressed her alcohol addiction and commenced work-related study.

- The mother establishing and maintaining clear legal and physical boundaries between herself and the children and their father.

- The family recruiting a student as paying boarder to help redress their serious financial difficulties, to avoid loss of the treasured family home.

- The family becoming more responsive to one another's needs, especially for space and privacy and with sharing household chores.

- Family members agreeing to stay in close contact with one another, through text messaging and other means.

- Family members coming to believe that they are actually an 'extraordinary family' with strengths and resources, not just an ordinary family with many problems.

- Family members allowing others, including the practitioner and the researcher, into the home; this shift in trust and intimacy seemed to mirror the developing intrafamilial trust.

- Lucy having a positive response to a session with her mother and Tho. Marjorie, Sally and Nigel are all hoping that this step will pave the way for Lucy to access needed services from community agencies and rejoin her family.

- The family feeling welcomed, affirmed, empowered and supported by the centre. This appears consistent with the agency's philosophy and mission statement as described by the manager.

## Identifying sensitive outcomes through participant action research

This study illustrates that collaborative investigation over time, by families, practitioners, managers and researchers can identify the steps along the way to long-term or larger outcomes. These sensitive or proximal outcomes are critical turning points in the change process; such minimal shifts can often be overlooked or their import minimized, when indeed they should be amplified and celebrated. Knowledge of such outcomes is vital for the practitioner, the program manager, the researcher and, most importantly, for family members (Hill 2004). This quintessentially post-modern 'way of knowing' is not especially new (Hartman 1990; Mayer and Timms 1970), yet it grows ever more important in a political climate dominated by economic rationalism. Within the academy, and in the field, there is pressure to demonstrate effectiveness, the 'evidence base for practice'. Notwithstanding intense ongoing debate around what constitutes such evidence, it would seem that intensive auditing of small and larger changes resultant from interventions is at least as defensible as other types of evidence; one might argue that it is far more defensible than many (Gray and McDonald 2006; McNamara and Neve 2009).

I have, however, been mindful throughout the conduct of the study described here that ungrounded hypothesizing in relation to change and difference can lead to false identification of sensitive outcomes; identified steps along the way to larger outcomes must drawn directly from the data and clearly articulated as a shared reality of the key stakeholders (Strauss and Corbin 1998). Throughout the course of this study, I have attempted to remain firmly focused on the unfolding narrative as voiced by the participants (McNamara 2009). This has proved, it would appear, an effective means of militating against departures from inferential accuracy in identifying outcomes (Curtin and Fossey 2007).

The social justice imperative, to give something back to families as part of the reciprocity of collaboration, seems consistent with participatory approaches to research (Charmaz 2005; Munford and Sanders 2003; O'Neil 2001). All family members involved in this study seemed pleased to receive copies of videotaped family therapy sessions and research interviews at the conclusion of data collection. The mother expressed considerable sadness that she had been unable to maintain accurate records of her children's development since serious family problems took over her energy and attention. The research videos met a need she now felt to record new-found strengths in her family's narrative. Family members have also actively sought updates on progress of the cross-national study, of which this research has been one part (Berry *et al.* 2006). As Wadsworth points out, participatory action research is 'not simply an exotic variant of consultation. It is active co-research, by and for those to be helped' (1998, p.14).

Tho invited the family engaged in this study to regard itself as 'extraordinary'. As a researcher I have found not only the family extraordinary but also the practitioner, the centre manager and the service itself. To ensure that the strengths and achievements of the family are acknowledged, it has been essential that my impressions be directly expressed as part of the process. This appears consistent with the spirit of participatory research (Hill 2004; Wadsworth 1998) and what Hammond (1998) describes as 'appreciative enquiry'.

## Conclusions

Research teams, which include the researched (our erstwhile subjects), the researched for (service users, caregivers, administrators) and the researchers hold exciting promise for future investigations of family and children's services (Wadsworth 1998). The clarity with which the steps on the way toward larger or long-term outcomes were identified by this team of collaborative investigators is especially promising. The study also illustrates the potential of participant action research to make a difference; this can occur when action is researched, changed and re-researched by all participants working together.

## Acknowledgements

I would like to acknowledge the commitment made by all engaged in this study which was based at Berry Street, Victoria, Australia. I am most appreciative of all who teamed up with me to explore these 'newer ways of knowing'. The family members, the practitioner and the centre manager have embraced with me the challenges and opportunities associated with longitudinal participant action research.

## Notes

1.  The British feminist researcher Vivienne Griffiths (1984) argues that drama is a feminist research strategy. She points out that it is collaborative (involving collective story-building); it enables people to find their voice (both verbal and nonverbal); it is concrete (rather than abstract); and it is context-dependent. All of these features would also appear to be intrinsic to participant action research.

# Afterword
# Cross-National Perspectives and Ideas

## Mark Ezell

At the 2004 Annual Meeting of the Society for Social Work Research, Thomas Insel, Director of the National Institute for Mental Health, discussed the length of time between science and service – that is, how long it takes before a discovery is widely used in practice (Insel 2004). He explained that the time lag between the production of evidence and its application in general aviation is 48 hours; in most of medicine, 17 years; and with mental disorders, forever. How long does it take child welfare practitioners to incorporate the use of new discoveries in their practice? Is enough relevant child welfare research being conducted, and done so with enough rigor, that practice will be improved at a rate faster than that for mental disorders and medicine? Not only do all the editors and chapter authors hope we are making progress, but we are all highly committed to improving child welfare practice and research post-haste.

This volume represents the efforts of child and family researchers from various countries to produce evidence that can quickly become part of everyday child and family services. The authors meet at least annually as members of the International Association for Outcome-Based Evaluation and Research on Family and Children's Services to discuss and plan child welfare research and its applications to practice and policy. These dialogues, cross-national comparisons and collaborative research projects are sure to quicken the time it takes to translate this new knowledge into everyday use. Child welfare practitioners, researchers and clients all over the world should benefit from the generosity of time, energy, resources and spirit of the Fondazione Emanuela Zancan, which helped start and continues to support the International Association. We also acknowledge the tireless dedication of Anthony Maluccio, Cinzia Canali and Tiziano Vecchiato, our fearless leaders, who founded and continue to lead the Association.

In his remarks mentioned above, Dr. Insel wisely reminds us that evidence of an intervention's effectiveness is only one piece of the puzzle of reducing the lag between science and service. Other factors that are important to address include increasing the knowledge and behaviors of practitioners, as well as improving our abilities to access and engage families. Progress will be enhanced as our understanding of the dissemination of innovations and implementation strategies increase. Our capacity to implement new and improve existing programs will advance as we increase our knowledge of agency requisites for effective services, such as agency climate, culture and structure. Finally, Dr. Insel suggests that the environment within which agencies operate and families receive services needs to change so that policy makers can identify new and different financing approaches and the stigma of 'clienthood' is reduced. It is clear from the work in this volume that the members of the International Association have embraced Dr. Insel's bold research agenda and are more than up to the challenge.

## Stepping back

To appreciate this volume fully, it is useful to step back from a chapter-by-chapter view and consider the whole and where it came from. This collection of essays is extraordinary if for no other reason than the singular focus on child and family services. The authors conduct their research with the great desire that their findings will have an impact on child and family policy, program design and everyday professional practice; and they hope that the influence occurs sooner rather than later. Their strong desire to make positive differences in the lives of children and families binds them together across hemispheres, time zones and languages. Their shared hopes create a remarkably positive synergy and a sense of community that is unique. It is easy for one to see how this synergy and sense of community have influenced their thinking and their contributions.

The work described in each chapter occurred in the context of a particular society and culture. Change is the only constant, as each country varies in its emphasis on evidence-based practice; the sources, levels and mechanisms of funding; the extent and nature of public–private partnerships; and the ever-changing configurations of service systems. That is not to say that homogeneity exists within any given country. As one appreciates the variations of dynamic contexts that the authors represent, it is easy to see both how captivating and challenging cross-national research is.

The chapters address a wide range of topics and vary in their focus from micro to macro. Important and vexing methodological issues that confront researchers of children and family services are the subjects of several chapters. The authors of numerous chapters concentrate on identifying 'sensitive outcomes' of family/community centers by using case study approaches. These authors take Fein and Staff's (1994) advice and look closely into the 'black box' of services (referring to a metaphor for multiple interventions that are not clearly specified). Adding to an already unique collection of chapters, are other presentations including the analysis of conversations with foster care alumni, and, at the other end of the spectrum, macro comparisons of the child welfare systems in numerous countries with administrative data.

## Recent trends in evaluation research

Outcome-based researchers are likely to be acquainted with several noteworthy trends in evaluation research, which are briefly reviewed here. These include the evidence-based practice (EBP) movement, the continuing need for complementary types of evaluation, and emerging protocols for the reporting of research.

### Evidence-based practice movement

The growing acceptance of outcome-based research and the current advocacy for evidence-based practice in social work, child welfare and social work education are intertwined. As Roberts and Yeager (2004, p.v) highlight:

> Evidence-based practice is based on systematic reviews of a body of research and evaluation studies on a particular treatment or intervention practice. Hand-in-hand with the movement toward evidence-based practice has been a search for methodologically rigorous practice-based research and empirical evidence resulting from the studies.

As others have indicated, evidence-based practice greatly depends on and is enhanced by thorough outcome evaluation.

The evidence-based practice movement in social work, although increasingly accepted, has been met with scrutiny and criticism. As a result, a long list of warnings and caveats is developing. Rubin and Babbie (2010) include a good discussion of 'controversies and misconceptions' about EBP in their widely used research book. Usher and Wildfire (2003) make good points about at least two concerns regarding EBP: first, that 'we should acknowledge its limitations and be modest about claims concerning the scientific bases of many practices in the field' (p.599); and, second, that we should question the recurring implication that researchers alone will set the research agenda and take us away from important partnerships among researchers, policy makers and practitioners.

Those of us engaged in outcome-based research should take these concerns to heart. We should continue to create and nurture collaborations with practitioners, as many of the researchers represented in this volume have done. For example, Brandon (Chapter 11) and others who conduct case studies to identify sensitive outcomes can only do this kind of work with the full cooperation of agencies and practitioners. Who better than practitioners can contribute to the interpretation of findings and implementation of lessons learned? Moreover, although we always strive for scientific rigor, we know that agency-based research involves compromises of design, sampling and measurement. It is incumbent on researchers to discuss these compromises fully as they seek to generalize findings.

Other commentators, such as Ainsworth and Hansen (2002), embrace 'evidence-based practice as ethical practice' (p.36) and point out that agencies with a research-resistant culture need to change, as do schools of social work. Additionally, these authors confront the thorny issue of what constitutes evidence and remind readers that tedious arguments about qualitative versus quantitative research should be avoided: 'This should not be an ideological battle for one side to win and the other to lose, as both approaches have much to contribute' (p.38). Ainsworth and Hansen (2002) also call for curriculum reform in schools of social work. As they indicate, since most social work researchers are educators as well, it is a curious phenomenon that so many of our graduates 'think that it is acceptable to practice primarily from a foundation of personal beliefs, political or religious ideology rather than empirical research' (p.45). This is not acceptable. Amen![1]

## *Need for complementary types of evaluation*

For years and years, evaluation of and accountability for social work programs focused on such program outputs as the number of clients served or the number of bed-days per month. Convincing the field to focus on outcomes started as an uphill battle but seems to have turned the corner on its way to social work gospel. (Of course, the insistence by many funders of social work programs, such as the United Way, helped greatly to legitimize the efforts to define and measure client outcomes.) As is often the case when the pendulum changes direction and swings back, it can swing too far. One danger with the enthusiasm for outcomes-based evaluation is that process evaluations and fidelity studies will become low priority. As various contributors to this volume remind us, without these types of studies, outcome-based research loses its value because 'program designers and practitioners cannot know whether the program intended is really the program that was implemented' (Thomlison 2003, p.561).

Outcome researchers can estimate the degree to which performance benchmarks have been achieved, but without formative evaluation, program managers are not given the tools to improve performance. Our research needs to guide management practice as well as direct practice, as Munford, Sanders and Maden (Chapter 13) remind us.

These different types of research complement one another and, resources permitting, one type should not be abandoned for another. The reality of human service programs is that each usually comprises several services (e.g. assessment, crisis intervention, and referral) delivered by many different staff who have varying levels of education and experience. It is rarely the case, therefore, that any two clients will receive the exact same 'package' of services delivered in exactly the same way. Besides measuring outcomes, this reality requires that researchers dig very deeply in order to identify the critical change mechanism in an intervention. There is far too little of this level of understanding.

Although all of us call for more and more outcome-based evaluation, formative evaluation, fidelity studies and looking inside the black box, I am cognizant of a disappointing trend that weighs heavily on the conduct of research in the area of child and family services. Research funding is harder to acquire than ever before. Ever since the Reagan administration's national devolution of much social service funding and policy-making from the national government to the states in the USA, the commitment to fund evaluations of new programs and policies has diminished. As states make cuts in social services, research funding competes with service funding and usually loses. In a high proportion of jurisdictions, whether the decisions are made at a legislative and/or executive level, priority is given to the funding of services and frontline workers at the cost of evaluation and middle management. Both of these are false economies; there is little appreciation that evaluation can contribute to improved effectiveness and efficiency. Middle management, greatly misunderstood and disrespected, provides important types of supervision and quality control. I would go so far as to suggest that some of the child fatalities in child welfare could be traced back, in part or in whole, to the lack of supervision of practitioners and the absence of programmatic quality control.

## *Protocols for reporting research*

Like EBP with its roots in health care, another practice is emerging from health care that social work researchers should consider – the establishment of protocols for reporting research. During the 1990s, an international group of biomedical researchers and editors published the CONSORT (Consolidated Standards of Reporting Trials) statement, which was revised in 2001 (Moher, Shulz and Altman 2001). Its goal was to improve the reporting of randomized control trials to the point of complete transparency. As a marker of its significance, several medical journals simultaneously published the statement.

Even though randomized control trials are rare in social work and child welfare, readers still need to have enough information to assess the quality of the research: 'Empirical evidence indicates that not reporting the information is associated with biased estimates of treatment effect' (Moher, Schulz and Altman 2001, p.1987). The CONSORT statement includes a checklist of items to report as well as a flow diagram of the progress of subjects through the intervention. Figure A.1 includes an abbreviated list, without descriptors, of these items. In 2006, the editorial board of the US journal, *Social Work Research*, began encouraging authors to refer to the CONSORT Statement when reporting empirical findings (Jenson 2006).

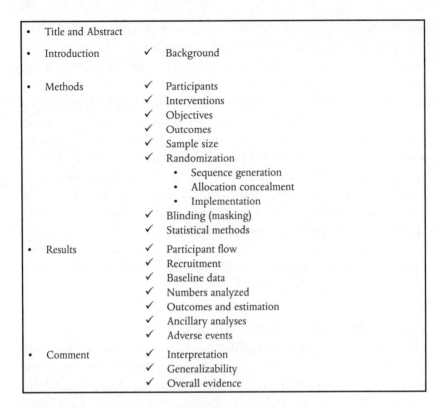

FIGURE A.1 **Items to include in reports of research**
*Source:* Adapted from Moher, Schulz and Altman 2001

In the field of community psychology, Sarason (2003) also points out that descriptions of community interventions are inadequate. He asserts that researchers should present more information about the 'before the beginning' phase. He uses Congress as an analogy to make his point: the inside story is what frequently explains why a proposed law passes or fails, and if passed, why it might not accomplish as much as hoped. As Sarason emphasizes, we need to know the stage preceding implementation 'if we are to begin to understand how outcomes were influenced or not influenced by the ups and downs, errors of omission and commission, the predictable and the unpredictable, the adaptations and compromises that were made' (p.211).

In addition, elsewhere I have recommended that researchers at least describe and possibly measure agency level factors and the characteristics of agencies' task environments (Ezell 2005). This includes such aspects as describing the educational background and attitudes of caseworkers and supervisors, agency auspice and the service density of the immediate task environment.

## Issues for the future

Despite the quality and range of chapters and topics in this volume, there are other issues that researchers might include in their future work. I make these suggestions to serve as a springboard for the future and not as criticisms of the work contained herein. For example, how do power and authority play out in programs, and what are the dynamics involved when most clients are involuntary? Second, how much did these programs cost and what are the ways that the levels of funding (and, of course, the availability of other types of resources) influence operations and outcomes? Third, how has cultural/societal history specifically influenced the design of policy, programs and the structure of the service systems?

In addition, as important as agencies and programs are to the operation of child welfare systems, the authority of the court is the legitimizing force that permits intervention into families (at least in the US). The nature and extent of this power define the leverage often needed to gain client cooperation, as well as the penalties/consequences for failing to cooperate.[2] Researchers rarely discuss or analyze this important aspect of intervention. What are the consequences if a family member, especially a parent, refuses to participate in a program? How real is an involuntary client's cooperation? Should the use of authority and/or negative consequences be viewed as one aspect of the intervention? In what other explicit and subtle ways does the 'hand of the state' operate in a program? Are practitioners aware of these forces, and how do they use them, if at all? How do different types of clients experience authority as they receive services? Certainly, the court-derived authority is not the only kind of power operating in these service transactions. Social class, gender and cultural differences, among others, create power differentials as well.

Although almost every chapter in this volume includes a description of the policy and historical context of service delivery, there is little or no discussion of cash and resource expenditures or any estimates of the cost of services per client. In the future, especially because of the cross-national nature of this work, a valuable point of comparison would be knowing if similar programs are operating on very little money and using volunteers versus being better financed programs with professional staff. Such a comparison could lead to a possible explanation for variation in client outcomes. If an intervention is implemented in two different settings, one well financed and the other on a tighter budget, is it really the same intervention?

For cultural reasons, certain programmatic alternatives are more and less acceptable in different countries, thereby making each country's continuum of services different.[3] For example, until very recently adoption was almost unheard of in Australia, whereas in the US it has been much more acceptable and frequently used. Because of differing availabilities of adoptive placements, out-of-home care of all types is likely to operate quite differently in these two countries. Although this example demonstrates distinct cultural differences, how culture influences policy, program design and the continuum of services is usually subtler. Since researchers struggle to see how their culture may impact services, one great benefit of the International Association is that the differences are much more apparent as we make comparisons. As we add to the work represented in this book, researchers in the International Association might consider developing the anthropology of child welfare, where the influence of culture, past and present, on program and policy design is analyzed in a comparative fashion.

## Conclusion

This volume represents a step forward in the development of empirically validated interventions in the field of child and family services. One of its unique contributions is that we hear the voices of researchers from diverse countries throughout the world, as they analyze similar types of programs influenced – and made different – by their geographic locations. This work thus promises to advance our knowledge of service effectiveness and to confirm the importance of cross-national research.

## Notes

1. Other writers also call for the integration of evidence-based practice with social work education (Edmond *et al.* 2006).

2. Many people argue that clients are not cooperating with programs when power and authority has been used to leverage it. When they do not have real choice, they are acquiescing.

3. It is likely that social welfare ideological differences shape service systems in addition to culture. The two might have an interactive influence on child welfare systems.

# References

Abidin, R. (1995) *Parenting Stress Index.* Lutz, Florida: Psychological Assessment Resources.

Adoption and Foster Care Analysis and Reporting System (AFCARS) (2005) *The AFCARS Report for 2003.* Washington, DC: US Department for Health and Human Services.

Agar, M. (2004) 'An anthropological problem, a complex solution.' *Human Organization 63,* 4, 411–18.

Agar, M. (2006) 'An ethnography by any other name.' *Forum: Qualitative Research 7,* 4, Art. 36. Available at www.qualitative-research.net/index.php/fqs/article/view/177/396, accessed 9 August 2010.

Ainsworth, F. and Hansen, P. (2002) 'Evidence based social work practice: A reachable goal?' *Social Work & Social Sciences Review 10,* 2, 35–48.

Ainsworth, F. and Maluccio, A.N. (1998) 'The policy and practice of family reunification.' *Australian Social Work 51,* 1, 3–7.

Aldgate, J. (1980) 'Identification of Factors influencing Children's Length of Stay in Care.' In J. Triseliotis (ed.) *New Developments in Foster Care and Adoption.* London: Routledge and Kegan Paul.

Aldgate, J., Jones, D.P.H., Rose, W. and Jeffery, C. (2006) *The Developing World of the Child.* London: Jessica Kingsley Publishers.

Aldgate, J., Rose, W. and McIntosh, M. (2007) *Changing Directions for Children with Challenging Behaviour and their Families: Evaluation of Children 1st Directions Projects.* Edinburgh: Children 1st.

American Humane Association, Children's Division, American Bar Association, Center on Children and the Law, Annie E. Casey Foundation, Casey Family Services *et al.* (1998) *Assessing Outcomes in Child Welfare Services: Key Philosophical Principles, Concepts for Measuring Results, and Core Outcome Indicators.* Englewood, CO: American Humane Association, Children's Division.

Ammerman, R.T. (1990) 'Predisposing child factors.' In R.T. Ammerman and M. Hersen (eds) *Children at Risk: An Evaluation of Factors Contributing to Child Abuse and Neglect.* New York: Plenum Press.

Anderson, R.A., Crabtree, B.F., Steele, D.J. and Reuben, R.M. (2005) 'Case study research: The view from complexity science.' *Qualitative Health Research 15,* 5, 669–85.

Armbruster, P., Sukhodolsky, D. and Michalsen, R. (2004) 'The impact of managed care on children's outpatient treatment: A comparison study of treatment outcome before and after managed care.' *American Journal of Orthopsychiatry 74,* 1, 5–13.

Australian Institute for Health and Welfare (2005) *Child Protection Australia 2003–4.* Available at www.aihw.gov.au/publications/cws/cpa03-04/cpa03-04-c04.pdf, accessed 9 August 2010.

Axelrod, R. and Tesfatsion, L. (2006) 'A guide for newcomers to agent-based modeling in the social sciences.' *Staff General Research Papers, 12515,* Iowa State University, Dept. of Economics. Available at http://ideas.repec.org/p/isu/genres/12515.html, accessed 9 August 2010.

Baartman, H. (1996) *Opvoeden kan zeer doen. Over oorzaken van kindermishandeling, hulpverlening en preventie.* Utrecht: SWP (in Dutch).

Baartman, H. (2005) 'Kindermishandeling: De politiek een zorg?' In H. Baartman, R. Bullens and J. Willems (eds) *Kindermishandeling: De politiek een zorg.* Utrecht: SWP (in Dutch).

Bal, S., Crombez, G., Van Oost, P. and Debourdeaudhuij, I. (2003) 'The role of social support in well-being and coping with self-reported stressful events in adolescents.' *Child Abuse and Neglect 27*, 1377–1395.

Baldwin, S., Wallace, A., Croucher, K., Quilgars, D. and Mather, L. (2002) *How Effective are Private and Public Safety Nets in Assisting Mortgagors in Unforeseen Financial Difficulties to Avoid Arrears and Repossessions? Review Protocol.* York: University of York.

Barreteau, O. (2003) 'Our companion modeling approach.' *Journal of Artificial Societies and Social Simulation 6*, 1. Available at http://jasss.soc.surrey.ac.uk/6/2/1.html, accessed 9 August 2010.

Barsky, A.E. (2009) 'The legal and ethical context for knowing and using the latest child welfare research.' *Child Welfare 88*, 2, 69–92.

Barth, R.P. (1990) 'On their own: The experience of youth after foster care.' *Child and Adolescent Social Work Journal 7*, 5, 419–46.

Baskin, K. (2004) *Complexity, Stories and Knowing: International Workshop on Complexity and Philosophy.* Rio de Janeiro, Brazil. Available at http://isce.edu/ISCE_Group_Site/web-content/ISCE_Events/Rio_2005/Rio_2005_Papers/Baskin.pdf, accessed on 26 July 2010.

Batavick, L. (1997) 'Community-based family support and youth development: Two movements, one philosophy.' *Child Welfare 76*, 5, 639–663.

Batchelor, J., Gould, N. and Wright, J. (1999) 'Family centres: A focus for the children in need debate.' *Child and Family Social Work 4*, 197–208.

Bebbington, A. and Miles, J. (1989) 'The background of children who enter local authority care.' *British Journal of Social Work 19*, 5, 349–78.

Becker-Lausen, E. and Mallon-Kraft, S. (1997) 'Pandemic outcomes: The intimacy variable.' In J. Jasinski and G. Kaufman Kantor (eds) *Out of the Darkness: Contemporary Perspectives on Family Violence.* Thousand Oaks, CA: Sage Publications.

Belotti, V. (ed.) (2009) *Accogliere bambini, biografie, storie e famiglie.* Firenze: Istituto degli Innocenti.

Belsky, J. (1997) 'Determinants and consequences of parenting: Illustrative findings and basic principles.' In W. Hellinckx, M. Colton and M. Williams (eds) *International Perspectives on Family Support.* Aldershot, England: Arena, Ashgate Publishing Limited.

Ben-Arieh, A., Zionit, Y. and Berman, Z. (2008) *The State of the Child in Israel: A Statistical Abstract.* Jerusalem, Israel: National Council for the Child.

Bernstein, N. (2000) *A Rage to Do Better: Listening to Young People from the Foster Care System.* San Francisco, CA: Pacific News Service.

Berry, M. (1997) *The Family at Risk: Issues and Trends in Family Preservation Services.* Columbia: University of South Carolina Press.

Berry, M., Brandon, M., Fernandez, E., Grietens, H., Lightburn, A., McNamara, P.M., Munford, R., Palacio-Quintin, E., Sanders, J., Warren-Adamson, C. and Zeira, A. (2006) 'Identifying sensitive outcomes of interventions in community-based centres.' *International Journal of Child and Family Welfare 9*, 1–2, 2–10.

Berry, M., Bussey, M. and Cash, S. (2001) 'Evaluation in a dynamic environment: Assessing change when nothing is constant.' In E. Walton, P. Sandau-Beckler and M. Mannes (eds) *Balancing Family-Centered Services with Child Well-being.* New York: Columbia University Press.

Berry, M., Charlson, R. and Dawson, K. (2003) 'Promising practices in understanding and treating child neglect.' *Child and Family Social Work 8*, 1, 13–24.

Bessell, S. (2006) 'Research with children: The time for debate is now.' *Communities, Families, Children, Australia 1*, 1, 43–9.

Biehal, N. (2005) *Working with Adolescents: Supporting families, Preventing Breakdown.* London: British Agencies for Adoption and Fostering.

Biehal, N. (2006a) 'Reuniting children with their families: Reconsidering the evidence on timing, contact and outcomes.' *British Journal of Social Work 37*, 5, 807–23.

Biehal, N. (2006b) *Reuniting Looked After Children with their Families.* London: National Children's Bureau.

Biehal N. (2008) 'Preventive services for adolescents: Exploring the process of change.' *British Journal of Social Work 38*, 3, 444–61.

Biehal, N., Ellison, S., Baker, C. and Sinclair, I. (2010) *Belonging and Permanence: Outcomes in Long-Term Foster Care and Adoption*. London: British Agencies for Adoption and Fostering.

Boaz, A., Ashby, D. and Young, K. (2002) *Systematic Reviews: What Have They Got to Offer Evidence-Based Policy and Practice?* Working paper 2. London: ESRC UK Centre for Evidence Based Policy and Practice, Queen Mary College, University of London.

Bouwmeester-Landweer, M. (2006) *Early Home Visitation in Families at Risk for Child Maltreatment.* Rotterdam: Optima Grafische Communicatie Rotterdam.

Brandon, M. (2006) 'Confident workers, confident families: Exploring sensitive outcomes in family centre work in England.' *International Journal of Child and Family Welfare 9*, 79–91.

Brandon, M. and Connolly, J. (2006) 'Are intensive family preservation services useful? A study in the United Kingdom.' *Family Preservation Journal 9*, 56–69.

Bronfenbrenner, U. (1979) *The Ecology of Human Development: Experiments by Nature and Design.* Cambridge, MA: Harvard University Press.

Bullock, R., Courtney, M., Parker, R., Sinclair, I. and Thoburn, J. (2006) 'Can the corporate state parent?' *Children and Youth Services Review 28*, 1344–58 (reprinted in *Adoption and Fostering 30*, 4, 6–19).

Bullock, R., Gooch, D. and Little, M. (1998) *Children Going Home: The Reunification of Families.* Aldershot: Ashgate.

Bullock, R., Little, M. and Millham, S. (1993) *Going Home: The Return of Children Separated from their Families.* Aldershot: Dartmouth.

Canali, C. and Rigon, P. (2002) 'Evaluating Outcomes for Children with Multiple problems.' In T. Vecchiato, A.N. Maluccio and C. Canali (eds) *Evaluation in Child and Family Services: Comparative Client and Program Perspective.* New York: Aldine de Gruyter.

Canali, C. and Vecchiato, T. (2010) 'Assessing the life space of children living in multi-problematic families.' *International Journal of Child and Family Welfare* (submitted).

Canali, C., Vecchiato, T. and Whittaker, J.K. (eds) (2008) *Conoscere i bisogni e valutare l'efficacia degli interventi per bambini, ragazzi e famiglie in difficoltà.* Padova: Fondazione Zancan.

Canavan, J., Dolan, P. and Pinkerton, J. (2000) *Family Support: Direction from Diversity.* London: Jessica Kingsley Publishers.

Caragata, L. and Sanchez, M. (2002) 'Globalisation and global need: New imperatives for expanding international Social Work education in North America.' *International Social Work 45*, 2, 217–238.

Casey Family Programs (2001) *It's My Life: A Framework for youth transitioning from Foster Care to Successful Adulthood.* Seattle, WA: Casey Family Programs.

Casey Family Programs (2003) *Family, Community, Culture: Roots of Permanency – A Conceptual Framework on Permanency from Casey Family Programs.* Seattle, WA: Casey Family Programs.

Casey Family Programs and Foster Care Alumni of America (2008) *Strategic Sharing.* Available at www.casey.org/Resources/Publications/StrategicSharing.htm, accessed on 12 December 2009.

Center for the Advancement of Collaborative Strategies in Health, New York Academy of Medicine (2005) *Sample Questionnaire for the Partnership Self-Assessment Tool.* Available at www.partnershiptool.net/samplePAT.htm, accessed on 8 February 2005.

Cerezo, M. (1997) 'Abusive family interaction: A review.' *Aggression and Violent Behavior 8*, 215–40.

Chambers, D.E., Wedel, K.R. and Rodwell, M.K. (1992) *Evaluating Social Programs.* Boston, MA: Allyn & Bacon.

Chambon, A. (1994) 'Dialogical analysis of case materials.' In E. Sherman and W. Reid (eds) *Qualitative Research in Social Work.* New York: Columbia University Press.

Charmaz, K. (2005) 'Grounded theory in the 21st Century: A qualitative method for advancing social justice research.' In N. Denzin and Y. Lincoln (eds) *The SAGE Handbook of Qualitative Research (Third Edition).* Thousand Oaks, CA: Sage.

Chaskin, R. (2004) 'Community-based practice in support of youth, families and community change: The case of the Southwest youth collaborative. A case-study summary.' Paper presented at the Fourth International Seminar on Outcome-Based Evaluation in Child and Family Services – Cross-National Research Initiatives. Abano Terme, Italy (September 2004).

Cheever, K. and Hardin, S. (1999) 'Effects of traumatic events, social support, and self-efficacy on adolescents' self-health assessments.' *Western Journal of Nursing Research 21*, 5, 673–84.

Child & Family (2008) *The Child in Flanders.* Brussels: Kind & Gezin.

Children's Workforce Development Council (2008) *The State of the Children's Social Care Workforce.* Leeds: Children's Workforce Development Council.

Chinman, M., Hunter, S., Ebener, P., Paddock, S., Stillman, L., Imm, P. and Wandersman, A. (2008) 'The Getting to Outcomes demonstration and evaluation: An illustration of the prevention support system.' *American Journal of Community Psychology 41,* 3/4, 206–24.

Chow, J. (1999) 'Multiservice centers in Chinese American immigrant communities: Practice, principles and challenges.' *Social Work 44,* 1, 70–81.

Cleaver, H. (2000) *Fostering Family Contact.* London: The Stationery Office.

Colton, M.J., Roberts, S. and Williams, M. (eds) (2002) 'Residential care: Last resort or positive choice? Lessons from around Europe.' *International Journal of Child and Family Welfare 5,* 3, 65–140.

Compton, B.R. and Galaway, B. (2005) *Social Work Processes (Seventh Edition).* Pacific Grove, CA: Brooks/Cole.

Connell, J. and Kubisch, A. (1999) 'Applying a theory of change approach to the evaluation of comprehensive, community initiatives: Progress, prospects and problems.' In K. Fullbright-Anderson, A. Kubisch and J. Connell (eds) *New Approaches to Evaluating Comprehensive Community Initiatives,* Volume 2: Theory, Measurement and Analysis. Washington, DC: Aspen Institute.

Coohey, C. and Braun, N. (1997) 'Toward an integrated framework for understanding child physical abuse.' *Child Abuse & Neglect 21,* 1081–94.

Cook, R., Fleishman, E. and Grimes, V. (1991) *A National Evaluation of Title IV-E Foster Care Independent Living Programs for Youth.* Phase 2 Final Report. Rockville, MD: Westat Corporation.

Cook, R.J. (1994) 'Are we helping foster care youth prepare for their future?' *Children & Youth Services Review 16,* 3–4, 213–29.

Corning, P.A. (1993) *The Synergism Hypothesis: A Theory of Progressive Evolution.* London: Blond & Briggs.

Courtney, M.E., Dworsky, A., Cusick, G.R., Keller, T., Havlicek, J., Perez, A. *et al.* (2007) *Midwest Evaluation of Adult Functioning of Former Foster Youth: Outcomes at Age 21.* Chicago, IL: University of Chicago, Chapin Hall Center for Children.

Courtney, M., Piliavin, I. and Grogan-Kaylor, A. (1995) *The Wisconsin Study of Youth Ageing Out of Out-of-home Care: A Portrait of Children About to Leave Care.* Report to the Wisconsin Department of Health and Social Services. Madison, WI: School of Social Work, University of Wisconsin-Madison.

Cousins, J.B., Donohue, J.J. and Bloom, G.A. (1996) 'Collaborative evaluation in North America: Evaluators' self-reported opinions, practices, and consequences.' *Evaluation Practice 17,* 207–26.

Crittenden, P. (2008) *Raising Parents: Attachment, Parenting and Child Safety.* Cullompton: Willan Publishing.

Crnic, K.A. and Greenberg, M.T. (1990) 'Minor parenting stresses with young children.' *Child Development 61,* 1628–37.

Curran, M.C. and Pecora, P.J. (1999) 'Assessing youth perspectives of family foster care: Selected research findings and methodological challenges.' In P. Curtis, D. Grady and J. Kendall (eds) *The Foster Care Crisis: Translating Research into Policy and Practice.* Lincoln, NE: University of Nebraska Press.

Curtin, M. and Fossey, E. (2007) 'Appraising the trustworthiness of qualitative studies: Guidelines for occupational therapists.' *Australian Occupational Therapy Journal 54,* 1, 88–94.

Curtis, P.A., Grady, D., Jr. and Kendall, J.C. (eds) (1999) *The Foster Care Crisis: Translating Research into Policy and Practice.* Lincoln, NE: University of Nebraska Press.

Dagenais, C., Nault-Brière, F., Didier D. and Dutil, J. (2008) 'Implementation and effects of a service coordination program for youths and their families in complex situations: A mixed evaluation design.' *Children and Youth Services Review 30,* 8, 903–13.

Dawson, K. and Berry, M. (2002) 'Engaging families in child welfare services: An evidence-based approach to best practice.' *Child Welfare 81,* 2, 293–317.

De'Ath, E. (1989) 'The family center approach to supporting families.' *Child Welfare 67,* 2, 197–207.

Del Valle, J.F., Lopez, M., Montserrat, C. and Bravo, A. (2009) 'Twenty years of foster care in Spain: Profiles, patterns and outcomes.' *Children and Youth Services Review 31,* 847–53.

Denzin, N. and Lincoln, Y. (2005) *The Handbook of Qualitative Research (Third Edition).* Thousand Oaks, CA: Sage.

Department for Education and Skills (2003a) *The Children Act Report 2002.* London: The Stationery Office.

Department for Education and Skills (2003b) *Every Child Matters.* London: Stationery Office.

Department for Education and Skills (2005) *National Statistics for the Year 2005.* London: The Stationery Office.

Department of Health (1998a) *The Quality Protects Programme: Transforming Children's Services* LAC (98) 26. London: Department of Health.

Department of Health (1998b) *Modernising Social Services: Promoting Independence, Improving Protection, Raising Standards.* London: The Stationery Office.

Department of Health (1999) *The Government's Objectives for Children's Social Services.* London: Department of Health.

Department of Health (2000a) *Adoption: A New Approach.* London: The Stationery Office.

Department of Health (2000b) *The Children Act Report 1995–1999.* London: The Stationery Office.

Department of Health (2001a) *The Children Act Report 2000.* London: Department of Health.

Department of Health (2001b) *The Children Act Now: Messages from Research.* London: The Stationery Office.

Department of Health and Social Security (1985) *Decision-Making in Child Care: Recent Research Findings and their Implications.* London: The Stationery Office.

Department of Health, Cox, A. and Bentovim, A. (2000) *The Family Assessment Pack of Questionnaires and Scales.* London: The Stationery Office.

DePoy, E. and Gilson, S. (2003) *Evaluation Practice: Thinking and Actions Principles for Social Work Practice.* Pacific Grove, CA: Brooks/Cole.

DeVoe, E.R. and Kantor, G.K. (2002) 'Measurement issues in child maltreatment and family violence prevention programs.' *Trauma, Violence and Abuse 3,* 1, 15–39.

Dickens, J., Howell, D., Thoburn, J. and Schofield, G. (2007) 'Children starting to be looked after by local authorities in England: An analysis of inter-authority variation and case-centred decision-making.' *British Journal of Social Work 37,* 597–617.

Dinkmeyer, D., McKay, G., McKay, J. and Dinkmeyer, D. Jr. (1998) *Parenting Teenagers: Systematic Training for Effective Parenting of Teens.* Minneapolis, MN: American Guidance Services.

Dixon-Woods, M., Fitzpatrick, R. and Roberts, K. (2001) 'Including qualitative research in systematic reviews: Opportunities and problems.' *Journal of Evaluation in Clinical Practice 7,* 125–33.

Dolev, T., Benbenishty, R. and Timar, A. (2001) *Decision Committees in Israel: Their Organization, Work Processes, and Outcomes.* Jerusalem, Israel: JDC-Brookdale.

Donzelli, A. and Sghedoni, D. (1998) *Le linee guida tra conoscenze, etica ed interessi.* Milano: Franco Angeli.

Dore, M. and Lightburn, A. (2006) 'Evaluating community-based clinical practice.' In A. Lightburn and P. Sessions (eds) *Handbook of Community-Based Clinical Practice.* New York: Oxford University Press.

Dubow, E. and Tisak, J. (1989) 'The relation between stressful life events and adjustment in elementary school children: The role of social support and social problem-solving skills.' *Child Development 60,* 6, 1412–23.

Durning, P. (1992) 'L'enfant, enjeu des interactions entre familles naturelles, milieux de suppléance familiale et travailleurs sociaux.' *Communautés éducatives 80,* 51–60.

Durning, P. (2007) 'The construction of socio-educational interventions.' In H. Grietens, E. Knorth, P. Durning, J. Dumas (eds) *Promoting Competence in Children and Families: Scientific perspectives on resilience and vulnerability.* Leuven: European Scientific Association on Residential and Foster care for Children and Adolescents (EUSARF).

Eayrs, C.B. and Jones, R.S. (1992) 'Methodological issues and future directions in the evaluation of early intervention programmes.' *Child: Care, Health and Development 18,* 1, 15–28.

Edmond, T., Megivern, D., Williams, C., Rochman, E. and Howard, M. (2006) 'Integrating evidence-based practice and social work field education.' *Journal of Social Work Education 42,* 2, 377–96.

Everitt, A. and Hardiker, P. (1996) *Evaluating for Good Practice.* Basingstoke: Macmillan Education.

Eysenck, H.J. (1995) 'Meta-analysis squared – Does it make sense?' *American Psychologist 50,* 110–11.

Ezell, M. (2004) 'The influences of inter- and intra-agency factors on client outcomes in child welfare.' Paper presented at the Fourth International Seminar on Outcome-Based Evaluation in Child and Family Services – Cross-National Research Initiatives. Abano Terme, Italy (September 2004).

Ezell, M. (2005) 'Advances in program evaluation: Associating agency-level factors with child and family outcomes.' (In Italian). In C. Canali, A.N. Maluccio and T. Vecchiato (eds) *La valutazione di outcome nei servizi per l'eta evolutiva e la famiglia: Apprendere dal confronto delle experienze.* Padova, Italy: Fondazione Zancan.

Fablet, D. (1993) 'Dispositifs innovants de suppléance familiale et prévention de l'exclusion.' *Connexions 62,* 91–106.

Fablet, D. (2005) *Suppléance Familiale et Interventions Socio-Educatives: Analyser les Pratiques des Professionnels.* Paris: L'Harmattan.

Farmer, E. and Parker, R. (1991) *Trials and Tribulations.* London: Her Majesty's Stationery Office.

Farmer, E., Sturgess, W. and O'Neill, T. (2009) *The Reunification of Looked After Children with Their Parents.* Report to the Department for Children, Schools and Families. Bristol: University of Bristol.

Fein, E. and Staff, I. (1994) 'Inside the black box: An exploration of service delivery in a family reunification program.' *Child Welfare 73,* 3, 195–214.

Fergusson, D.M., Grant, H., Horwood, L.J. and Ridder, E.M. (2005) 'Randomized trial of the Early Start program of home visitation.' *Pediatrics, 116,* 803–9.

Fernandez, E. (2004) 'Effective outcomes to promote child and family wellbeing: A study of outcomes on interventions through children's family centres.' *Child and Family Social Work 9,* 91–104.

Fernandez, E. (2006) 'How children experience fostering: Participatory research with children.' *Child and Family Social Work 12,* 4, 349–59.

Fernandez, E. and Barth, R.P. (eds) (2010) *How Does Foster Care Work? International Evidence on Outcomes.* London: Jessica Kingsley Publishers (in press).

Fetterman, D.M. and Wandersman, A. (2004) *Empowerment Evaluation Principles in Practice.* New York: Guilford Press.

Fisher, M. (2002) 'The Social Care Institute for Excellence: The role of a national institute in developing knowledge and practice in social care.' *Social Work and Social Sciences Review 10,* 36–64.

Fisher, M., Marsh, P. and Phillips, D. (1986) *In and Out of Care.* Batsford: British Agencies for Adoption and Fostering.

Fook, J. (1996) *The Reflective Researcher: Social Workers' Theories of Practice Research.* Sydney: Allen and Unwin.

Foster Care Alumni of America (2009) *FLUX: Life After Foster Care.* Available at www.fostercarealumni.org, accessed 9 August 2010.

Frame, L., Berrick, J.D. and Brodowski, M.L. (2000) 'Understanding reentry to out-of home care for reunified infants.' *Child Welfare 79,* 4, 339–69.

Fraser, M., Pecora, P. and Haapala, D. (1991) *Families in Crisis: The Impact of Intensive Family Preservation Services.* New York: Aldine de Gruyter.

Fraser, M.W., Walton, E., Lewis, R.E., Pecora, P.J. and Walton, W.K. (1996) 'An experiment in family reunification: Correlates of outcomes at one-year follow-up.' *Children and Youth Services Review 18,* 335–61.

Friedman, R. and Israel, N. (2008) 'Research and evaluation implications: Using research and evaluation to strengthen systems of care.' In B. Stroul and B. Blau (eds) *The System of Care Handbook.* Baltimore, MD: Paul Brookes.

Friere, P. (1985) *The Politics of Education, Culture, Power and Liberation.* Basingstoke, England: Macmillan.

Frost, N. (2002) 'A problematic relationship? Evidence and practice in the workplace.' *Social Work and Social Sciences Review 10,* 38–50.

Gambrill, E. and Shlonsky, A. (2000) 'Risk assessment in context.' *Children and Youth Services Review 22,* 813–37.

Gardner, R. (1998) *Family Support.* Birmingham: Venture Press.

Gaudin, J.A., Polansky, N., Kilpatrick, A. and Shilton, P. (1996) 'Family functioning in neglectful families.' *Child Abuse & Neglect 20,* 6, 363–77.

Geeraert, L. (2004) *Vroegtijdige preventie van kindermishandeling. Literatuurstudie en empirische exploratie van vroegtijdige preventieprogrammema's voor gezinnen met een risico van fysieke kindermishandeling en/ of verwaarlozing* (Unpublished PhD thesis). Leuven: Katholieke Universiteit Leuven, Centre for Disability, Special Needs Education, and Child Care (in Dutch).

Geeraert, L., Van den Noortgate, W., Grietens, H. and Onghena, P. (2004) 'The effects of early prevention programmes for families with young children at risk for physical child abuse and neglect: A meta-analysis.' *Child Maltreatment 9,* 277–91.

Gelles, R.J. (2000) 'How evaluation research can help reform and improve the child welfare system.' *Journal of Aggression, Maltreatment and Trauma 4,* 1, 7–28.

Gilbert, R., Spatz Widom, C., Browne, K., Fergusson, D., Webb, E. and Janson, S. (2008) 'Burden and consequences of child maltreatment in high-income countries.' *The Lancet 373,* 68–81.

Gilligan, R. (2004) 'Promoting resilience in child and family social work: Issues for social work practice.' *Social Work Education 23,* 1, 93–104.

Ginsberg, L. (2001) *Social Work Evaluation Principles and Methods.* Boston, MA: Allyn & Bacon.

Glaser, B. and Strauss, A. (1967) *The Discovery of Grounded Theory: Strategies for Qualitative Research.* Chicago: Aldine Publishing Co.

Glass, N. (2001) 'What works for children – the political issues.' *Children and Society 15,* 14–20.

Goldspink, C. and Kay, R. (2003) 'Organisations as self-organising and self-sustaining systems: A complex and autopoietic systems perspective.' *International Journal of General Systems 32,* 5, 459–74.

Goodman, R. (1997) 'The Strengths and Difficulties Questionnaire: A research note.' *Journal of Child Psychology and Psychiatry 38,* 5, 581–86.

Grahame-Smith, D. (1995) 'Evidence based medicine: Socratic dissent.' *British Medical Journal 310,* 1126–27.

Gray, M. and McDonald, C. (2006) 'Pursuing good practice.' *Journal of Social Work 61,* 7–20.

Green, B.L., Mulvey, L., Fisher, H.A. and Woratschek, F. (1996) 'Integrating program and evaluation values: A family support approach to program evaluation.' *Evaluation Practice 17,* 261–72.

Grietens, H., Geeraert, L. and Hellinckx, W. (2004) 'A scale for home visiting nurses to identify risks of physical abuse and neglect among mothers with newborn infants.' *Child Abuse & Neglect 28,* 321–37.

Grietens, H. and Hellinckx, W. (2003) 'Predicting disturbed parental awareness in mothers with a newborn infant: Test of a theoretical model.' *Infant and Child Development 12,* 117–28.

Griffiths, V. (1984) 'Feminist research and the use of drama.' *Women's Studies International Forum 7,* 5, 511–519.

Grimshaw, J.M. and Russell, I.Y. (1993) 'Effect of clinical guidelines on medical practice: Asystematic review of rigorous evaluations.' *Lancet 342,* 1317–22.

Gutbrandsson, B. (2006) *Rights of Children at Risk and in Care.* Strasbourg: Council of Europe Publishing.

Haigh, R. (1999) 'The quintessence of a therapeutic environment – five universal qualities.' In P. Campling and R. Haigh (eds) *Therapeutic Communities: Past, Present and Future.* London: Jessica Kingsley Publishers.

Hammond, S. (1998) *The Thin Book of Appreciative Enquiry.* Plano, TX: Thin Books Publishing Co.

Hampton, J.R. (1997) 'Evidence-based medicine, practice variations and clinical freedom.' *Journal of Evaluation in Clinical Practice 3,* 123–31.

Handley, K., Horn, S., Kaipuke, R., Maden, B., Maden, E., Stickey, B., Munford, R. and Sanders, J. (2009) *The Spinafex Effect: Developing a Theory of Change for Communities.* Wellington, New Zealand: The New Zealand Families Commission.

Hartman, A. (1990) Editorial: Many ways of knowing. *Social Work 35,* 1, 3–4.

Hawe, P., Shiell, A. and Riley, T. (2009) 'Theorizing interventions as events in systems.' *American Journal of Community Psychology 43,* 267–76.

Hearn, B. (1995) *Child and Family Support and Protection: A Practical Approach.* London: National Children's Bureau.

Hellinckx, W., Grietens, H., Geeraert, L., Moors, G. and Van Assche, V. (2001) *Risico op kindermishandeling? Een preventieve aanpak.* Leuven/Leusden: Acco (in Dutch).

Hensey, D., Williams, J. and Rosenbloom, L. (1983) 'Intervention in child abuse: Experience in Liverpool.' *Departmental Medicine and Child Neurology 25,* 606–11.

Heron, J. and Reason, P. (2001) 'The practice of co-operative inquiry: research 'with' rather than 'on'people.' In P. Reason and H. Bradbury (eds) *Handbook of Action Research: Participation, Enquiry and Practice.* London: Sage.

Hess, P., McGowan, B. and Botsko, M. (2000) 'A preventive services program model for preserving and supporting families over time.' *Child Welfare 79,* 227–65.

Hess, P., McGowan, B. and Botsko, M. (2003) *Nurturing the One: Supporting the Many.* New York: Columbia University Press.

Hetherington, R. and Piqvardt, R. (2001) 'Strategies for survival: users' experiences of child welfare in three welfare regimes.' *Child and Family Social Work 6,* 239–248.

Hill, M. (ed) (1999) *Effective Ways of Working with Children and their Families.* Gateshead, England: Jessica Kingsley Publishers.

Hill, S. (2004) 'Doing collaborative research: Doing what feels right and makes sense.' *International Journal of Social Research Methodology 7,* 2,109–26.

Hoagwood, K., Burns, B.J. and Weisz, J.R. (2002) 'A profitable conjunction: From science to service in children's mental health.' In B.J. Burns and K. Hoagwood (eds) *Community treatment for youth: Evidence-based interventions for severe emotional and behavioral disorders.* New York: Oxford University Press.

Hormuth, P. (2001) *All Grown Up, Nowhere to Go: Texas Teens in Foster Care Transition.* Austin, TX: Center for Public Priorities.

Horvath, A.O. and Greenberg, L.S. (1989) 'Development and validation of the Working Alliance Inventory.' *Journal of Counseling Psychology 36,* 223–33.

Horwitz, R.I. (1996) 'The dark side of evidence-based medicine.' *Cleveland Clinic Journal of Medicine 63,* 320–23.

Howe, D. (1995) *Attachment Theory for Social Work Practice.* Basingstoke, England: Macmillan.

Howe, D., Brandon, M., Hinings, D. and Schofield, G. (1999) *Attachment Theory, Child Maltreatment and Family Support: A Practice and Assessment Model.* Basingstoke, England: Macmillan.

Hunt, J. and Macleod, A. (1999) *The Best-Laid Plans. Outcomes of Judicial Decisions in Child Protection Cases.* London: The Stationery Office.

Insel, T.R. (2004) 'Science to Service: Mental Health Care after Decade of the Brain.' Presentation at the Meeting of the Society for Social Work Research, New Orleans, LA. January 16, 2004.

Jenson, C., Pine, B.A., Spath, R. and Kerman, B. (2009) 'Developing strong helping alliances in family reunification.' *Journal of Public Child Welfare 3,* 4, 331–3.

Jenson, J.M. (2006) 'Changes in publication practices for Social Work Research.' *Social Work Research 30,* 2, 67–9.

Jergeby, U. and Soydan, H. (2002) 'Assessment processes in social work practice when children are at risk: A comparative cross-national vignette study.' *Journal of Social Work Research and Evaluation 3,* 2, 127–44.

Johnson, M., Stone, S., Lou, C., Vu, C., Ling, J., Mizrahi, P. and Austin, M. (2006) *Family Assessment in Child Welfare Services: Instrument Comparisons.* Berkeley, CA: Center for Social Services Research.

Jones, M.A. (1985) *A Second Chance for Families, Five Years Later: Follow-Up of a Program to Prevent Foster Care.* New York: Child Welfare League of America.

Kamerman, S.B. and Kahn, A.J. (1995) 'Innovations in toddler day care and family support services: An international overview.' *Child Welfare 7,* 6, 1281–1300.

Kazdin, A.E. and Weisz, J.R. (2003) *Evidence-based Psychotherapies for Children and Adolescents.* New York: Guilford Press.

Kerman, B., Wildfire, J. and Barth, R.P. (2002) 'Outcomes for young adults who experienced foster care.' *Children & Youth Services Review 24,* 5, 319–44.

Knorth, E.J. (2008) 'Il futuro dell'assistenza di tipo residenziale: risultati della ricerca.' In C. Canali, T. Vecchiato and J.K. Whittaker (eds) *Conoscere i bisogni e valutare l'efficacia degli interventi per bambini, ragazzi e famiglie in difficoltà.* Padova: Fondazione Zancan.

Kolko, D. (1996) 'Physical abuse.' In J. Briere, L. Berliner, J. Bulkley, C. Jenny and T. Reid (eds) *The APSAC Handbook on Child Maltreatment.* Thousand Oaks, CA: Sage Publications.

Krugman, R. (1999) 'National call to action: Working toward the elimination of child maltreatment. The politics.' *Child Abuse & Neglect 23*, 963–7.

Lahti, J. (1982) 'A follow-up study of foster children in permanent placements.' *Social Service Review 56*, 556–71.

Lasker, R.D. and Weiss, E.S. (2001) 'Partnership synergy: A practical framework for studying and strengthening the collaborative advantage.' *Millbank Quarterly III–IV,* 179–205.

Lasker, R.D. and Weiss, E.S. (2003) 'Creating partnership synergy: The critical role of community stakeholders.' *Journal of Health and Human Services Administration 26,* 1, 119–39.

Lau, U.K. (2003) 'Social service for single parent families in Hong Kong: A paradox.' *Child and Family Social Work 8,* 1, 47–52.

Leon, A.M. (1999) 'Family support model: Integrating service delivery in the twenty-first century.' *Families in Society 80,* 1, 14–24.

Lew, A. and Bettner, B. (1996) *A Parent's Guide to Understanding and Motivating Children.* Newton Center, MA: Connexions Press.

Lewis, R.E., Walton, E. and Fraser, M.W. (1995) 'Examining family reunification services: a process analysis of a successful experiment.' *Research on Social Work Practice 5,* 259–82.

Liberati, A. (2005) (ed.) *Etica, Conoscenza e sanitá: Evidence based Medicine fra Ragione e Passione.* Roma: Pensiero Scientifico Editore.

Lightburn, A. (1992) 'Special needs adoptive families' mediation of chronic illness and handicap.' In J. Gilgun, K. Daly and G. Handel (eds) *Qualitative Methods in Family Research.* Newbury Park, CA: Sage.

Lightburn, A. (2002) 'Family Service Centers: Lessons from national and local evaluations.' In A. Maluccio, C. Canali and T. Vecchiato (eds) *Assessing Outcomes in Child and Family Services – Comparative Design and Policy Issues.* New York: Aldine de Gruyter.

Lightburn, A. and Kemp, S. (1994) 'Family support programmes: Opportunities for community-based practice.' *Families in Society 75,* 1, 16–26.

Lightburn, A. and Sessions, P. (eds) (2006) *Handbook of Community-Based Clinical Practice.* Oxford: Oxford University Press.

Lightburn, A. and Warren-Adamson, C. (2006) 'Evaluating family centres: The importance of sensitive outcomes in cross-national studies.' *International Journal of Child and Family Welfare 9,* 1–2, 11–25.

Lindsey, D. (2004) *The Welfare of Children.* New York: Oxford University Press.

Lindsey, D., Martin, S. and Doh, J. (2002) 'The failure of intensive casework services to reduce foster care placements: An examination of family preservation studies.' *Children and Youth Services Review 24,* 743–75.

Littell, J.H. (2005) 'Lessons from a systematic review of effects of multisystemic therapy.' *Children and Youth Services Review 27,* 4, 445–463.

Lurie, J. and Clifford, G. (2005) *Parenting a Young Child with Behavior Problems.* Trondheim, Norway: NTNU Social Research Unit.

McAuley, C., Pecora, P.J. and Whittaker, J.K. (eds) (2009) 'High risk youth: Evidence on characteristics, needs and promising interventions.' *Child & Family Social Work 14,* 2, 129–242.

Macdonald, G. (2003) *Using Systematic Reviews to Improve Social Care.* London: Social Care Institute for Excellence (SCIE).

McMahon, L. and Ward, A. (2001) *Helping Families in Family Centres: Working at Therapeutic Practice.* London: Jessica Kingsley Publishers.

MacMillan, H.L., Wathen, C.N., Barlow, J., Fergusson, D.M., Leventhal, J.M. and Taussig, H.N. (2009) 'Interventions to prevent child maltreatment and associated impairment.' *The Lancet 373,* 250–66.

McMillen, J.C., Rideout, G.B., Fisher, R.H. and Tucker, J. (1997) 'Independent living services: The views of former foster youth.' *Families in Society: The Journal of Contemporary Human Services 78,* 471–9.

McNamara P. (2006) 'Mapping change in a child and family centre in Melbourne.' *International Journal of Child and Family Welfare 9,* 1–2, 41–52.

McNamara, P. (2007) 'Keeping families safe from violence.' *Eureka Street 17,* 20, 45–7.

McNamara, P. (2008a) 'Comment: Sorrowing in the sisterhood.' *Australian and New Zealand Journal of Family Therapy 29*, 1, 48–50.

McNamara, P. (2008b) 'Changed forever: A victim's friends reflect on intimate partner homicide.' *Journal of Family Studies 14*, 2–3, 198–217.

McNamara, P. (2009) 'Feminist ethnography: Storytelling that makes a difference.' *Qualitative Social Work 8*, 2, 161–77.

McNamara, P. and Neve, E. (2009) 'Engaging Italian and Australian Social workers in evaluation.' *International Social Work 52*, 1, 9–22.

Mahler, M., Bergman, A. and Pine, F. (1975) *The Psychological Birth of the Human Infant.* New York: Basic Books.

Maluccio, A.N., Abramczyk, L.W. and Thomlison, B. (1996) 'Family reunification of children in out-of-home care: Research perspectives.' *Children and Youth Services Review 18*, 287–305.

Maluccio, A.N. and Fein, E. (1983) 'Permanency planning: Aredefinition.' *Child Welfare 62*, 195–201.

Maluccio, A.N., Pine, B.A. and Warsh, R. (1994) 'Protecting children by preserving their families.' *Children and Youth Services Review 16*, 295–307.

Maluccio, A.N., Canali, C. and Vecchiato, T. (2002) (eds) *Assessing Outcomes in Child and Family Services: Comparative Design and Policy Issues.* New York: Aldine de Gruyter.

Maluccio, A.N. and Whittaker, J.K. (1997) 'Learning from the family preservation initiative.' *Children and Youth Services Review 19*, 1–2, 5–16.

Maluccio, A.N. and Whittaker, J.K. (2002) 'Le risposte per l'infanzia all'esterno della famiglia negli Usa: Una revisione critica.' *Studi Zancan 6*, 36–80.

Manalo, V. and Meezan, W. (2000) 'Toward building a typology for the evaluation of services in family support programs.' *Child Welfare 79*, 4, 405–429.

Manby, M. (2005) 'Evaluation of the impact of the Webster-Stratton Parent–Child Videotape Series on Participants in a Midlands Town in 2001–2002.' *Children and Society 19*, 316–28.

Mancini, J.A., Marek, L.I., Byrne, R.A. and Huebner, A.J. (2004) 'Community-based program research: Context, program readiness, and evaluation usefulness.' *Journal of Community Practice 12*, 1/2, 7–21.

Mason, J. (1996) *Qualitative Researching.* London: Sage.

Mathews, K.M, White, M.C. and Long, R.G. (1999) 'Why study the complexity sciences in the social sciences.' *Human Relations 52*, 4, 439–62.

Mayer, J. and Timms, N. (1970) *The Client Speaks.* London: Routledge and Keegan Paul.

Mazzucchelli, F. (ed.) (2008) *Il diritto di essere bambino: famiglia, società e responsabilità educativa.* Milano: Franco Angeli.

Mika, K.L. (1996) *Program Outcome Evaluation: A Step-by-Step Handbook.* Milwaukee, WI: Families International, Inc.

Miles, M.B. and Huberman, A.M. (1994) *Qualitative Data Analysis: An expanded sourcebook. (Second Edition).* Thousand Oaks, CA: Sage Publications.

Millham, S., Bullock, R., Hosie, K. and Little, M. (1986) *Lost in Care: The Problem of Maintaining Links between Children in Care and their Families.* Aldershot: Gower.

Milner, J.S. (2000) 'Social information processing and child physical abuse: Theory and research.' In D.J. Hansen (ed.) *Motivation and Child Maltreatment.* Lincoln: University of Nebraska Press.

Ministry of Labor and Social Affairs (1998) *National Plan for Children at Risk and Domestic Violence.* Jerusalem, Israel: Ministry of Labor and Social Affairs.

Moher, D., Schulz, K.F. and Altman, D. (2001) 'The CONSORT statement: Revised recommendations for improving the quality of reports of parallel-group randomized trials.' *Journal of the American Medical Association 285*, 15, 1987–91.

Moran, P., Ghate, D. and Van der Merwe, A. (2004) *What Works in Parenting Support: A Review of the International Evidence.* DfES Research Report RR574. London: Policy Research Bureau.

Moro, A.C. (1991) *Il bambino è un cittadino.* Milano: Mursia.

Moro, A.C. (2006) *Politiche per l'infanzia e la famiglia. il contributo di Alfredo Carlo Moro.* Padova: Fondazione Zancan.

Morrison, T. (2007) 'Emotional intelligence, emotion and social work: Context, characteristics, complications and contribution.' *British Journal of Social Work 37*, 2, 245–63.

Mulroy, E.A. and Lauber, H. (2004) 'A user-friendly approach to program evaluation and effective community interventions for families at risk of homelessness.' *Social Work 49*, 44, 573–85.

Munford, R. and Sanders, J. (eds) (2003) *Making a Difference in Families: Research that Creates Change.* Sydney, Australia: Allen and Unwin.

Munford, R., Sanders, J. and Madden, B. (2006) 'Small steps and giant leaps at Te Aroha Noa.' *International Journal for Child and Family Welfare 9*, 1–2, 102–9.

Munro, E., Stein, M. and Ward, H. (2005) 'Comparing how different social, political and legal frameworks support or inhibit transitions from public care to independence in Europe, Israel, Canada and the United States.' *International Journal of Child and Family Welfare 8*, 4, 197–8.

Naples, N. (2003) *Feminism and Method: Ethnography, Discourse Analysis, and Activist Research.* New York: Routledge.

National Statistics and Department of Health (2002) *Children Looked After by Local Authorities. Year Ending 31 March 2001.* London: Department of Health.

National Statistics and Department of Health (2003) *Children Looked After by Local Authorities. Year Ending 31 March 2002.* London: Department of Health.

National Statistics and the Department for Children, Schools and Families (2009) *Children Looked After by Local Authorities: Year ending 31 March 2008.* London: The Stationery Office.

Nelson, K., Landsman, M. and Deutelbaum, W. (1990) 'Three models of family-centered preventive services.' *Child Welfare 69*, 1, 3–19.

Neve, E. and McNamara, P. (2007) 'La formazione degli assistenti sociali alla valutazione: Australia e Italia a confronto.' *Studi Zancan 6*, 26–60.

Newberger, C.M. (1983) 'Parental awareness and child abuse: A cognitive-developmental analysis of urban and rural samples.' *American Journal of Orthopsychiatry 53*, 512–24.

Nollan, K.A., Wolf, M., Ansell, D., Burns, J., Barr, L., Copeland, W. and Paddock, G. (2000) 'Ready or not: Assessing youth's preparedness for independent living.' *Child Welfare 79*, 2, 159–78.

O'Neil, D. (2001) *Owning my Own Record: I Look Back to See What Worked. Research Undertaken with Ten Client Families at St. Lukes.* Bendigo: St Luke's Family Service.

Olds, D.L., Eckenrode, J., Henderson, C.R. Jr. *et al.* (1997) 'Long-term effects of home visitation on maternal life course and child abuse and neglect. Fifteen year follow-up of a randomized trial.' *Journal of the American Medical Association 278*, 637–43.

Packman J. and Hall, C. (1998) *From Care to Accommodation: Support, Protection and Control in Child Care Services.* London: The Stationery Office.

Palacio-Quintin, E. (2006) 'A case study of a community-based family support centre in Quebec.' *International Journal for Child and Family Welfare 9*, 1–2, 60–9.

Palareti, L., Berti, C., Bastianoni, P. (2006) 'Valutare le comunità residenziali per minori: la costruzione di un modello ecologico.' *Psicologia della salute 1*, 123–35.

Palmonari, A. (2008) 'I servizi per bambini e ragazzi in difficoltà: innovazioni e valutazioni.' In C. Canali, T. Vecchiato and J.K. Whittaker (eds) *Conoscere i bisogni e valutare l'efficacia degli interventi per bambini, ragazzi e famiglie in difficoltà.* Padova: Fondazione Zancan.

Patton, M.Q. (2008) *Utilization-Focused Evaluation (Fourth Edition).* Thousand Oaks, CA: Sage.

Pawson, R. and Tilley N. (1997) *Realistic Evaluation.* London: Sage.

Pecora, P.J., Kessler, R.C., Williams, J., Downs, A.C., English, D., White, J. *et al.* (2010) *What Works in Family Foster Care? Identifying Key Components of Success from an Alumni Follow-up Study.* Oxford, England: Oxford University Press.

Pecora, P.J., Kessler, R.C., Williams, J., O'Brien, K., Downs, A.C., English, D. *et al.* (2005) *Improving Family Foster Care: Findings from the Northwest Foster Care Alumni Study.* Seattle, WA: Casey Family Programs.

Pew Commission on Children in Foster Care (2004) *Fostering the Future: Safety, Permanence and Well-being for Children in Foster Care.* Philadelphia, PA: Pew Charitable Trusts.

Phillips, B., Ball, C., Sackett, D., Badenoch, D., Straus, S., Haynes, B. and Dawes M. (2001) *Oxford Centre for Evidence-based Medicine Levels of Evidence.* Oxford: Centre for Evidence-based Medicine.

Pine, B.A. and Healy, L.M. (2007) 'New Leadership for the Human Services: Involving and Empowering Staff through Participatory Management.' In J. Aldgate, L.M. Healy, B. Malcolm, B.A. Pine, W. Rose and J. Seden (eds) *Enhancing Social Work Management: Theory and Best Practice from the UK and the USA.* London: Jessica Kingsley Publishers.

Pine, B.A., Healy L.M. and Maluccio, A.N. (2002) 'Developing measurable program objectives – a key to evaluating family reunification programs.' In T. Vecchiato, A.N. Maluccio and C. Canali (eds) *Evaluation in Child and Family Services: Comparative Client and Program Perspectives.* New York: Aldine de Gruyter.

Pine, B.A., Spath, R. and Jenson, C. (2005) *Report on the Use of Parent–Child Visiting in the Casey Family Services Family Reunification Program.* West Hartford, CT: The University of Connecticut School of Social Work.

Pine, B.A., Spath, R., Jenson, C. and Werrbach, G. (2004) *The Use of Groups in the Casey Family Services Family Reunification Program: Evaluators' Report.* West Hartford, CT: The University of Connecticut School of Social Work.

Pine, B.A., Spath, R., Maguda, A., Werrbach, G. and Jenson, C. (2006) *Collaboration between the Casey Family Services Family Reunification Program and its State Agency Partners: Evaluators Report.* West Hartford, CT: The University of Connecticut School of Social Work.

Pine, B.A., Spath, R., Werrbach, G., Jenson, C. and Kerman, B. (2009) 'A better path to permanency for children in out-of-home care.' *Children and Youth Services Review 31,* 1135–43.

Pinkerton, J. and Katz, I. (2003) 'Perspective through international comparison in the evaluation of family support.' In I. Katz and J. Pinkerton (eds) *Evaluating Family Support: Thinking Internationally, Thinking Critically.* Chichester, England: Wiley.

Pithouse, A., Holland, S. and Davey, D. (2001) 'Assessment in a specialist referred family centre: Outcomes for children.' *Children in Society 15,* 302–14.

Pithouse, A., Lindsell, S. and Cheung, M. (1998) *Family Support and Family Centre Services.* Aldershot, England: Ashgate.

Pithouse, A. and Tasiran, A. (2000) 'Local authority family centre intervention: A statistical exploration of services as family support or family control.' *Child and Family Social Work 5,* 129–141.

Poertner, J. (2000) 'Managing for service outcomes: The critical role of information.' In R. Patti (ed.) *The Handbook of Social Welfare Management.* Thousand Oaks, CA: Sage.

Popay, J. and Dunston, R. (2001) *Protocol Implementation Process Methods Group,* Campbell Collaboration. Available at www.duke.edu/web/c2method/ProcImplGrou.htm, accessed 9 August 2010.

Provincia di Torino (1984) *Quattro mura di umanità. Atti del Convegno nazionale sulle comunità alloggio.* Torino: Provincia di Torino.

Quinton, D., Rushton, A., Dance, C. and Mayes, D. (1997) 'Contact between children placed away from home and their birth parents: Research issues and evidence.' *Clinical Child Psychology and Psychiatry 2,* 393–413.

Reason, P. and Bradbury, H. (eds) (2001) *Handbook of Action Research: Participative Inquiry and Practice.* New York: Sage Publications.

Reilly, T. (2003) 'Transition from care: States and outcomes of youth who age out of foster care.' *Child Welfare 82,* 6, 727–746.

Richardson, J. and Joughin, C. (2002) *Parent Training Programmes for the Management of Young Children with Conduct Disorders: Findings from Research.* London: Gaskell.

Roberts, A.R. and Yeager, K.R. (2004) *Evidence-based Practice Manual: Research and Outcome Measures in Health and Human Services.* New York: Oxford University Press.

Roberts, A.R. and Yeager, K.R. (eds) (2006) *Foundations of Evidence-Based Social Work Practice.* New York: Oxford University Press.

Rogosch, F., Cicchetti, D., Shields, S. and Toth, S. (1995) 'Parenting dysfunction in child maltreatment.' In M.H. Bornstein (ed.) *Handbook of Parenting. Volume 4.* Mahwah, New Jersey: Lawrence Erlbaum Associates.

Rose W. (2006) 'The Developing World of the Child: Children's Perspectives.' In J. Aldgate, D.P.H. Jones, W. Rose and C. Jeffery (eds) *The Developing World of the Child.* London: Jessica Kingsley Publishers.

Rose, W., Aldgate, J., McIntosh, M. and Hunter, H. (2009) 'High-risk children with challenging behaviour: Changing directions for them and their families.' *Child and Family Social Work 14,* 178–88.

Rosen, A. (1993) 'Systematic planned practice.' *Social Service Review 67*, 1, 84–100.

Rosen, A. and Proctor E.K. (2003) *Developing Practice Guidelines for Social Work Interventions: Issues, Methods and Research Agenda.* New York: Columbia University Press.

Rosenthal, R. (1984) *Meta-analytic Procedures for Social Research.* Beverly Hills, CA: Sage Publications.

Royse, D., Thyer, B.A., Padgett, D.K. and Logan, T.K. (2006) *Program Evaluation: An Introduction.* Belmont, CA: Thompson.

Rubin, A. and Babbie, E. (2008) *Research Methods for Social Work (Sixth Edition).* Belmont, CA: Brooks/Cole-Thomson Learning.

Rubin, A. and Babbie, E. (2010) *Research Methods for Social Work (Seventh Edition).* Belmont, CA: Brooks/Cole.

Ruch, G., (2004) *Reflective Practice in Contemporary Child Care Social Work.* Doctoral Thesis, University of Southampton, England (unpublished).

Rutter, M., Tizard, J. and Whitmore, K. (1970) *Education, Health and Behaviour.* London: Longmans.

Sackett, D.L., Straus S.E., Richardson, W.S., Rosenberg, W. and Haynes R.B. (2000) *Evidence-Based Medicine: How to Practice and Teach EBM.* Philadelphia: Churchill Livingstone.

Sacks, F.M., Pfeffer, M.A., Moye, L.A., Rouleau, J.L. *et al.* (1996) 'The effects of pravastatin on coronary events after myocardial infarction in patients with average cholesterol levels. Cholesterol and Recurrent Events Trial investigators.' *New England Journal of Medicine 3*, 335, 14, 1001–9.

Sanders, J. and Munford, R. (2010) *Working with Families: Strengths-based Approaches.* Wellington, New Zealand: Dunmore Publishing.

Sanders, M.R., Pidgeon, A.M., Gravestock, F., Connors, M.D., Brown, S. and Young, R.W. (2004) 'Does parental attributional retraining and anger management enhance the effects of Triple P–Positive Parenting Program with parents at risk of child maltreatment?' *Behavior Therapy 35*, 513–35.

Sanders, R. and Roach, G. (2007) 'Effectiveness of referred access family support services.' *Children and Society 12*, 161–71.

Sarason, S.B. (2003) 'The obligations of the moral-scientific stance.' *American Journal of Community Psychology 31*, 4, 209–11.

Schofield, G., Thoburn, J., Howell, D. and Dickens, J. (2007) 'The search for stability and permanence: Modelling the pathways of long-stay looked after children.' *British Journal of Social Work 37*, 619–42.

Schon, D. (1983) *The Reflective Practitioner: How Professionals Think in Action.* London: Temple Smith.

Scott, D. and O'Neil, D. (1996) *Beyond Child Rescue: Developing Family-centred Practice at St. Luke's.* Sydney: Allen and Unwin.

Scottish Intercollegiate Guideline Network (2008) *SIGN 50: A Guideline Developers' Handbook.* Edinburgh: Scottish Intercollegiate Guideline Network (SIGN).

Seaman, P., Turner, K., Hill, M., Stafford, A. and Walker, M. (2005) *Parenting and Children's Resilience in Disadvantaged Communities.* London: National Children's Bureau/Joseph Rowntree Foundation.

Selwyn, J. and Sturgess, W. (2003) 'Achieving permanency through adoption: Following in the US footsteps?' *Adoption and Fostering 26*, 40–49.

Silverman, D. (1993) *Interpreting Qualitative Data.* London: Sage.

Sinclair, I., Baker, C., Wilson, K. and Gibbs, I. (2005) *Foster Children: Where They Go and How They Get On.* London: Jessica Kingsley Publishers.

Sinclair, R., Garnett, L. and Berridge, D. (1995) *Social Work and Assessment with Adolescents.* London: National Children's Bureau.

Small, A., Cooney, S. and O'Connor, C. (2009) 'Evidence-informed program improvement: Using principles of effectiveness to enhance the quality and impact of family-based prevention programs.' *Family Relations 58*, 1, 1–13.

Smith, M. (2006) 'Early Interventions with Young Children and their Parents in the UK.' In C. McAuley, P. Pecora and W. Rose (eds) *Enhancing the Well-being of Children and Families through Effective Interventions: International Evidence for Practice.* London: Jessica Kingsley Publishers.

Smith, T. (1996) *Family Centres and Bringing up Young Children.* London: Her Majesty's Stationery Office.

Snow, D.A. and Anderson, L. (1991) 'Researching the homeless.' In J.R. Feagin, A.M. Orum and G. Sjoberg (eds) *A Case for the Case Study.* Chapel Hill, NC: University of North Carolina Press.

Snowden, D. and Boone, M. (2007) 'A leader's framework for decision making.' *Harvard Business Review*, November, 69–76.

Social Work Task Force (2009) *Building a Safe Confident Future: Final Report of the Social Work Task Force.* London: Department for Children, Schools and Families.

Socialstyrelsen (2004) *Barn och unga – isatser ar 2003.* Stockholm, Sweden: Socialstyrelsen.

Spath, R. and Pine, B.A. (2004) 'Using the case study approach for improved programme evaluations.' *Child and Family Social Work 9*, 57–63.

Spath, R., Pine, B.A., Jenson, C. and Werrbach, G. (2002) *Casey Family Services Family Reunification Program Case Study Report.* West Hartford, CT: The University of Connecticut School of Social Work.

Spencer, L., Ritchie, J., Lewis, J. and Dillon, L. (2003) *Quality in Qualitative Evaluation: A Framework for Assessing Research Evidence.* Government Chief Social Researcher's Office Occasional Papers Series No. 2. London: Prime Minister's Strategy Unit, The Cabinet Office.

Stacey, R. (2003) *Complexity and Group Process.* Hove, NY: Routledge.

Stein, T.J. and Gambrill, E.D. (1979) 'The Alameda project: A two-year report and one-year follow-up.' *Child Abuse and Neglect 3*, 521–8.

Stradling, B. and MacNeil, M.M. (2007) *Delivering Integrated Children's Services for Children in Highland: An Overview of Challenges, Developments and Outcomes.* Highland: University of the Highlands and Islands Millenium Institute, Highland.

Straus S.E. and McAlister, F.A. (2000) 'Evidence-based medicine: A commentary on common Criticisms.' *JAMC 163*, 7, 837–41.

Straus, S.E., Richardson, W.S., Glasziou, P. and Haynes, R.B. (2005) *Evidence-based Medicine: How to Practice and Teach EBM (Third Edition).* Edinburgh: Churchill Livingstone.

Strauss, A. and Corbin, J. (1998) *Basics of Qualitative Research: Techniques and Procedures for Developing Grounded Theory.* Thousand Oaks, CA: Sage Publications.

Swenson, C.C., Randall, J., Henggeler, S.W. and Ward, D. (2000) 'The outcomes and costs of an interagency partnership to serve maltreated children in state custody.' *Children's Services: Social Policy, Research, and Practice 3*, 191–209.

Taussig, H.N., Clyman, R.B. and Landsverk, J. (2001) 'Children who return home from foster care: A 6-year prospective study of behavioral health outcomes in adolescence.' *Pediatrics 108*, 10, 1–7.

Terling, T. (1999) 'The efficacy of family reunification practices: Reentry rates and correlates of reentry for abused and neglected children reunited with their families.' *Child Abuse and Neglect 23*, 1359–70.

Thoburn, J. (1980) *Captive Clients: Social Work with Families of Children Home on Trial.* London: Routledge and Kegan Paul.

Thoburn, J. (2002) 'Outcomes of permanent substitute family placement for children in care.' In T. Vecchiato, A.N. Maluccio and C. Canali (eds) *Evaluation in Child and Family Services: Comparative Client and Program Perspectives.* New York: Aldine de Gruyter.

Thoburn, J. (2003) 'Esiti per minori in affidamento permanente a una famiglia sostitutiva.' In C. Canali, A.N. Maluccio and T. Vecchiato (eds) *La valutazione di efficacia nei servizi alle persone.* Padova, Italy: Fondazione Zancan.

Thoburn, J. (2007) *Globalisation and Child Welfare: Some Lessons from a Cross-national Study of Children in Out-of-home Care.* Norwich: UEA Social Work Monographs. Available at http://www.uea.ac.uk/swp/people/jthoburn.

Thoburn, J. (2010) 'Achieving safety, stability and belonging for children in out-of-home care: The search for 'what works' across national boundaries.' *International Journal of Child and Family Welfare* (in press).

Thomas, M., Chenot, D. and Reifel, B. (2005) 'A resilience-based model of reunificiation and rentry implications for out-of-home care services.' *Families in Society 86*, 2, 235–43.

Thomlison, B. (2003) 'Characteristics of evidence-based child maltreatment interventions.' *Child Welfare 72*, 5, 541–69.

Timmermans, S. and Mauck, A. (2005) 'The promises and pitfalls of evidence-based medicine.' *Health Affairs 24*, 18–28.

Torres, R.T., Preskill, H.S. and Piontek, M.E. (1997) 'Communication and reporting: Practices and concerns of internal and external evaluators.' *Evaluation Practice 18*, 2, 105–25.

Tunstill, J. (2003) 'Political and technical issues facing evaluators of family support.' In I. Katz and J. Pinkerton (eds) *Evaluating Family Support: Thinking Internationally, Thinking Critically.* Chichester, England: Wiley.

Tunstill, J., Aldgate, J. and Hughes, M. (2007) *Improving Children's Services Networks: Lessons from Family Centres.* London: Jessica Kingsley Publishers.

Turner, J. (1993) 'Evaluating family reunification programs.' In B.A. Pine, R. Warsh and A.N. Maluccio (eds) *Together Again: Family Reunification in Foster Care.* Washington, DC: Child Welfare League of America.

UNICEF (2002) *A World Fit for Children.* New York: UNICEF.

UNICEF Innocenti Research Centre (2007) *Child Poverty in Perspective: An Overview of Child Well-being in Rich Countries. Report Card 7.* Florence: UNICEF Innocenti Research Centre.

US Department of Health and Human Services, Administration for Children and Families, Children's Bureau (2003) *Child Welfare Outcomes 2001: Annual Report to Congress.* Washington, DC: US Government Printing Office.

US Department of Health and Human Services, Administration on Children, Youth and Families (2009a) *Child Maltreatment 2007.* Washington, DC: US Government Printing Office. Available at www.acf.hhs. gov/programs/cb/pubs/cm07/index.htm, accessed on 14 December 2009.

US Department of Health and Human Services, Administration for Children and Families, Children's Bureau (2009b) *Preliminary FY 2008 Estimates as of October 2009* (16). Washington DC: US Department of Health and Human Services. Available at www.acf.hhs.gov/programs/cb/stats_research/afcars/ tar/report16.htm, accessed 9 August 2010.

US Department of Health and Human Services, Administration for Children and Families, Children's Bureau (2009c) *Trends in Foster Care and Adoption: FY 2002–FY 2007.* Available at www.acf.hhs.gov/ programs/cb/stats_research/afcars/trends.htm, accessed 9 August 2010.

Usher, C.L. and Wildfire, J.B. (2003) 'Evidence-based practice in community-based child welfare systems.' *Child Welfare 72,* 5, 597–614.

Utting, D., Monteiro, H. and Ghate, D. (2007) *Interventions for Children at Risk of Developing Antisocial Personality Disorder.* London: Policy Research Bureau.

Van Bueren, G. (2008) *Child Rights in Europe.* Strasbourg: Council of Europe.

Vecchiato, T. (2007) 'Nuove prospettive della progettazione personalizzata e della valutazione di outcome.' *Giornale di Gerontologia LV,* 5, 403–406.

Vecchiato, T., Maluccio, A.N. and Canali, C. (2002) (eds) *Evaluation in Child and Family Services: Comparative Client and Program Perspectives.* New York: Aldine de Gruyter.

Vecchiato, T. and Mazzini E.L.L. (eds) (2008) *L'integrazione sociosanitaria: risultati di sperimentazioni e condizioni di efficacia.* Padova: Fondazione Zancan.

Vecchiato, T., Bezze, M., Canali, C., Neve, E. and Pompei, A. (2009) 'La valutazione dei soggetti e delle risorse nello spazio di vita.' *Studi Zancan 6,* 95–109.

Vecchiato, T., Canali, C. and Innocenti, E. (eds) (2009) *Le risposte domiciliari nella rete integrata dei servizi sociosanitari.* Padova: Fondazione Zancan.

Veerman, J.W. and van Yperen, T.A. (2007) 'Degrees of freedom and degrees of certainty: A developmental model for the establishment of evidence-based youth care.' *Evaluation and Program Planning 30,* 212–21.

Vinnerljung, B., Oman, M. and Gunnarson, T. (2005) 'Educational attainments of former child welfare clients: A Swedish national cohort study.' *International Journal of Social Welfare 14,* 1, 265–76.

Wade, J., Biehal, N., Farrelly, N. and Sinclair, I. (2010) *Outcomes for Children Placed for Reasons of Abuse or Neglect: The Consequences of Staying in Care or Returning Home.* Report to Department for Children, Schools and Families. York: University of York.

Wadsworth, Y. (1998) *What is Participatory Action Research?* Action Research International. Paper 2 (November 1998). Available at www.scu.edu.au/schools/gcm/ar/ari/p-ywadsworth98.html, accessed 9 August 2010.

Walton, E., Fraser, M.W., Lewis, R.E. and Pecora, P.J. (1993) 'In-home family-focused reunification: an experimental study.' *Child Welfare 72,* 473–87.

Wandersman, A. (2001) 'Program development, evaluation, and accountability.' In L.H. Ginsberg (ed.) *Social Work Evaluation: Principles and Methods.* Boston, MA: Allyn & Bacon.

Warren, C. (1997) 'Family support and the journey to empowerment.' In C. Cannan and C. Warren (eds) *Social Action with Children and their Families: A Community Development Approach.* London: Routledge.

Warren-Adamson, C. (2001) *Family Centres and their International Role in Social Action.* Aldershot: Ashgate.

Warren-Adamson, C. (2002a) 'Applying a parenting scale in family resource centres – Challenges and lessons.' In T. Vecchiato, A.N. Maluccio and C. Canali (eds) *Evaluation in Child and Family Service: Comparative Client and Program Perspectives.* New York: Aldine de Gruyter.

Warren-Adamson, C. (2002b) 'What's Happening in France? The settlement and social action centre: Exchange as empowerment.' In C. Warren-Adamson (ed.) *Family Centres and their International Role in Social Action.* Aldershot: Ashgate Publishing.

Warren-Adamson, C. (2006) 'Family Centres: A review of the literature.' *Child and Family Social Work 11,* 171–82.

Warren-Adamson, C. and Lightburn, A. (2004) 'Sensitive outcomes and the development of practice protocols for evaluation.' Paper presented at the Fourth International Seminar on Outcome-Based Evaluation in Child and Family Services – Cross-National Research Initiatives. Abano Terme, Italy (September 2004).

Warren-Adamson, C. and Lightburn, A. (2006) 'Developing a community-based model for integrated family centre practice.' In A. Lightburn and P. Sessions (eds) *The Handbook of Community-Based Clinical Practice,* New York: Oxford University Press.

Warren, K., Franklin, C. and Streeter, C.L. (1998) 'New directions in systems theory: Chaos and complexity.' *Social Work 43,* 4, 357–72.

Webster-Stratton, C. (1992) *The Incredible Years: A Trouble-Shooting Guide for Parents of Children Aged 3–8.* Toronto: Umbrella Press.

Webster-Stratton, C. (2000) *The Incredible Years: A Trouble Shooting Guide for Parents of Children aged 3–8.* Toronto: Umbrella Press.

Webster-Stratton, C. and Taylor, T.K. (1998) 'Adopting and Implementing Empirically Supported Interventions: A Recipe for Success.' In A. Buchanan and B.L. Hudson (eds) *Parenting, Schooling and Children's Behaviour.* Aldershot: Ashgate.

Weisz, J.R. and Gray, S. (2008) 'Evidence-based psychotherapies for children and adolescents: Data from the present and a model for the future.' *Child and Adolescent Mental Health 13,* 54–65.

Whittaker, J.K. (2009) 'Evidence-based Intervention and services for high-risk youth: A North American perspective on the challenges of integration for policy, practice and research.' *Child & Family Social Work 14,* 166–77.

Wigfall, V. and Moss, P. (2001) *More than the Sum of the Parts: A Study of a Multi-agency Child Care Network.* London: National Children's Bureau and Joseph Rowntree Foundation.

Wise, S. (2003) 'The child in family services: Expanding child abuse prevention.' *Australian Social Work 56,* 3, 183–96.

Wolcott, H. (2001) *Writing Up Qualitative Research (Second Edition).* Thousand Oaks, CA: Sage Publications.

Wulczyn, F., Kogan, J. and Jones Harden, B. (2003) 'Placement stability and movement trajectories.' *Social Services Review 77,* 2, 212–36.

Zeira, A. (2002) 'Promoting self-evaluation of programs for children at risk and their families.' In T. Vecchiato, A.N. Maluccio and C. Canali (eds) *Evaluation in Child and Family Services: Client and Program Perspectives.* New York: Aldine de Gruyter.

Zeira, A. (2004) 'New initiatives in out-of-home placements in Israel.' *Child and Family Social Work 9,* 3, 305–7.

Zeira, A. (2010) 'Testing practice wisdom in child welfare.' In: S.B. Kamerman, S. Phipps and A. Ben-Arieh (eds) *From Child Welfare to Child Well-Being: An International Perspective on Knowledge in the Service of Making Policy.* New York: Springer.

Zeira, A., Canali, C., Vecchiato, T., Jergeby, U., Thoburn, J. and Neve E. (2008) 'Evidence-based social work practice with children and families: A cross-national perspective.' *European Journal of Social Work 11,* 1, 57–72.

Zigler, E., Taussig, C. and Black, K. (1992) 'Early childhood intervention. A promising preventative for juvenile delinquency.' *American Psychologist 8,* 997–1006.

# Contributors

**Jane Aldgate**, OBE, is Professor of Social Care at The Open University. She has researched a wide range of child welfare issues, including family support and services for looked-after children. Recent books include co-editing *The Developing World of the Child* (JKP, 2006) and, with Miranda McIntosh, *Looking After the Family: A Study of Children Looked after in Kinship Care in Scotland* (Astron, 2006). Jane is currently seconded to the Scottish Government in Edinburgh, working on Getting It Right for Every Child, a coordinated multi-agency framework for assessment, planning and action for children.

**Marianne Berry** is Director of the Australian Centre for Child Protection at the University of South Australia in Adelaide. She is a National Research Fellow of the United States Children's Bureau, and has published extensively in the area of protective and supportive services to children, youth and families. She is a founding member of the International Association of Outcome-Based Evaluation and Research in Family and Children's Services.

**Nina Biehal** is a professor at the University of York, leading a research team whose work focuses on vulnerable children. She has a background in social work and has published on a wide range of child care topics, mainly focusing on children in and on the edge of care. Her work includes studies of outcomes in long-term foster care and adoption, outcomes of reunification for maltreated children and of leaving care, as well as studies of runaways from care and abuse by foster carers. She has also undertaken evaluations of preventive work with adolescents, treatment foster care and social pedagogy.

**Marian Brandon** is a reader in social work and Director of Post-qualifying Programmes at the University of East Anglia. She has a background in social work and has published widely on child maltreatment, family support and the effects of parental behaviour on children's well-being. She works on national and international studies and conducts analyses of cases of child death and serious injury through abuse for the English and Welsh Governments.

**Cinzia Canali** is senior researcher at the Fondazione Emanuela Zancan, Padua (Italy), a study centre active in the field of human services. She is mainly involved in projects related to evaluative research and evaluation of services, with particular attention to children and families services. She is involved in multi-site research in Italy about children at risk of out-of-home placement. Also she collaborates with Italian Caritas for the national report on poverty and social exclusion (published every year). She is an associated member of the International Association for Outcome-Based Evaluation and Research on Family and Children's Services and is involved in the coordination of its activities.

**Mark Ezell**, Ph.D., is Professor of Social Work at the University of North Carolina Charlotte. His teaching and research interests include management practice, child welfare contracting, juvenile justice, advocacy, research, and program evaluation. He has published widely on these topics in professional journals and presented numerous papers throughout the world. In 1997, he was selected by the US Children's Bureau as a Child Welfare Research Fellow and received funding for research related to child welfare contracting. He published his book – *Advocacy in the Human Services* (Wadsworth) – in October 2000.

**Arron K. Fain** was a Youth Advocate with the Casey Family Programs Field Office in Austin, Texas, and is currently a full-time college student (USA).

**Hans Grietens** is professor at the University of Groningen (the Netherlands) and (until August 2010) at the University of Leuven (Belgium). He is involved in research on outcomes of services provided to children in public care, with particular interest in child maltreatment issues. He is the president of the European Scientific Association on Residential and Foster Care for Children and Adolescents (EUSARF) and the editor of the *International Journal of Child & Family Welfare*.

**Kate E. Holmes**, MPA, is an independent consultant and an entrepreneur. As a consultant Kate provides support to a variety of non-profits including community development, education and child welfare organizations. Kate assists organizations with organizational capacity, strategy development and project planning. Kate received her Master degree from the Evans School of Public Affairs at the University of Washington.

**Anita Lightburn**, Ed.D., is Professor of Social Work at Fordham University Graduate School of Social Service, and Director of the Beck Institute for Religion and Poverty. Current program evaluation and intervention research focuses on capacity building in faith communities, family support and leadership development in child welfare and community mental health from a complexity science perspective. Her experience in local, national and cross-national evaluations includes family support, school-based mental health, early childhood intervention and community-based systems of care. Publications and current work focus on innovations in community-based practice.

**Patricia McNamara** is Senior Lecturer in the School of Social Work and Social Policy at La Trobe University in Melbourne, Australia. Over the past 20 years she has engaged in a range of Australian and cross-national studies of child, adolescent and family well-being. She has, most recently, conducted research into family violence, staff support in youth justice and adolescent mental health. She currently leads a consortium of government and community service organizations in a major study of respite foster care in the Australian State of Victoria. She is a foundation board member of the International Association for Outcome-Based Evaluation and Research in Family and Children's Services.

**Bruce Maden** is the Chief Executive of Te Aroha Noa Community Services, an integrated multidisciplinary community development agency situated in Palmerston North, New Zealand. He has qualifications in social work, psychology and Christian studies. Bruce has strong interests in family therapy, strengths-based practice, adult learning, working with social complexity, collaborative practice, bicultural practice, community development, counselling and social work education, practice research and spiritual direction. Bruce is a visionary leader and innovative thinker who believes deeply that communities must be involved in the development of the services influencing their lives and in discovering solutions to the issues affecting them.

**Anthony N. Maluccio** is Professor Emeritus in the School of Social Work, University of Connecticut, USA. He has published extensively in the fields of child and family social work, child welfare and foster care. He has conducted a range of research projects in the areas of adoption, permanency planning, family foster care, family reunification, family preservation and residential treatment of children and youths, through grants from federal agencies, state agencies and private foundations. He has been a Fulbright Senior Scholar in Italy at the University of Padova and Fondazione Zancan as well as in England at the University of Oxford. He is co-founder and president of the International Association for Outcome-Based Evaluation and Research on Family and Children's Services.

**Robyn Munford** is Professor of Social Work, School of Health and Social Services, Massey University, New Zealand. She has qualifications in social work, disability studies and sociology, and is the co-leader of a FRST-funded longitudinal project researching young people's pathways to resilience. Robyn has extensive experience in disability and family research, including research on family well-being using participatory and action research methodologies, and has published internationally on this research. She has recently completed an action research project that explored social and community work practice in community-based settings. Robyn has published widely on social and community work theory and practice, including strengths-based practice, disability studies, community development and bicultural practice, research methods, research ethics, children and young people, and family well-being.

**Anne E. Nicoll** provides program evaluation and research consultation to non-profit educational and human service agencies across the United States. She has held a lecture appointment with the University of Washington School of Social Work where she taught advanced research methods. She served as a researcher and Director of Quality Management with the Casey Family Program, Seattle, Washington, and as Director of the Evaluation Center within the Northwest Institute for Children and Families at the University of Washington, School of Social Work. Dr. Nicoll holds an M.S.W. from the University of Utah and a Ph.D. in Social Welfare from the University of Washington.

**Kirk O'Brien**, Ph.D., is the Director of Foster Care Research at Casey Family Programs in Seattle, Washington, where he has worked since 2001. His primary responsibilities include managing, evaluating and providing consultation on studies of youth in and alumni formerly in foster care, and studies evaluating strategies to help youth exit foster care by safely achieving permanence. Dr. O'Brien received his B.A. in Psychology from Emory University and received his doctorate in Developmental Psychology (with a specialty in quantitative methods) from the University of Houston. His professional interests include the Transtheoretical Model, family systems theory, and quantitative methods.

**Peter J. Pecora** is Managing Director of Research Services at the Casey Family Programs and Professor of Social Work at the University of Washington, Seattle. He has researched and published extensively in the field of child and family outcomes. He was a line worker and later a program coordinator in a number of child welfare service agencies in Wisconsin. He has also served as an expert witness for a number of states. He has co-authored the books *Evaluating Family Based Services* and *The Child Welfare Challenge*, journal articles and book chapters on child welfare programs design, administration and research. He has led a study of foster care alumni with the states of Oregon and Washington in conjunction with Harvard Medical School and the University of Michigan.

**Barbara A. Pine** (Social Work, 1978) is now Professor Emerita at the University of Connecticut from which she retired after 26 years of service. While at the School of Social Work, her teaching, research, scholarship and consulting were in three main areas: child welfare, social work administration and professional ethics. Her recent scholarship has focused on family reunification after a child's placement in foster care.

**Colleen Reed** is co-director of the Institute of Gerontology. She has conducted research in late-life depression, family care-giving, health services utilization and program evaluation. She is the principal investigator of a three-year research and training project funded by the Colorado Health Foundation focusing on evidence-based practice in settings providing social services to older residents of the state. She also was the principal investigator of PROGRESS, an innovative program partially funded by the John A. Hartford Foundation and aimed at training future leaders in geriatric social work. Her prior experience includes clinical social work with individuals and families, mental health treatment, and social work care management primarily with Latino families and gay, lesbian and bisexual individuals and families. At GSSW, she teaches a social work skills course, a course on assessment and intervention with older adults, and courses on practice evaluation and research.

**Wendy Rose**, OBE, is a senior research fellow at The Open University and a former senior civil servant advising on children's policy in England. She works on national and international development and research projects, and is seconded to the Scottish Government as a professional adviser. Recent books include co-editing *The Developing World of the Child* (JKP, 2006), with Colette McAuley and Peter Pecora, *Enhancing the Well-being of Children and Families through Effective Interventions* (JKP, 2006), and, with Colette McAuley, *Child Well-being: Understanding Children's Lives* (JKP, 2010).

**Jackie Sanders** is an Associate Professor in the School of Health and Social Services, Massey University, New Zealand. She has qualifications in sociology and children's studies and is co-leader of an international, longitudinal study of vulnerable young people's pathways and transitions that is funded by the New Zealand Foundation for Research, Science and Technology (FRST). Jackie has worked as a health service planner and as a manager of non-profit family service organisations. She has undertaken youth, family and child well-being research for 16 years and published extensively in these areas. She maintains an active involvement with community organisations that work with young people and families.

**Robin Spath** is Assistant Professor and Chair of the Women and Children in Families Substantive Area at the University of Connecticut School of Social Work. Dr. Spath has extensive experience in research and program evaluation, as well as administrative and direct practice experience in child welfare and family violence. She has given presentations and authored and co-authored a number of publications on topics related to child welfare, family violence, and research methodology.

**June Thoburn** CBE is an Emeritus Professor of Social Work at the University of East Anglia, Norwich, England. She has researched widely on most aspects of child and family social work. Recently she has published on services to minority ethnic and indigenous children and on alternative routes to permanence for children who need out-of-home care. She has a particular interest in cross-national comparisons of child welfare legislation, services and outcomes.

**Tiziano Vecchiato** is the Director of the Fondazione Emanuela Zancan, Padua (Italy), a centre for research on social, health and educational services, since 1992. As President of one section of the Italian National Health Council in Rome (1997–2002), he was engaged in issues of planning and evaluating human services. He coordinates the Italian reports on social exclusion in collaboration with Italian Caritas. At European level, he collaborates with the European Economic and Social Committee (EESC) section, Employment, Social Affairs and Citizenship. He is member of EUSARF and vice-president of the International Association for Outcome-Based Evaluation and Research on Family and Children's Services.

**Chris Warren-Adamson** is Visiting Senior Research Fellow at the University of Southampton. He teaches social work at the University of Brighton where he is part of a complexity theory study group, as well as playing a part in a wider complexity theory interest group enabled by the International Association of Outcome-Based Evaluation and Research on Family and Children's Services. He has a long-term career interest in collective approaches to child and family support – child and family centres, family group conferencing, day and residential group care, community and neighbourhood initiatives, networks of family placement, and making sense of the need for a 'containing' base as a prerequisite for professional child and family social work practice.

**Catherine Roller White**, MA, is a Research Analyst at Casey Family Programs, where she was worked since 2004. She coordinates studies of youth in foster care and alumni of foster care; these studies describe youth and alumni outcomes and examine how experiences in foster care can be improved to improve outcomes. In addition, she coordinates evaluations of interventions to help youth in foster care achieve permanency. She has authored and co-authored numerous journal articles and chapters related to well-being outcomes for youth and young adults who have been or are currently in foster care. Her primary areas of interest are in education and mental health.

**James K. Whittaker** is The Charles O. Cressey Endowed Professor Emeritus at the University of Washington School of Social Work, Seattle, where he has served as a member of senior faculty since 1970. His research and teaching interests encompass child and family policy and services, and the integration of evidence-based practices into contemporary child and family services agencies. A frequent contributor to the professional literature, Dr. Whittaker is author/co-author/editor of eight books and nearly 100 peer review papers and book chapters. In all, Professor Whittaker's works have been translated into eight languages including Danish, Dutch, German, French, Italian, Korean and Japanese.

**Anat Zeira** is an associate professor at the School of Social Work and Social Welfare at the Hebrew University of Jerusalem and a founding member of the International Association of Outcome-Based Evaluation and Research on Family and Children's Services. Her main areas of interest are related to evidence-based social work practice with children and at-risk youth and their families. Recently her research has focused on the transition to adulthood of care leavers. She has published widely in professional journals and presented numerous papers at international conferences. Through her studies and publications she emphasizes the importance of systematic monitoring and evaluation by practitioners and its dissemination in the field.

# Subject Index

# Author Index